WITHDRAWN

The Politics of Precaution

**Other Books Published in Cooperation with
the International Food Policy Research Institute**

IFPRI

*Sustainability, Growth, and Poverty Alleviation: A Policy and Agroecological
Perspective*
Edited by Steven A. Vosti and Thomas Reardon

Famine in Africa: Causes, Responses, and Prevention
By Joachim von Braun, Tesfaye Teklu, and Patrick Webb

Paying for Agricultural Productivity
Edited by Julian M. Alston, Philip G. Pardey, and Vincent H. Smith

*Out of the Shadow of Famine: Evolving Food Markets and Food Policy in
Bangladesh*
Edited by Raisuddin Ahmed, Steven Haggblade, and Tawfiq-e-Elahi
Chowdhury

Agricultural Science Policy: Changing Global Agendas
Edited by Julian M. Alston, Philip G. Pardey, and Michael J. Taylor

*Land Tenure and Natural Resource Management: A Comparative Study of
Agrarian Communities in Asia and Africa*
Edited by Keijiro Otsuka and Frank Place

The Politics of Precaution

Genetically Modified Crops in Developing Countries

ROBERT L. PAARLBERG

Published for the International Food Policy Research Institute

The Johns Hopkins University Press
Baltimore and London

The Johns Hopkins University Press
2715 North Charles Street
Baltimore, Maryland 21218-4363
www.press.jhu.edu

International Food Policy Research Institute
2033 K Street, NW
Washington, D.C. 20006
(202) 862-5600
www.ifpri.org

LIBRARY OF CONGRESS CATALOGING-IN-PUBLICATION DATA
Paarlberg, Robert L.
    The politics of precaution : genetically modified crops in developing countries / Robert L.
Paarlberg.
        p.   cm.
    Includes bibliographical references (p.   ).
    ISBN 0-8018-6668-5 (cloth : alk. paper) — ISBN 0-8018-6823-8 (pbk. : alk. paper)
    1. Crops—Genetic engineering—Government policy—Developing countries.   I. Title.
SB123.57 .P33   2001
631.5′233′091724—dc21   2001029424

A catalog record for this book is available from the British Library.

Contents

Tables

Foreword

The potential revolution in farming made possible by genetically modified (GM) crops has created an international divide in policies toward this new technology. Whereas farmers in Argentina, Canada, and the United States adopted GM crops quickly and are now growing them commercially, most other countries in the world have taken a much more precautionary approach, ranging from restrictions of various kinds to outright bans.

In *The Politics of Precaution: Genetically Modified Crops in Developing Countries,* Robert L. Paarlberg presents the first clear picture of how some developing countries are dealing with the shifting scientific and policy environment surrounding GM crops. As this book makes clear, GM crop policy does not consist of a simple thumbs-up or thumbs-down on a single issue. In fact, GM crops raise a number of policy issues: What is a country's legal stance toward intellectual property rights? What are its regulations on biosafety and food safety? How will GM crops fit into a country's trade policies? And is it willing to invest its own public funds in research on GM crops for its farmers? By considering all these facets of GM crop policy, Paarlberg offers a comprehensive view of how some developing countries are managing the new technology.

In particular, Paarlberg describes the range of policy choices made by four developing countries—Brazil, China, India, and Kenya. Of these four countries, only China as of 2001 had officially approved the commercial planting of GM crops. The other three have pursued a precautionary approach, in some cases over the objections of their own farmers. These countries, Paarlberg shows, are responding not necessarily to scientific evidence but rather to political and social pressures from international environmental and nongovernmental organizations and donors outside their borders.

This study should be of great interest to anyone who follows the international debate over GM foods and crops, including policymakers, researchers, students, and those in the international private sector. Paarlberg's findings are also presented in a shorter form in a 2020 Vision discussion paper called *Governing the GM Crop Revolution,* published by IFPRI in 2001.

Per Pinstrup-Andersen
Director General, International Food Policy Research Institute

Preface and Acknowledgments

I remember exactly where I was when I decided to undertake this research project. It was July 1998 and I was in the South Building cafeteria at the U.S. Department of Agriculture, talking with Montague Yudelman, my longtime friend and tutor on matters linked to agricultural development. I was telling Monty I had just finished co-authoring a book on agricultural policy reform in the United States and I was looking for a new project to ensure productive use of my upcoming sabbatical leave from teaching at Wellesley College. I knew I wanted to spend this year traveling in Asia, Africa, and Latin America, learning about the policy challenges facing agriculture in the tropics and talking with officials at the national level about the constraints and opportunities they were facing. I asked Monty for any suggestions he might have regarding new policy issues in agricultural development that I might consider as a focus for my work. He answered, without hesitation: "Genetically modified crops."

Until that moment I had tried to avoid the issue of GM crops, hoping to postpone learning about this new farming technology until some of the scientific uncertainties and ideological controversy attached to it had died away. Monty knew the controversy was not going to die down. He sensed this new technology might hold out unique promise for some poor farmers in tropical countries, yet it was not reaching these farmers. He persuaded me it might be useful for a political scientist to invest some time in understanding why.

At that time much had already been written about policies toward genetically modified crops in the United States and Europe. Advocates were also writing about what the policies of developing countries *should* be toward GM crops. Yet little was available describing the actual policy choices of governments in the developing world so far, and why they were making those choices. This, I concluded, was a research project I could profitably undertake. Since Wellesley would generously cover my salary, and since the Weatherhead Center at Harvard University would generously continue to provide me with a research appointment and an office, all I needed was financial support and administrative assistance for my travel. The International Food Policy Research Institute (IFPRI) and Winrock International solved these two problems admirably. IFPRI offered to pay my travel expenses if I would agree to draft a short version of my findings by the end of 2000 for their 2020 Vision discussion paper series, and Winrock International offered some additional financial support through a small grant from the Rockefeller Foundation plus valuable assistance on the ground at several of the research stops I was planning to make in Nairobi, Delhi, and Beijing.

My research effort took me on four separate trips to Kenya, Brazil, India, and China to gather documents and talk with dozens of government policy officials, international civil servants, scientists, corporate executives, and leaders of nongovernmental organizations. My goal in these conversations was to learn what policies had been set in place toward GM crops in those countries, and why. I learned that answering this question obliged me to classify policy choices in each of these four countries in five different areas: intellectual property rights, biological safety, trade, food safety, and public research investments. This book is the final product of that research and classification effort.

I enjoy this kind of work because it allows me to speak with and learn from such a wide variety of accomplished professionals who are struggling with policy issues of vital significance to the future prosperity and well-being of hundreds of millions of still destitute farmers in the developing world. It is a privilege to be welcomed as a visitor and a pleasure to encounter almost everywhere patterns and practices of local hospitality that I wish my own country could someday embrace. In most cases I will never be able adequately to repay the generosity. All I can do here is to mention the names of some of those who were especially helpful to me during my 1999–2000 research effort and express the wish that we will meet again soon.

In Nairobi I had particularly valuable help from John Wafula, W. M. Mwangi, Florence Wambugu, Harris Mule, John Lynam, Joseph DeVries, J. O. Ochanda, John Mugabe, Moses Onim, Steve Collins, G. N. W. Thitai, Charity Kabutha, Stephen Gacugia, and Gerhard van't Land.

In Brasilia and São Paulo I was helped most by Francisco Reifschneider, Maria Jose Amstalden Sampaio, Carlos Magno Campos da Rocha, Simone Scholze, Eliana Fontes, Lucile Oda, Mauro Carneiro, Andrea Lazzarini Salazar, and Mariana Pooli.

In Delhi and Hyderabad, I had essential assistance from Maria Brown, Gaurav Laroia, V. L. Chopra, B. Venkateswarlu, H. P. Singh, Ellora Mubashir, J. P. Mishra, N. P. Sarma, E. A. Siddiq, R. D. Kapoor, P. K. Ghosh, and Raju Barwale.

In Beijing, I was fortunate to have help from Lu Mai, Ke Bingsheng, Zhang Chonghua, Yang Tingting, Qian Keming, Gong Xifeng, Chen Xiwen, Feng Lu, Du Ying, Phillip W. Laney, Wang Dehui, Wang Qinfang, Peng Yufa, Wang Canfa, and Huang Jikun.

For overall guidance and counsel I have profited on multiple occasions from talking to Calestous Juma, Carl Pray, Per Pinstrup-Andersen, C. S. Prakash, Lowell Hardin, Aarti Gupta, Rob Horsch, Gary Toenniessen, and Julian Kinderlerer. For help at IFPRI in publishing my earlier discussion paper version of this work I am indebted to Heidi Fritschel and especially to my longtime friend Rajul Pandya-Lorch. Large institutional debts are owed to IFPRI, Winrock, the Rockefeller Foundation, Wellesley College, and the Weatherhead Center at Harvard University. Don Paarlberg, my father and my greatest personal inspiration, was the first person to read the original rough draft of this manuscript from cover to cover, much to my pleasure. Deepest thanks of all go to my wife, Marianne Perlak, who understood the importance I attached to doing this job right and who kindly forgave all the other things I stopped doing well while the project was under way.

A project covering as much ground as this will certainly contain factual errors. I hope my readers will forgive these and feel free to point them out, as they are my own responsibility.

The Politics of Precaution

1 Introduction: The Challenge of the GM Crop Revolution

The genetic modification of plants and animals has been the foundation of all modern agriculture. For 10,000 years human societies have modified natural species through crude practices such as seed selection and controlled breeding. Yet the fundamental principles of heredity did not become known until the mid-nineteenth century, when Gregor Mendel's work with garden peas was first published in an obscure Austrian journal in 1866. This knowledge dramatically enhanced the efficiency of genetic modification through controlled breeding, leading early in the twentieth century to the development of modern hybrid seed varieties for important food crops such as maize, and then by mid-century to high-yielding "green revolution" seed varieties for wheat and rice.

In 1953 science moved toward a far deeper understanding of the molecular foundation of plant and animal genetics with the discovery of the double helical structure of the DNA molecules that are the critical constituents of genes. Genes are segments of DNA that contain enough information to produce a polypeptide strand or protein, which in turn determines the traits expressed in the organism. With this discovery, the human project of modifying species could now be undertaken at the molecular level through engineered gene transfers.

In 1973, scientists began engineering actual recombinations of DNA molecules by moving specific genes carrying desired traits from a source organism into the DNA of a living target organism. Compared with the slow and imprecise processes of conventional breeding, in which all of the genes of the parent organisms must repeatedly be recombined, recombinant DNA (rDNA) provided life scientists with a faster, more powerful, and potentially more precise method. This technique also differed from all previous practices of life modification because it permitted the controlled movement of discrete genetic traits across species. Other techniques for creating entirely new organisms, such as chemical or physical mutagenesis, were not as controlled or predictable. And other techniques for mixing the DNA of sexually incompatible species in nature, such as wide-hybrid crossing, did not have the same range among species.

Terms such as "genetic engineering," "genetic manipulation," "genetic transformation," or "transgenesis" were initially favored to describe this new genetic modification technique. More recently the technique has been referred to less precisely but more simply as "genetic modification," or GM. Several different methods of rDNA gene insertion are currently available, including "gene guns" using DNA-coated metal microprojectiles; the use of a "disarmed" (or benign) plasmid from the plant pathogen *Agrobacterium tumefaciens* as a vector; or direct uptake of DNA by protoplasts of plant cells (Serageldin and Persley 2000).

The first generation of GM crops was developed in the private sector in the 1980s, field tested early in the 1990s, and released by government regulators for commercial use beginning in the mid-1990s. Commercial success was initially elusive. The very first GM plant approved for commercial development was the Calgene Corporation's extended shelf life tomato ("Flavr Savr"), which won approval from the Food and Drug Administration (FDA) in the United States in 1994. For reasons unrelated to its transgenic properties this product was not a commercial success in the United States; the processed paste from this first GM tomato was nonetheless marketed profitably for a time in Europe by the company Zeneca.

The GM crops that first gained widespread use by farmers were maize, cotton, potato, soybean, and canola varieties engineered to resist pests or viruses or to tolerate some herbicides. Most of these new GM crops carried only one new agronomic trait—such as resistance to insects or to specific herbicides—although some varieties of maize and cotton were modified to carry both herbicide and insect resistance traits. Virus resistance was also incorporated into some of these early GM crops, including tomatoes, potatoes, and tobacco. The private seed companies that designed these new crops did so with the needs of farmers uppermost in mind; the great attraction was a reduced need to purchase and spray toxic chemicals plus reduced soil tillage time or cost.

These GM techniques were part of a larger shift in the world of agriculture toward what is called "precision farming," which employs a combination of information technology and biotechnology to reduce indiscriminate use of chemical and water inputs. The preeminent precision farming technology is the use of the Global Positioning System (GPS) with satellite tracking and onboard computer monitoring to help farmers adjust fertilizer applications with greater precision to the differing soil needs of specific areas of their fields. The result is a less wasteful pattern of fertilizer application, which both lowers farming costs and reduces fertilizer pollution of surface water and ground water. Other precision technologies include the use of lasers to level farm fields and the automated linking of local crop sprinkler control systems to rainfall forecasts, both of which can reduce wasteful use of irrigation water. Genetically modified (GM) crops are the most recent component of this precision revolution. By using GM crops, farmers have been able to reduce sprayings of herbicides and insecticides and also cut back on their own labor inputs, including soil-disturbing tillage practices. It is the altered genetic information coded into the DNA of a GM crop that facilitates these money-saving efficiencies. The first generation of pest- and herbicide-tolerant GM crops won final approval from regulators and were released for commercial use in a half dozen countries almost simultaneously in 1995–1996. The new GM crops performed as advertised. Between 1996 and 2000, however, the planting of these crops took hold quickly in some countries yet scarcely at all in others. In the United States, Argentina, and Canada widespread planting began almost immediately, and by 2000 roughly 54 percent of the soybean area in the United States and 95 percent of Argentine soybean area was planted to GM varieties. GM cotton planting spread even farther, covering 72 percent of cotton area in the United States by 2000. GM corn planting spread as well, accounting for as much as one-third of the U.S. crop in 1999, but then declining slightly in 2000. This small decrease in GM corn planting in the United States (and also in Canada) in 2000 was offset by a significant increase in GM corn planting in Argentina, up from 5 percent to an estimated 20 percent of the national crop (James 2000b).

Farmers in the United States, Argentina, and Canada were attracted to these new GM varieties primarily because they permitted significant cutbacks in pesticide or herbicide sprays and reduced other crop management requirements. The GM seeds cost more than conventional varieties because of a "technology fee" that seed companies applied to the purchase price so as to recoup their research and development costs. In some cases the purchase of these GM varieties also carried contractual obligations not to use or sell the grown seeds of these crops. Many farmers nonetheless found them an attractive commercial option. Farmers planting herbicide-tolerant GM soybeans in the United States, for example, could gain roughly US$6 per acre in the form of reduced herbicide costs, despite technology fees and no change in yields. By switching to GM soybeans farmers did increase their use of one kind of herbicide (glyphosate) significantly, but they reduced their use of other more toxic and more persistent synthetic herbicides even more significantly (OECD 2000).

While farmers in the United States, Argentina, and Canada were going ahead with this GM crop revolution, farmers in most other countries were not. As of 2000, the United States alone planted 69 percent of the world's GM crops (in terms of acreage); Argentina's share was 23 percent, and Canada's 7 percent. The other countries of the world together planted less than 2 percent (James 2000b). Other countries in which some minor plantings of GM crops could be found were Australia, Bulgaria, China, France, Germany, Mexico, Romania, South Africa, Spain, and Uruguay. Some countries in Europe (such as Portugal) that earlier had started to plant GM crops had ceased doing so by 2000.

One reason for this clustering of GM crop acreage in just three relatively prosperous Western hemisphere countries was a decision by the private companies selling GM seeds to focus first on their best-paying customers. Successful farmers in the United States, Canada, and Argentina had the purchasing power and the commercial seed buying habits to constitute an instantly lucrative market. The crops they produced (soybeans, maize, cotton) were thus among the first to be transformed with GM techniques by the private companies that were leading in the development and production of GM seeds. Because the GM crop revolution so far has been pushed forward primarily by private international companies responding to market forces, poor farmers in tropical countries were initially less attractive as commercial customers, so the private companies did not invest in developing GM varieties of tropical subsistence crops such as cassava, millet, or cowpeas.

Yet this is not the only reason the GM crop revolution has so far been confined to only a few countries. Commercial farmers in dozens of countries—rich and poor alike—grow soybeans, maize and cotton, and in many of these countries the pest and disease problems encountered are similar to those in the United States, Canada, and Argentina. Pest and disease problems are especially prevalent in developing countries, where weeds, insects, and viral disease often reduce potential crop production by 50 percent or more (Yudelman, Ratta, and Nygaard 1998). As limited as they may be, the improved crop traits provided by the first commercial products of the GM revolution should have been attractive to farmers beyond just a few countries.

Governmental policy restrictions are now as significant as limited product lines in holding back the GM crop revolution in most countries outside the Western hemisphere. Regulatory authorities in many developing countries, in particular, have not yet approved the release of any GM crops for use by their own farmers. Rather than doing everything possible to get their hands on this powerful new technology, officials in many developing countries have taken decisions that tend to slow the entry of GM crops into their own farming sectors. A central purpose of this book is to document and explain this emerging pattern of policy resistance to GM crops among some developing-country government authorities.

One reason the planting of GM crops spread quickly in the United States after 1995 was a relatively permissive regulatory environment. After some hesitation in the 1980s, authorities in the United States decided to screen GM crops for food safety and biological safety (biosafety) using essentially the same regulatory standards and regulatory institutions already in place for non-GM foods and crops. This decision drew criticism from opponents of the new technology, but it allowed official approvals of new GM crops to go forward rapidly. Canada and Argentina followed this U.S. lead. In Europe GM crops came to be regulated under separate statutes, yet the regulatory outcome at first was the same: official approval following standardized case-by-case reviews of scientific evidence for known risks. Between 1992 and 1998, European Union regulators approved some 18 different GM products for commercial use, including vaccines and flowers as well as crops (Birchard 2000).

This permissive regulatory approach toward GM crops began to come under strong challenge in Europe after 1996. One reason was a crisis in public confidence over food safety regulation brought on by "mad cow disease" (bovine spongiform encephalopathy, or BSE). For a decade, senior UK officials had reassured consumers that eating beef from diseased animals was safe, but in 1996 it became clear that consumption could lead in some cases to a fatal illness called Creutzfeldt-Jakob Disease (CJD).[1] This discovery forced the slaughter of 4 million cows in Britain and shredded public confidence in all official food safety pronouncements. The BSE crisis had no link to GM crops, but it sensitized consumers and the media throughout Europe to food safety dangers exactly at the moment GM foods were first appearing on supermarket shelves. EU regulators tried to reassure Europeans that GM foods had been tested and were officially deemed safe, but this time the public were not about to trust official pronouncements.[2]

Consumer anxieties over GM foods in Europe were soon heightened by organized media campaigns against the new technology waged by green party leaders, organic farmers, and environmental nongovernmental organizations (NGOs). These campaigns generated further consumer anxiety and led by 1997 to separate EU labeling requirements for GM foods and eventually to preemptive actions by private supermarket chains to remove foods with GM content from their shelves voluntarily (European Commission 2000a). In 1998 the European Union announced a moratorium on new approvals of GM crops for commercial release. This had a secondary effect of halting imports into the European Union of any bulk commodity shipments that might contain new GM varieties not yet registered in the European Union (for example, corn imports from the United States). By 2000, 14 applications were pending in the European Union for new GM crop approvals, yet no new approvals were being granted.

European governments justified these stricter regulatory measures toward GM crops and foods on several grounds. First, they invoked the "precautionary principle," which they said should apply when assessing technologies for risk under conditions of scientific uncertainty. This principle had been widely

---

1. As late as 1995 Britain's Conservative Prime Minister John Major had told the House of Commons there "is no scientific evidence that BSE can be transmitted to humans or that eating beef causes it in humans." By 2000, consumption of BSE beef had led to the death of 77 Britons from CJD; many more are likely to become ill and die in the future given the long incubation period of CJD.

2. Public health officials in the European Union have continued to endorse GM crops as safe. In 2000 the EU Commissioner for Health and Consumer Protection, David Byrne, reiterated that, "[r]ight around the world, the scientific evidence is that there is no problem with GMOs over and above any other food" (Birchard 2000, 322).

popularized in international environmental policy circles particularly since the Rio Earth Summit Conference of 1992.[3] GM foods may not test positive for known risks, but the novelty of the GM transformation process suggests the possibility of entirely new risks that conventional testing routines might not catch. Using this thinking, governments in Europe have been willing to block new applications of the technology without any positive evidence of risk. The requirement that consumers be informed through labeling when purchasing foods containing previously approved GM materials was justified on the basis of a consumer's "right to know." Elements of this more cautious European policy approach to GM crops and foods spread to Japan and to the other industrial countries of East Asia and the Pacific in 1999–2000.

These divergent policies toward GM technologies in rich countries have created a complicated policy choice problem in the developing world (Serageldin and Persley 2000). Should governments in the developing world follow the more permissive U.S. approach toward GM crop technologies, or the more precautionary EU approach? Developing-country officials have come under pressure to adopt either one set of policies or the other. These conflicting pressures are brought to bear consciously through bilateral donor agencies, international organizations, private business firms, philanthropic foundations, and international NGOs. Industrial world pressures are also imposed on developing countries unconsciously through private international commodity markets, which alter crop prices in poor countries based on changing consumer tastes toward GM foods in rich countries.

Officials in the developing world confront several additional dilemmas when deciding whether to fall in line behind the United States or Europe in their regulatory approach to GM crops and foods. On the one hand, imperatives to boost agricultural production are much stronger in most developing countries than in either the United States or Europe, which seems to argue for the more permissive U.S. approach. On the other hand, developing countries tend to have weaker technical and regulatory capacities within their own borders, which could make it more difficult for them to use GM crop technologies efficiently and safely, arguing perhaps for the more cautious European approach. The industry-driven U.S. approach may not suit developing-country circumstances because of possible conflicts between the commercial interests and property rights claims of the private international firms now developing GM crops and the meager financial resources and seed-saving habits of farmers in poor tropical countries. Yet the European approach may also be inappropriate, since farmers and consumers in poor countries are not yet as wealthy and well fed as Europeans, and they face on-farm resource protection

---

3. There is no single consensual statement of this principle. Numerous "soft" and "hard" variants are currently in use and under discussion (Soule 2000).

challenges that are quite distinct from those faced by farmers in rich countries (Paarlberg 1994).

This study does not advise officials in developing countries how to resolve such policy choice dilemmas. It does, however, seek to draw an accurate map of the choices they will have to make, and then review the choices actually made in 1999–2000 by several prominent developing countries. The method used is to subdivide the problem of policy choice toward GM crops into five areas: intellectual property rights (IPR) policy, biosafety policy, trade policy, food safety and consumer choice policy, and public research investment policy. Within each of these areas a spectrum of possible policy choices is then described, ranging from those that might do the most to speed the development and planting of GM crops to those that might do the most to slow the spread of GM crops. Chapter 2 explains and justifies this classification scheme in the abstract.

The next four chapters of this book then employ this scheme to classify actual policy choices about GM crops and foods in 1999–2000 in four important developing countries: Kenya, Brazil, India, and China. These policy choices are all relatively new, some are still untested in practice, and many are still evolving. In some cases the process of choice has been complicated by political or legal challenge, or by internal jurisdictional controversy. A rough and provisional classification of these choices—as tending either to promote or to prevent the spread of GM crop technologies—can nonetheless be described.

One important finding from this study is that Kenya, Brazil, and India have all recently adopted national policies that are slowing the spread of GM crops within their own borders. In some respects these policies are even more cautious than those adopted in Europe. Farmers in most European countries still may legally plant at least some GM crops if they wish, and imports of some GM commodities are still permitted. Yet, as of mid-2001, authorities in Kenya, Brazil, and India had not approved commercial planting of any GM crops or the routine commercial importation of GM commodities.

This degree of caution is surprising given the unmet food production needs of some of these countries and given the prevalence within these countries of precisely the crop pest and crop disease problems that GM crops have been designed to address. It is all the more surprising that each of these three countries has slowed the planting of GM crops primarily in the name of biological safety, which otherwise is not a high policy priority.

Of the developing countries examined in this study, only China had approved any kind of commercial GM crop production by mid-2001. China began commercial production of GM crops in 1997, partly on the strength of a determined national GM crop research program. Yet what sets China apart is not just its research program, because Brazil and India have also invested significantly in an independent GM crop research capacity; nor is it stronger

IPR guarantees to private companies, since China has at times antagonized international seed companies by failing to control IPR piracy in the area of crop biotechnology. What set China most clearly apart from Kenya, Brazil, and India was its decision to implement a biosafety policy that was permissive rather than precautionary. China's biosafety screening process focused only on demonstrated risks to the environment from GM crops, rather than on hypothetical or unknown risks.

The final chapter in this book seeks to explain such policy differences so far in Kenya, Brazil, India, and China. The explanation is based in part on the differential ability of these countries to resist international influence. China has gone ahead with some GM crops while others held back partly because pressures from international media campaigns, donor agencies, and NGO advocacy are not as heavily felt within the political system of China as within the political systems of Kenya, Brazil, and India. China is not as dependent on the international donor community as Kenya, so it faces less international donor pressure to design and implement highly cautious biosafety procedures for GM crops. China is not as significant an exporter of food to Europe as Brazil, so it faces less commodity market pressure to remain a GM-free source of supply. And China's political system is not as open to international NGO influence as that of either Brazil or India, so it is less likely to be challenged by internationally connected anti-GM activist networks when it decides to field test or release a GM crop for commercial use.

The recent international controversy regarding GM crops has generated numerous writings that address the hypothetical costs, risks, or benefits of this new technology. This study does not attempt either to summarize or to second-guess that large and still growing body of analysis. Our subject here is not the technology itself but the policy choices made by governments in the developing world toward the technology. It is sometimes assumed that, in the modern age of globalization, developing countries will have no choice: they will have to accept whatever technologies are presented to them by the industrial world. Yet, in the case of GM crop technologies, the industrial world has become deeply divided. This division should give poor countries more room to make an independent choice of their own. Yet it also ensures that a higher than usual level of controversy will be injected, from abroad as well as at home, into the choice-making process.

2   Classifying Policies toward GM Crops and Foods

Powerful new technologies often require governments to make new and unfamiliar policy choices. So it is with technologies for the genetic modification of agricultural crops, particularly in the developing world. This chapter introduces one method of classifying the most important policy choices governments in the developing world must make toward genetically modified (GM) crops and foods. Subsequent chapters then use this classification scheme to examine and compare actual policy choices made in 1999–2000 by Kenya, Brazil, India, and China.

Policy choices toward GM crops and foods could be classified in many different ways. One approach would be to examine which institutions in society are permitted to control the new technology, and to consider in particular the issue of public versus private sector control. Another approach would be to classify how government decisions are made, whether by employing authoritarian or technocratic or democratic policy procedures. Yet another approach would be to ask who benefits from the new technology—for example, farmers or consumers, or rich versus poor. Here I employ a method of classification that struggles with a more fundamental problem: does policy toward the new technology tend to promote its use or to prevent its use? In the case of a technology as new and controversial as GM crops and foods, this promotion versus prevention question has to be faced before any of the more derivative policy questions come into play.

There are, of course, gradients between promotion and prevention. Here I shall describe a scale of four possible postures toward GM crops and foods overall. Policies designed to accelerate the spread of GM crop and food technologies within the borders of a nation I shall call "promotional." Policies that attempt to be neutral toward the new technology, intending neither to speed nor to slow its spread within the nation's borders, I shall call "permissive." Policies intended to slow the spread of GM crops and foods for various public reasons but without banning the technology entirely will be called "precautionary." Finally, governments might opt to block or ban entirely the spread of this new technology within their borders; this I shall label a "preventive" policy posture.

9

Governments can choose between being promotional, permissive, precautionary, or preventive in several separately important policy areas. Five such areas will be singled out in this study:

- Intellectual property rights. Governments everywhere must decide whether or not to grant within their borders intellectual property rights (IPRs)—such as patents or plant breeders' rights—to the inventors of GM crops. Developing-country governments seeking access to GM crop technologies may have to grant IPRs in some form to the private seed and biotechnology companies that have emerged as leading purveyors of the new technology. If no IPR protection is offered, the private companies might keep the technology away.
- Biosafety. When screening GM crops for safety to the biological environment, hurdles of varying heights can be imagined. Governments wishing to promote GM crop technologies within their borders could set the biosafety hurdle extremely low. Those wishing to prevent the planting of GM crops could set the hurdle impossibly high.
- Trade. Governments wishing to promote GM technology could encourage (or at least not restrict) the import of GM seeds into their country. Governments wishing to prevent adoptions of the technology could impose import bans or laborious case-by-case import approval procedures.
- Food safety and consumer choice. The planting of GM crops could be promoted through a food safety policy that draws no significant distinction between the GM variety of a food and its conventional counterpart, thereby requiring no separate consumer safety testing. Alternatively, the planting of GM food crops could be discouraged or blocked entirely through a policy that sets a much higher safety standard for GM foods, or perhaps requires complete segregation of GM from non-GM foods in commercial market channels.
- Public research investment policy. Developing-country governments interested in promoting GM technologies may have to invest their own treasury funds. They could use such funds as an alternative to depending on the private sector, instead developing appropriate GM crop varieties within their own national agricultural research systems and then using national extension services to spread those home-grown GM technologies to farmers. At the other extreme, governments wishing to block the technology could decide to prohibit public research on the genetic engineering of new plants or animals.

Because GM crop technologies are still so new, explicit policy choices have not yet been made in all of these areas by some developing countries. The result, however, can be an implicit choice. For example, if a government's existing food testing or labeling policies have not been updated to take the presence of GM crops into account, the implication will be official acceptance of those crops as comparable to non-GM crops in their consumer safety aspects. Governments may also on occasion make choices toward GM crops with other issues in mind. In the area of intellectual property, for example, a government skeptical toward private companies might decide to deny IPRs within its borders to inventors of all new plant varieties—conventionally bred as well as genetically engineered. Alternatively, a government might decide to create a new national IPR system for plant breeders not specifically to promote GM crops but instead out of a larger international legal obligation within the World Trade Organization (WTO). The classification scheme offered here captures these unintended and derived policy choices toward GM crops, as well as those that were intended and GM-specific.

In order to guide the classification and analysis in the following chapters with as much precision as possible, I now provide greater detail on what a promotional, permissive, precautionary, or preventive policy (intended or otherwise) might look like within each of the five policy areas listed above.

Intellectual Property Rights

During the Green Revolution of the 1960s and 1970s governments in the developing world did not feel compelled to provide private companies or private plant breeders with exclusive intellectual property rights to the sale or use of new crop technologies. The new high-yielding varieties then being offered to developing-country farmers had been developed by breeders working for philanthropic or public research institutions. The new seeds were not developed and sold by private companies; instead they were given away through international assistance programs, distributed by public extension agencies and development NGOs, and sold at subsidized prices through government seed companies.

In the GM crop revolution it is private companies that have taken the lead so far. When public funding for international agricultural research faltered in the 1980s, the initiative in developing most new GM crops fell to private seed and biotechnology companies. These companies do not normally behave like philanthropic foundations or public sector extension services. In order to recover their expensive private investments in the development of GM seeds, they seek IPR protections to exclude competitors from selling these seeds to farmers.

The private corporate argument for IPRs is straightforward. Without some guarantee of enforceable intellectual property rights, private companies may have little incentive to invest shareholder assets in the creation of new technologies because commercial competitors will be able to copy the technology and then share in the benefit without paying any of the original research costs. This may be especially true of animal and plant technologies, which are unique because they can be self-copying whenever the animals and plants reproduce naturally. Some recent historical evidence from the industrial world supports this corporate viewpoint. Private companies historically made few investments in crop improvement, precisely because crops were self-copying and IPRs were so difficult to protect. Companies began investing heavily in crop research only after corn hybridization technology was developed in the United States in the 1930s (Lele, Lesser, and Horstkotte-Wessler 2000). The kernels produced by these new hybrid corn plants were valuable for feed or food use, but the desirable traits did not survive when the kernels were replanted. This natural biological IPR protection guarantee was the incentive private investors needed, so private sector investments in corn research subsequently increase dramatically. Partly as a consequence, commercial yields for corn in the United States have increased more than twice as much as for wheat since the 1940s—by 255 percent for corn compared with 119 percent for wheat (Warren 1998). Farmers had to buy hybrid seeds every year but they did so eagerly because of the much higher yields. If a natural means to appropriate value (such as hybridization) does not exist, there is a danger that private companies will underinvest in new crop technologies. This, presumably, is why governments seeking to promote new technologies must step in to provide minimal IPR guarantees.

Governmental IPR guarantees in the area of crops can take two forms: patents or plant breeders' rights. Patents are the familiar legal device governments use to provide inventors with a temporary right (for example, for 20 years from the date of application) to exclude others from making, using, selling, or importing an invention.[1] Yet patent protection for agricultural plants is permitted by only a few governments, led by the United States. Plant breeders' rights (PBRs) are a far more common form of IPR in the area of agricultural crops. Many nations have plant variety protection laws that grant plant breeders the right to control the commercial use of their own new varieties for a fixed number of years, while at the same time allowing other breeders to use the new varieties as an initial source of variation in their own work. The stated purpose of all such IPR systems is not to slow the use of new inventions but rather to grant inventors a right to control temporarily (and hence profit from) the circumstances in which their inventions will be used commercially by others.

Strong IPR guarantees have been one reason for high rates of new farm crop development in the United States. Since 1930 the United States has enacted a sequence of plant variety protection laws to provide PBRs. And since 1980 the United States has also provided full patent protection for agricultural crop inventions, under the terms of the 1980 *Diamond v. Chakrabarty* Supreme

---

1. The invention must be new, as defined by the patent law, and if it has been described in a printed publication anywhere or was in public use prior to the date of the application a patent cannot be granted (Nelson et al. 1999).

Court decision. Naturally occurring living beings cannot be patented, but patent protection is now available for any organism altered by human intervention. This new patent protection option in the United States gave private U.S. companies a stronger incentive to invest in the development of commercially useful GM crops. The incentive was then made even stronger when subsequent court interpretations allowed inventors in the United States to seek full patent protection even down to the level of individual genes or gene sequences. By 2000, the United States patent office had issued patents on about 6,000 separate genes.[2] From the standpoint of U.S. patent law, the inventive use of a gene was treated just like the inventive use of any other chemical found in nature. Strong IPR protection is one reason companies headquartered in the United States—such as Monsanto and DuPont—became the early world leaders in the development of commercially applicable GM crop innovations.

For developing countries, the relationship between a strong IPR protection policy and GM crop development or dissemination is not so clear, however. Strong IPRs may help stimulate GM crop innovations by private companies, but those same IPRs can make it more difficult to get new GM crop technologies into the hands of poor developing-country farmers, who may not be able to afford the high price of privately sold GM seeds. Scientists in developing-country institutes may also have problems negotiating the terms under which they can develop and bring to market new crop technologies of their own incorporating GM innovations privately patented elsewhere. In negotiating license terms with patent holders, developing-country scientists will have some leverage of their own, derived from their greater access to local germplasm and their strong connections to local seed distribution systems. Yet they may still find it difficult to enter into advantageous research partnerships with the international companies that have developed most GM crops. The companies may grant them a license to use proprietary GM technologies for research purposes only or with onerous conditions (for example, that any new discoveries that might emerge will be owned by the company). The developing-country crop research institutes that thrived during the earlier Green Revolution, thanks to the free international exchange of germplasm, have struggled under the current gene revolution to find a way to work with foreign corporate or university-based patent holders.

Strong IPRs may even get in the way of the innovative process itself. Increased patenting of upstream research can stifle subsequent downstream innovation and commercial product development (Conway 1999). As patents proliferate, more legal cooperation is needed among separate companies or

---

2. Roughly 1,000 of these patents are for human genes (Pollack 2000). It would not have been possible for the United States to embrace this extreme version of IPR protection without the development of DNA mapping techniques, which allow each newly developed plant trait to have its own unique genetic "fingerprint."

universities to bring each new commercial GM crop package to the market. Commercializing a single insecticidal GM plant in the United States can require separate patents for the plant itself, the transformation technology, the selectable marker employed, the gene coding for an insecticidal protein, the promoter, and the various regulatory elements and modifications needed to express genes in plant cells (Sehgal 1999). If separate companies hold these patents, legal gridlock can ensue, resulting in a "tragedy of the anticommons." Simply administering an IPR system of this kind can become problematic as well.[3]

The patenting of GM crop inventions by private companies and universities can also slow down or complicate publicly or philanthropically funded efforts to innovate and extend GM crop technologies to poor farmers. This is illustrated in the case of so-called Golden Rice, a rice plant enhanced with beta carotene that is potentially valuable for addressing Vitamin A deficiencies in developing countries. The Rockefeller Foundation, together with the Swiss Federation and the European Union, sponsored the creation of this new GM plant in 1999 on the condition that it should be made freely available to subsistence farmers in poor countries. The Swiss scientists who developed this new GM plant, however, found themselves using 70 separate IPRs resting in the hands of 32 different patent holders (Potrykus 2000; ISAAA 2000). Even though the four most important private companies holding these patents agreed to make them available for Golden Rice on a royalty-free basis, and even though many developing countries can treat the technology as unencumbered within their own borders because their laws do not recognize the patents in question, the process of bringing this project to commercial completion will be legally complicated.

Some critics go further to argue that the development process in poor countries is fundamentally incompatible with the concept of IPR protection. IPRs are intended to facilitate formal transfers of technology and to create incentives for new innovations, but developing countries have historically relied on simpler expedients such as imitation and minor improvement, and these methods can be blocked by IPR guarantees (Chang 2001). Although the corporate arguments for IPRs are plausible, there is in fact little empirical evidence that stronger IPR regimes lead to increased domestic investments in research and development (R&D). This weak empirical case is acknowledged even by the World Bank, in a publication that nonetheless tends to welcome strengthened IPRs as a useful feature of the new global economy (World Bank 1999).

---

3. In 1996, the U.S. Patent and Trademark Office received an astonishing 500,000 separate applications for genetic patents and had to place restrictions on further applications (Enriquez and Goldberg 2000). To protect its ability to function, the U.S. patent office has had to consider new regulations preserving the patentability of fully characterized genes whose functions are known, but excluding uncharacterized gene fragments (such as expressed sequence tags, for which half a million patent applications are currently pending).

For purposes of policy classification here, I shall describe the most "promotional" policy a developing country could take toward GM crops as one that extends patent protection as well as plant variety protection to new GM crop varieties. This would mimic the IPR policy toward GM crops that has been adopted by the government of the United States.

A slightly less promotional IPR policy option would be to deny patent protection for life forms, but to offer plant variety protection for GM crops under a PBR system. This is the approach traditionally taken by most European governments, and it is strong enough to satisfy the most recent rules on intellectual property within the World Trade Organization. The conventional policy model for states taking this approach is to enact a plant variety protection law at home that satisfies the standards of the International Union for the Protection of New Varieties of Plants (known as UPOV), an international agreement on PBRs. The original UPOV agreement was reached in 1961, and it thus predates both the GM crop revolution and the more recent controversy over the patenting of life forms. There are currently two different UPOV agreements to which governments can adhere, a weaker 1978 version and a stronger 1991 version. For classification purposes I shall describe the IPR policies of states adhering to the 1991 version of UPOV as permissive toward GM crops, and the policies of states adhering to the weaker 1978 version as precautionary.

Under UPOV 1978, the balance is tilted less toward incentives to innovate or invest in new technologies and more toward options to use technologies that already exist. UPOV 1978 implicitly protects the traditional "farmer's privilege" to use and exchange (but not sell) seeds of protected plant varieties for propagation purposes on their own holdings. Private seed companies are understandably less enthusiastic about IPR systems that allow farmers to replant and exchange the seeds of protected varieties, so companies with valuable GM seeds to sell might seek to keep these varieties out of the hands of farmers in such countries (UPOV 1978).

The 1991 version of the UPOV Convention (UPOV 1991) provides IPRs for breeders that are nearly as strong as patent protection, and much stronger than those provided under UPOV 1978. UPOV 1991 leaves the farmer's privilege up to national laws, and hence less well preserved. It also increases the number of actions for which prior authorization from the breeder is required. The scope of actions for which prior authorization is required is expanded to include the use of harvested materials from protected varieties obtained from propagating material and so-called "essentially derived" varieties (Dutfield 1999, 20). Extending protection to essentially derived varieties was intended to prevent the practice of "cosmetic breeding" whereby breeders make only the slightest changes in a protected variety then make a claim of their own for IPRs (IDRC 2000). On the other hand, breeders themselves are still permitted to use protected varieties as an initial source of variation for the creation of genuinely new varieties, and then to market those *new* varieties without authorization from the original breeder (Dutfield 1999). PBR systems refer to this as the "breeder's exemption."

UPOV 1991 also permits member states to protect plant varieties with patents as well as PBRs. The United States follows this "double protection" option, but most European countries still expressly forbid patenting of plant varieties and operate under UPOV only.[4] The UPOV 1991 IPR standard is not quite as promotional as U.S. patent law, yet it provides quite strong IPRs to breeders. Now that UPOV 1978 has been superseded by UPOV 1991, developing-country governments need special dispensation from UPOV to accede to the less stringent 1978 version of the Convention. A number of developing countries have nevertheless followed this more cautious plant variety protection policy course (IDRC 2000). As of 2000, 14 developing countries had become formal parties to UPOV, and all were adherents to the weaker 1978 version of the Convention.

If developing-country governments want to adopt IPR policies designed completely to block the planting of GM crops within their own borders, they might decide to offer no IPRs at all for newly created varieties of plants. Nonexistent IPR guarantees are in fact widespread in the developing world, although slowing or blocking the spread of GM crop technologies has seldom been the primary motive. Many developing countries do not extend any IPR guarantees to plant breeders or to seed companies—out of tradition, and because crop variety development and seed production are still largely an individual farmer practice rather than a commercial business, and because it is a business commanded through the public sector rather than motivated through private market forces. The private international seed companies that are currently the custodians of so many GM crop technologies can be expected to view such nonexistent IPR policies with suspicion.

Simple assertions of state sovereignty also at times motivate this rejection by so many developing countries of private IPRs over plant varieties. The 1992 Convention on Biological Diversity (CBD), which was negotiated at the insistence of developing countries, assigns full legal control over the "indigenous germplasm" within their national borders to sovereign states alone (CBD 1992). Using the CBD, developing-country governments can seek rights of

---

4. In a controversial effort to harmonize rules in the European Union, the European Parliament in 1998 gave final approval to a provisional biotechnology patent directive which for the first time in European history did create a legal right to obtain patents for higher organisms such as plants and animals. The directive is weaker than U.S. patent law since it makes explicit allowance for the "farmer's privilege" to use farm-saved seeds of protected varieties, but it is stronger than a simple PBR approach because it does not include a provision guaranteeing a breeder's privilege to use patented biotechnology inventions as the initial source for creating other new varieties. The directive has been a lightning rod for criticism, and several EU member governments filed nullity suits against it (IDRC 2000).

access—perhaps through compulsory licensing—to the commercial benefits that might derive from any improved plant varieties (GM or otherwise) developed using their indigenous plant materials (Dutfield 1999, 25). Such claims can once again keep private investors or companies at a distance.[5] Alternatively, some developing-country governments have asserted that commercial rights over improved varieties of plants must always be shared with the communities of rural farmers who, through patient seed selection practices over the years, did the most to improve natural varieties. The "farmer's rights" asserted in this fashion again can undercut private corporate incentives to invest (Dhar and Rao 1999). Finally, some developing-country governments might find it objectionable on ethical grounds to grant intellectual property rights to commercial breeders who alter the nature of living things such as plants or animals. Whether the living things in question were altered through a genetic engineering technique (such as recombinant DNA) or through conventional plant breeding does not have to be the issue. The result can be the same: an IPR policy that blocks or slows down investments in the spread or innovation of new GM crops.

Private investments in the development of GM technologies can also be blocked if a government embraces an IPR protection policy on paper but refuses to enforce that policy, a practice of obvious concern to the international private sector. The U.S. International Trade Commission has estimated losses to U.S. corporations from IPR piracy in the late 1980s at US$40–60 billion annually (Dutfield 1999, 10). Private companies that have invested in the development of GM technologies may not wish to share them in countries where IPR piracy losses threaten to swamp any possible commercial gain.

Table 2.1 summarizes these four different policy postures toward GM crops within the area of IPRs. Developing-country choices among these various policies can be important for the future of GM crops even if GM was not the issue that drove the choice process. A variety of non-GM crop issues could have been more salient, including the desire of national plant breeders to upgrade PBRs simply for non-GM variety development purposes. Just as important, governments in the developing world are now also confronting a need to strengthen their IPR protection policies as a condition of participation in the WTO. An agreement on Trade-Related Aspects of Intellectual Property Rights (TRIPS) was concluded in the 1986–93 Uruguay Round of multilateral trade negotiations in the General Agreement on Tariffs and Trade (now the WTO). TRIPS was advanced in the Uruguay Round largely by the United States,

---

5. The United States at first refused to sign the CBD, for fear that it might require compulsory licensing if a patented product developed from the indigenous germplasm of a country was being sold to that country. The United States later did sign the CBD, as qualified by some unilateral interpretations. Even so, the U.S. Senate refused to ratify, so the United States still does not participate as a formal party.

TABLE 2.1 Intellectual property rights policies toward GM crops

Promotional policy	Permissive policy	Precautionary policy	Preventive policy
Full patent protection, plus plant breeders' rights (PBR) under UPOV 1991	PBR under UPOV 1991	PBR under UPOV 1978, which preserves farmer's privilege	No IPRs for plants or animals; or IPRs provided on paper that are not enforced

which values IPR protection partly because of the rapidly growing portion of its own exports that contain a high intellectual property content (up from 9.9 percent in 1947 to 27.4 percent by 1986). In order to protect itself from further piracy of the intellectual property content of these exports, the United States insisted that the final Uruguay Round agreement contain a requirement that all parties to the WTO honor IPRs, including IPRs for plant varieties. The TRIPS agreement came into effect on January 1, 1995. An additional five-year grace period for compliance (until January 1, 2000) was offered to all developing countries, with the "least developed countries" having until 2006 to comply. The WTO planned to begin reviewing developing-country legislation for TRIPS compliance in 2000–2001, but a number of developing countries were at the same time seeking a blanket extension of their transition periods.

This new IPR obligation in the WTO is significant, but the final TRIPS language on plant variety protection was not as strong as the United States would have liked. Article 27, Paragraph 3, of the TRIPS agreement does require members to provide for the protection of plant varieties, but this does not have to be done through U.S.-style patents. It can also be done through various unique alternative *sui generis* systems, including some relatively weak systems such as UPOV 1978. This *sui generis* loophole was strongly criticized by the U.S. Commissioner of Patents and Trademarks as "an international giant step backward as far as biotechnology is concerned" (Cantley 1996, 14). The TRIPS agreement also allows governments to exclude inventions from patentability when necessary to secure "*ordre public* or morality." These vague terms might well be interpreted inside the WTO on a case-by-case basis to include values such as human, animal, or plant life, and even environmental protection (Dutfield 1999).

Because of such loopholes, governments in the developing world do not have to adopt a fully promotional or even a permissive IPR policy toward GM crops in order to comply with TRIPS. A national plant variety law modeled after the 1978 version of UPOV, an approach classified here as "precautionary," is likely to be enough to satisfy the WTO (Dutfield 1999). In any case, small poor countries will probably not be the first to be charged with non-compliance, because the U.S. government is likely to take commercial significance into account when selecting cases for future legal action inside the WTO.

Biosafety Policy

A second area in which developing-country governments must make policy choices regarding GM crops is the area of biological safety, or biosafety. Possible risks to the biological environment should be a consideration when any new plant variety is introduced into a farming system, whether it is a GM plant or not. In most industrial countries, well-developed biosafety policies governing the movement or release of new plants into the environment were in operation long before the development of GM crops. For these industrial countries the challenge has been to decide how much additional care, if any, to impose on GM plants. In many developing countries, however, the formal screening of new crop plants for biosafety had not been a well-established procedure prior to the onset of the GM crop revolution. Screening had traditionally been viewed as a costly and technically demanding task, secondary in importance to boosting farm yields. For these countries the challenge has been to put in place biosafety policies strong enough to catch possible biohazards associated with GM crops, yet not so strong as to block the use of GM crops on speculative grounds alone, or so demanding as to exceed the technical or administrative capacity of government regulators.

A number of possible hazards to the biological environment must be considered whenever a new plant or animal species (GM or otherwise) is introduced into a farming ecosystem. These risks include harmful competition with or direct damage to desirable species, unwanted gene flow (including transgene flow) into close relative species, unwanted resistance to herbicides among weeds, unwanted resistance to insecticides among pests, the creation of new strains of viral pathogens, and possible loss in biodiversity. The GM crop traits most often associated with these risks are the herbicide tolerance trait found in several commercial GM soybean and canola varieties and the insecticidal trait found in a number of commercial GM varieties of maize, cotton, and potato. Fears are expressed that, if a trait for herbicide tolerance breeds into the wild relative of a GM crop through unintended gene flow, the wild relative could then itself develop enough herbicide tolerance to become a "superweed" more difficult for farmers to control. In the case of insecticidal GM traits such as the bacterium *Bacillus thuringiensis* (Bt), the fears most often expressed are that pest populations could eventually develop resistance to the trait, and therefore become more difficult to control, and that non-target species (for example, monarch butterflies) could suffer unintended damage perhaps by ingesting pollen containing the insecticidal trait (Winrock 2001).

Technical specialists continue to debate whether crops that have been transformed through recombinant DNA (rDNA) deserve to be screened more tightly for such hazards than conventional crops. Early opinion in the United States held that GM crops could be screened in essentially the same manner as conventional crops. In 1987 the United States National Academy of Sciences determined that "[t]here is no evidence that unique hazards exist either in the use of r-DNA techniques or in the transfer of genes between unrelated organisms. . . . The risks associated with the introduction of r-DNA organisms are the same in kind as those associated with the introduction in the environment of unmodified organisms and organisms modified by other genetic techniques" (cited in U.S. Congress Committee on Science 2000, 36). Several years later a similar view was endorsed by the Organisation for Economic Co-operation and Development (OECD 1993). This original approach began to lose political support, especially in Europe, soon after the first widespread commercial releases of GM crops in 1995–96. Groups opposed to GM crops began to highlight the possible superweed and pest resistance effects of such crops and to demand much tighter biosafety screening processes. It was in the context of this intensifying biosafety debate in the industrial world, in the middle and later years of the 1990s, that officials in many developing countries were forced for the first time to confront the issue.

In the developing world, the greatest rural biosafety hazards have traditionally come not from crops at all, but from various exotic wild species introduced intentionally or accidentally into farming ecosystems from distant regions. Crop plants (GM or otherwise) are seldom invasive because crops bred for human use are generally noncompetitive outside of their well-protected and cared-for farming environments. Wild exotics, on the other hand, can do devastating damage if introduced into farming environments in circumstances in which the natural competitors or the other species that usually control them are absent. By some estimates, such exotic species movements, having nothing to do with genetic engineering, currently generate losses to agriculture in the developing world of tens of billions of dollars annually (Bright 1999). Examples include losses from virus-carrying whiteflies in South and Central America, and from the exotic cattail weeds now strangling rice in the wetlands of northern Nigeria. In China, when *Spartina anglica* was introduced from Europe in 1963–64, it caused huge losses of biodiversity in fish ponds and shrimp ponds in southern coastal areas, and more than 200 indigenous species were made extinct.

Still, prudence requires that all agricultural crop plants be screened for possible unintended biohazards. Industrial countries have done this routinely for new varieties of both GM and non-GM agricultural crops, growing them initially in closed greenhouses, then in isolated field plots, and then subjecting them to testing in a variety of settings and climates prior to commercial registration and release (Nuffield Council on Bioethics 1999, 98). In the United States, most new varieties of crops, both GM and non-GM, are subjected to 50 or more site-years (number of sights times number of years) of testing for various performance and biosafety characteristics before being selected for seed production and farm use (U.S. Congress Committee on Science 2000).

When establishing their own biosafety policies, developing countries once again face a choice of whether to be promotional, permissive, precautionary, or preventive toward GM crops. Governments wishing to be fully promotional might impose either no biosafety screening at all for new crops (GM or otherwise) or just token screening for appearance's sake. One token screening procedure might be to grant biosafety approval to all new crops (GM or otherwise) that had received approval in some other country. Alternatively, field trials might be required only to learn the agronomic performance traits of crops while paying little attention to biosafety concerns. Such a lax approach might be adopted on grounds that poor countries, especially those with unmet food production needs and limited resources, cannot afford the same costly biosafety screening procedures that have been adopted by rich countries. Arguably these poor countries should concentrate on the real biohazards already posed by wild exotics, rather than the mostly hypothetical threats posed by human-developed crops (GM or otherwise). If only token biosafety testing or screening were required for GM crops, the commercial release of new GM seeds into the farming environment could take place without delay as soon as those transgenic seeds had been bred for the agronomic traits (such as color, yield, or cooking properties) desired by local farmers.

A slightly less promotional approach would be to screen new GM crops case by case for a full range of conventional biosafety risks, using standard scientific experiments to look for actual demonstrations of such risks based on the intended use of the new crop. Under this approach new GM crops would not be viewed as inherently more dangerous to the environment because of their novel transgenic nature. They would be screened much like non-GM crops. This would be a permissive approach to the regulation of GM crops in the sense that it would not set a higher biosafety standard for GM than for non-GM, yet it would not be a lax or a lenient approach so long as the common biosafety standard was set high enough.

One example of a permissive approach based on a high overall standard is the approach taken by the United States. The philosophy underlying this U.S. policy was originally set out by the U.S. Office of Science and Technology Policy in 1986, in its *Coordinated Framework for Regulation of Biotechnology.* Under this framework, biotechnology products are regulated according to their intended use, not according to how they are produced (for example, GM versus non-GM).[6] All new crops in the United States (GM and non-GM) are subjected to regulation for biosafety under the Animal and Plant Health Inspection Service

---

6. One minor exception can be found in a separate set of National rDNA Research Guidelines, which evolved in the United States in the 1970s to impose special precautions on rDNA research.

(APHIS) of the U.S. Department of Agriculture (USDA), which exercises its authority through a permit system. A company, a university, or a public sector research scientist wishing either to move or to field test a GM crop must obtain the necessary permits before proceeding, and to secure such permits must provide detailed information about the plant, including all new genes and gene products, their origin, the purpose of the test, how the test will be conducted, and the specific precautions that will be taken to prevent escape of pollen, plants, or plant parts from the field test site. An APHIS scientific reviewer evaluates the possible environmental impacts of the proposed test, including impacts on endangered or threatened species, and other non-target species. For GM crops with which it has had prior experience, APHIS has developed a notification procedure to simplify the process of obtaining a field trial permit. U.S. officials assert that in no instance to date has any GM plant approved for field testing by APHIS created an environmental hazard or exhibited any unpredictable or unusual biosafety behavior, compared with similar crops modified through conventional breeding methods (McCammon 1999).

After field testing and before new plants can be produced on a wider scale and then sold commercially in the United States, their creators must again petition APHIS for a "determination of non-regulated status." This requires the submission of still more information: field test results, information about in-direct effects on other plants, and data on the environmental consequences of introduction, including the adverse consequences. All petitions are published in the Federal Register and the public are given time to comment. APHIS then grants the petition only if it determines that the plant poses no significant risk to other plants in the environment and is as safe to use as more traditional varieties (USDA 2000c).

In the United States it is thus APHIS, rather than the Environmental Protection Agency (EPA), that performs the core environmental impact assessment function for new crop varieties, as required under the U.S. National Environmental Policy Act (U.S. Congress Committee on Science 2000). Only if a GM crop has been engineered to produce pesticidal substances (such as Bt) must EPA also give approval, under its larger regulatory mandate in the area of pesticides. In approving insecticidal GM crops the EPA may decide to impose crop management requirements designed to minimize pest resistance problems. To date, EPA asserts that it has found no documented case of environmental harm caused by a plant pesticide created through biotechnology (U.S. Congress Committee on Science 2000, 22).

The U.S. government practice of using traditional agencies such as APHIS and EPA to screen novel GM crops for biosafety strikes some as much too permissive. Critics seeking tighter biosafety regulations in the United States launched an early legislative effort in Congress to pass a bill that would govern GM organisms separately. This effort fell short in 1989, however, and since that time the United States has applied to GM products essentially the same laws it had previously applied to biohazards from non-GM crops and from chemicals. Procedurally, GM plants producing pesticidal substances (such as Bt) are regulated by the EPA under the Federal Insecticide, Fungicide and Rodenticide Act (FIFRA), which was originally designed to regulate conventional chemical pesticides.[7] The most extreme expression of this permissive practice of viewing GM as nothing new came in 1997 when the United States Department of Agriculture (USDA) proposed that GM foods might even qualify as "organic" if grown in the same manner as conventional organic foods. Under a wave of objections from organic farmers this proposed rule was abandoned by USDA and replaced by a definition of organic that specifically excluded GM crops.

In most of the industrial world beyond the United States and in most of the developing world there has been a greater readiness to view biohazard threats from GM crops as sufficiently distinct to require separate legislation and separate regulatory consideration. Biosafety legislation in most European countries, for example, clearly distinguishes between genetically modified organisms (GMOs) and non-GM organisms, and all organisms that originate from rDNA are subject to specific GMO regulations.[8] This distinction has not emerged from any scientific demonstration that GM crops pose a higher biosafety risk than conventional crops; it responds instead to the novelty of the transformation process and the accompanying possibility that conventional screening processes might not capture all the risks of this process. Despite this separate approach to screening GMOs for biosafety, a number of GM crops were approved for commercial use in the European Union between 1992 and 1998, including three canola varieties, four corn varieties, and one soybean variety. Only after GM crops became politically controversial did the nations of Europe begin placing such a high separate screening standard on GM crops as to bring new commercial releases to a halt. New approvals were halted in 1998, and in June 1999 the European Council recommended a thoroughly precautionary approach when dealing with notifications and authorizations for placing GM products on the market: so long as the effects of GM products on the environment or human health were not certain, new approvals should come to a halt (Nelson et al. 1999). In 2001 the European Union began moving toward a possible lifting of the approval freeze, but only by setting in place even more precautionary approval standards and processes.

---

7. Under FIFRA, the EPA is mandated to consider human safety, the fate of the substance in the environment, its effectiveness on target pests, and also any effects on so-called "non-target" species, so pesticidal GM crops do not escape extra EPA screening for biosafety on top of APHIS screening.

8. In the European Union, governmental screening of GM crops for biosafety is legislated and regulated at the national level. An EU-wide Council Directive (90/220) has been promulgated on the release of GM organisms, but all such EU directives (as opposed to regulations) need to be implemented through national legislation (Nelson et al. 1999).

This recent European approach of singling out GM crops for much tighter biosafety regulation on grounds of scientific uncertainty rather than on grounds of demonstrated risk is what I shall call here a precautionary approach. Under this approach, governments hold back on the field testing or commercial release of GM crops not just to avoid risks that are known and have been demonstrated, but also to avoid hypothetical risks that have not yet been demonstrated. We might expect this to be a favored strategy in some wealthier societies where the need to accept even a hypothetical biosafety risk is low because farmers have already become productive growing non-GM crops, and because consumers are already well fed. We might not expect such a highly precautionary biosafety approach to be favored in developing countries where farmers are not yet productive and where people are not yet well fed. Michael Lipton captures this expectation in the form of a rhetorical question:

> The probable costs of the (mostly remote) environmental risks from GM crops to developing countries, even with no controls, do not approach the probable gains of GM crops concentrated on the local and labour-intensive production of food staples. Are lower safety standards justified because, by producing more and better food and more jobs for the undernourished, or by reducing agrochemical use, GM crops save many more lives than they cost and improve more lives than they worsen? (Nuffield Council on Bioethics 1999, 73)

Some developing countries might nonetheless justify using a precautionary biosafety approach, perhaps by pointing to the especially valuable or vulnerable endowments of genetic resources that exist within their borders. Alternatively, poor countries with a weak technical capacity to distinguish between demonstrated biohazards and those that are only hypothetical might feel safer treating all of them as real.

At an even more cautious extreme, a fully preventive approach to GM crop biosafety could also be adopted by governments in developing countries. Under this approach, new GM crop varieties would not be screened case by case, either for demonstrated risks or for remaining uncertainties. Instead, the presence of risk would simply be assumed without testing, based on the novelty of the GM process alone. Permission to release GM crops into the environment would be denied on principle.

Table 2.2 summarizes these four different biosafety policies toward GM crops. How will developing countries make this biosafety policy choice? Given the imperative so many developing countries face to deliver improved social welfare benefits to the rural poor, given the somewhat lower priority these countries have traditionally assigned to environmental protection, and given the known biosafety costs associated with some conventional non-GM crop production systems (for example, spraying insecticides), we might expect most developing countries to adopt at least a permissive posture toward GM

TABLE 2.2 Biosafety policies toward GM crops

Promotional policy	Permissive policy	Precautionary policy	Preventive policy
No careful screening, only token screening, or approval based on approvals in other countries	Case-by-case screening for demonstrated risk, based on intended use of product	Case-by-case screening for scientific uncertainties as well as demonstrated risks, owing to the novelty of the GM process	No careful case-by-case screening; biosafety risk assumed because of GM process

crops in the area of biosafety policy. The case-study evidence to be presented in Chapters 3, 4, and 5 will go sharply against this expectation.

Trade Policy

Trade policies toward GM crops, especially on the import side, are a third area in which we can judge the decisions of governments to promote or to prevent the use of GM crop technologies. In developing countries where a local scientific capacity to generate GM crop technologies may still be absent, imports of transgenic plant materials or seeds may be the only way to get a GM crop revolution started. By the same token, blocking or regulating such imports may be the easiest way to stop GM technologies from spreading internally.

It will not always be easy to separate new restrictions on GM crop imports from the various other formal or informal crop import restrictions that most developing countries already have in place. Most countries, including poor countries, went into the current transgenic crop revolution with a full set of policies in place to govern imports of agricultural plants, seeds, and commodities, including restrictive animal and plant health protection policies known as sanitary and phytosanitary (SPS) policies. Plants destined for release into the environment cannot be imported in most countries without a period of quarantine or at least screening to check for the presence of pest infestations or crop disease. Commercial seed imports have tended to be restricted even more tightly in the developing world, partly out of a commercial motive to protect the domestic market for "infant" national seed industries. Foodgrain and other commodity imports also tend to be restricted in the developing world—typically through import license systems—as part of a larger policy effort to promote national self-sufficiency in basic food supplies. All of these restrictions preceded the GM crop revolution, so classifying additional import restrictions that might be targeted specifically at GM crops can call for some fine distinctions.

On the export side too, classifying developing-country trade policies toward GM crops can be difficult. This stems in part from the highly differentiated and still rapidly evolving international consumer response to GM foods. To the extent that international markets will accept GM food exports, developing countries seeking to boost exports may have a strong incentive to plant GM crops so as to lower production costs and remain internationally competitive with other exporters. To the extent that international markets reject GM foods, developing-country governments will have an incentive to keep GM products out of export channels and perhaps even block the planting of GM crops altogether, so as to keep their nation a GM-free source of supply.

On both the import and the export side, developing-country trade policies toward GM crops will also tend to be driven by internal policy choices in other areas, particularly biosafety and food safety. For example, a government that has adopted a highly precautionary internal biosafety policy toward GM crops might be expected to select an equally restrictive policy toward the import of GM seeds or plants. In the area of food safety and consumer choice, if a nation imposes strict labeling requirements on GM foods internally it can be expected to impose strict labeling requirements on GM food imports at the border as well.

With these considerations in mind, what would a promotional trade policy toward GM crops look like? A fully promotional trade policy would encourage the import of GM seeds or plants by imposing little or no screening on such imports. On the export side, the payoff from such a promotional policy might be greater agricultural productivity and export competitiveness, assuming consumer acceptance abroad. If importer resistance were encountered, the promotional response might be to seek a remedy through the WTO.

A permissive trade policy toward GM crops would impose SPS regulations on GM seed and plant material imports, but these regulations would be science-based in accordance with WTO standards and no more strict than the regulations imposed on non-GM seeds or plant materials. Restrictions on seed imports would be neutral between GM and non-GM. Some commercial restrictions on commodity imports might be imposed to promote local food production, but these would again be neutral between GM and non-GM commodities.

Governments following a precautionary import policy would impose a separate and more restrictive set of regulations on imports of GM plant materials and seeds, either on conventional SPS grounds or on some more expansive biosafety grounds. These special regulations might take the form of additional testing or information requirements, labeling requirements, or perhaps a prior notification requirement imposed on exporters. One framework importers might use to pursue a prior notification approach is contained in the January 2000 Cartagena Protocol on Biosafety, to be discussed below. For GM commodities destined for consumption rather than environmental release, specific information and labeling requirements could be imposed, including some that might require segregating GM from non-GM products in bulk commodity shipments.

If made strict enough, precautionary import regulations such as these could be such an inconvenience to exporters as to block virtually all movements of GM materials, seeds, or commodities into the country. If so, the policy might have to be reclassified as preventive rather than merely precautionary. A more direct way of taking a preventive approach would be to impose an outright import ban or an open-ended moratorium on the import of GM commodities, products, or plant materials. Some developing-country governments might decide to embrace a fully preventive trade policy toward GM crops as a means of avoiding the cost of having to segregate GM from non-GM commodities internally and as a way to keep the country entirely GM free, perhaps in hopes of boosting exports to foreign customers wary of eating GM foods. This could be seen as a rational choice even if large price premiums for non-GM commodities had not yet emerged on the world market. Given the practical difficulty a nation would face imposing product segregation or reverting to GM-free status once it had permitted the planting of GM crops, the mere possibility of future price premiums for non-GM commodities could motivate a decision to use import policy to remain GM free (IBAC 1999).

Table 2.3 describes the trade policy gradient from promotion to prevention of GM crops. When developing-country governments choose from among these various trade policies toward GM crops and materials, they will have to be aware of their larger trade policy obligations in several important international institutional settings, especially the WTO and the CBD. To what extent

TABLE 2.3 Trade policies toward GM crops

Promotional policy	Permissive policy	Precautionary policy	Preventive policy
Encourage import of GM seeds or plant materials through little or no regulation; use World Trade Organization to insist upon market access for GM crop exports	Regulate GM seeds and plant materials, but in accordance with World Trade Organization and no more tightly than non-GM	Regulate imports of GM seeds and materials separately from non-GM, and also more tightly; impose labeling requirements on imports of GM foods or commodities	Block all GM imports so as to remain GM free, either for non-trade purposes or in hopes of exporting GM free so as to capture export premiums

do these larger obligations constrain the trade policy choices developing countries can make about GM crops?

Within the WTO, it is permissible under the terms of the Sanitary and Phytosanitary (SPS) Agreement (negotiated in the 1986–93 Uruguay Round of multilateral trade negotiations) to impose import restrictions on GM crops and materials, or on other imports, but only if those restrictions are based on a scientific assessment of the risks; only up to the point necessary to achieve the public health or environmental goals in question; and only if the import restrictions in question are not arbitrarily or unjustifiably at variance with other government policy measures. Nations can use import policy to pursue any level of health or environmental protection they wish, but these import policies must be appropriate to that standard, they must be based on sound science, and they must be consistent with internal policies so as not to discriminate against trade (Roberts 1998). The more difficult question is whether governments can restrict imports when a new technology (such as genetic engineering) raises questions about public health and environmental safety that have not yet been answered fully by science. Article 5.7 of the SPS Agreement states that, if the relevant scientific evidence is "insufficient," governments may restrict imports on a provisional basis while they seek additional information about the risks posed by a recently identified hazard (Roberts 1998). The WTO is thus willing to tolerate temporary import restrictions that are *provisional* while new information is being sought, but it does not endorse the use of open-ended *precautionary* import restrictions as a substitute for gathering more information.

These WTO obligations under the SPS Agreement might seem to constrain developing-country governments wishing to select a precautionary or preventive import policy toward GM materials and crops, in the absence of scientific evidence connecting those materials or crops to new human or environmental risks. GM seed companies and governments in countries that are currently producing and exporting GM crops (such as the United States, Argentina, and Canada) are certainly hoping the SPS Agreement will operate in this fashion. For several reasons, however, developing-country governments actually retain considerable freedom in choosing their import policies toward GM crops and materials, despite the terms of this SPS Agreement.

First, the WTO has a long tradition of giving developing-country governments special and differential treatment compared with industrial-country governments (in Europe, for example). Developing countries tend to be given more room and more time to bring their import policies up to WTO standards. Second, GM crop exporters that might use the SPS Agreement to discipline importers will probably be watching the big commodity importers—especially the countries of industrial Europe and East Asia—more closely than the lower-income developing countries, most of which tend not to be large commercial importers of farm commodities. Third, developing countries may be able to choose precautionary or preventive import policies toward GM crops and materials in the years ahead because of language contained in the January 2000 Cartagena Protocol on Biosafety negotiated among the parties to the Convention on Biological Diversity (CoP CBD 2000).

This new Protocol on Biosafety was drafted specifically to govern international trade in living modified organisms (LMOs), including all transgenic organisms other than pharmaceuticals for humans. Because the Protocol was drafted and negotiated primarily by environment ministry representatives, it tends to favor environmental over commercial trade interests. In its preamble it explicitly endorses "the precautionary approach" toward protection of biological diversity, and in the body of the text it states repeatedly (in Articles 10 and 11) that "lack of scientific certainty due to insufficient relevant scientific information and knowledge" should not prevent states from taking precautionary import actions in the area of transboundary movements of LMOs.

The Protocol also creates some additional procedures and institutions that importing states can use, if they wish, to screen imports of GM crops and commodities more carefully according to a precautionary approach. Under an advance informed agreement (AIA) procedure created by the Protocol, before governments import any LMO intended for environmental release for the first time they are permitted to require prior notification from exporters of the identity and biosafety classification of the organism, its center of origin, including its habitats and where it may persist or proliferate, a description of its characteristics, the nucleic acid or modification introduced, the modification technique used, its intended use, the quantity to be transferred, a risk assessment report (as detailed in a separate annex of the Protocol), suggested methods for safe handling, and its regulatory status within the state of export, among other things. The costs of risk assessment under this procedure are to be borne by the exporter ("notifier"). For LMO shipments intended for direct use as food or feed or for processing, this AIA procedure does not apply, but potential exporters are nonetheless obliged under the Protocol to provide timely information about such LMOs (to a newly created international Biosafety Clearing-House) soon after putting them into the market. When LMOs are shipped internationally, labels will now be required (under Article 18) identifying the shipments as possibly containing LMOs and as "not intended for intentional introduction into the environment." The Conference of Parties of the CBD is to produce more precise identification requirements for such LMO shipments within two years after the Protocol enters into force. The Protocol was opened for signature in May 2000 and is to go into force after 50 countries have ratified it.

A casual reading of the language in this new Protocol on Biosafety might give the impression that GM crops and materials pose a distinct threat to importers, a bit like hazardous chemicals or toxic wastes. The environmental ministers who drafted the Protocol did indeed model the AIA procedure for LMOs on the "prior informed consent" procedure written into an earlier Basel

Convention on transboundary movements of hazardous wastes. There is thus ample room under the terms of this new Protocol for developing countries to select restrictive import policies toward GM crops, seeds, or plant materials.

It remains to be seen how the import-limiting steps and procedures endorsed by the new Protocol will come to be viewed alongside the less precautionary SPS rules of the WTO. The preamble to the Protocol does not resolve this matter, asserting ambiguously that the Protocol "does not imply a change in the rights and obligations of a Party under any existing international agreement" (such as the SPS Agreement), while also asserting that the Protocol is not "subordinate" to those other agreements. Exporters of GM crops, led by the United States, fought to insert a so-called "savings clause" in the operational part of the Protocol that would have upheld the authority of existing WTO rules, but they were blocked from doing so by the European Union and by most developing countries (*Inside U.S. Trade* 2000, 25). Particularly in light of the content of the new Protocol on Biosafety, it should be assumed that governments in the developing world will enjoy considerable international freedom to place selective restrictions on imports of GM crops and materials in a precautionary or even in a preventive manner if that should become their policy choice (Gupta 2000).

Food Safety and Consumer Choice

In Europe, Japan, and the United States, food safety and informed consumer choice issues tend to dominate the public debate over GM crops. These issues are also under debate within the developing world, though typically as a secondary concern to issues such as IPR, biosafety, or trade. Food safety is of course a serious problem in poor countries, but the principal hazards come from unclean water, a lack of refrigeration, or unsanitary conditions for food transport, storage, marketing, and preparation, not from the still mostly speculative risks associated with GM. In the poorest countries, concerns about food prices and simple food availability can loom much larger than food safety.

Eating any food can be dangerous because of natural allergic reactions, because of the natural toxicity of some foods (cyanogenic glycosides produce cyanide in cassava if it is not prepared properly), and most of all because of food contamination risks. Rich as well as poor countries confront these dangers. In the United States, the Centers for Disease Control and Prevention in Atlanta reported in 1999 that 76 million Americans suffered at least one food-borne illness annually, and 5,000 of these Americans died, often from diseases transmitted from undercooked meat or unwashed kitchen utensils or cutting boards (Stout 1999). The question governments now must confront is whether or not GM crops have created new food safety risks in addition to these existing risks.

Judging the "safety" of food is hardly an exact science. Through experimental testing it is possible to certify that some foods will be dangerous for human consumption, but certifying a complete *absence* of danger is (like any effort to prove a negative) beyond the capability of experimental science. Complicating any process of safety certification is the further problem that food ingredients safe to consume in some concentrations can become unsafe if the concentration increases; it is the dose that makes the poison. In practice, regulators tend to recognize foods as safe based not so much on laboratory science as on social history. If a food has been a familiar component of the human diet for some time without any known adverse effects, it comes to be "generally recognized as safe"—or GRAS, to use the terminology of the United States Food and Drug Administration (FDA). Whole foods (fruits, vegetables, and grains) that are GRAS usually receive minimal regulatory oversight.

The GM version of a food that is GRAS may not, of course, deserve the same classification. Genetic engineering—like conventional breeding—can transfer new or unfamiliar toxicants, nutrients, or allergenic proteins into an otherwise safe food. In the United States, as a result, the FDA has since 1992 required that all new ingredients introduced by genes in GM foods receive pre-market regulatory approval if the new ingredients are not substantially equivalent to those already in foods (Nelson et al. 1999). This substantial equivalence approach is controversial because it downplays the novelty of foods that have been altered only slightly through genetic engineering, yet it is the approach originally embraced by a range of technical specialists far beyond the United States. This approach was proposed in 1993 by the OECD and endorsed in 1996 by the Food and Agriculture Organization of the United Nations and the World Health Organization.

The GM foods that have been developed and placed onto the market for human consumption using this inexact approach have shown no evidence, so far, of being any less safe than their conventional counterparts. One study of consumer experiences with GM foods produced by the U.K. Nuffield Council on Bioethics reached the following conclusion in May 1999:

> We have not been able to find any evidence of harm. We are satisfied that all products currently entering the market have been rigorously screened by the regulatory authorities, that they continue to be monitored, and that no evidence of harm has been detected. (Nuffield Council on Bioethics 1999, 126–127)

This positive regulatory record was briefly marred in the United States in 2000 when a GM variety of Bt maize called StarLink approved by the EPA and FDA only for animal feed and not for human food use came to be intermingled in marketing channels with maize varieties that were approved for human food use. Regulators had refused to approve this GM variety for human consumption because it contained a protein not substantially equivalent to those already in the food supply. The protein was not a known allergen, but its slow digestion in the human gut was judged a source of risk if it were an allergen. The regulatory error came in assuming that a GM maize variety approved only for animal feed use could be released into the hands of private farmers with no danger of its leaking into human food use market channels. When some leakage was subsequently detected, efforts were made to withdraw StarLink corn from the market, but by then the low-level intermingling of some StarLink maize with approved varieties had spread widely, even into export channels. The discovery of unapproved StarLink in shipments to Japan prompted a temporary cutback in all Japanese imports of corn from the United States pending an agreement on new inspection procedures (DeCola 2000).

In this context, what are the policy options available to developing-country governments? If the goal is to promote planting of GM food crops, they might conclude from the record that GM foods have not yet been associated with any new consumer safety risks serious enough to warrant special treatment. GM food crops would then be regulated for food safety in the same manner and with the same degree of strictness as non-GM crops, and no separate labeling of GM foods would be required. This describes the regulatory approach toward GM foods taken by the United States. In 1992 the FDA issued a statement that foods derived from new plant varieties produced through biotechnology would be regulated under the existing federal Food, Drug, and Cosmetic Act (FD&C Act) to meet the same standards as those created through traditional means. Under this law, the FDA uses the characteristics of the food, not the processes used in its production, as the basis for regulation (ADA 1995). Direct consultations with the FDA were originally voluntary for food companies submitting applications for approval, but meeting the standards of the FD&C Act has always been a legal requirement. To demonstrate they have met these standards, industries must generate a substantial range of toxicologic and product safety data.[9] In April 2000, the FDA sought to strengthen consumer confidence in GM foods by tightening these procedures to require producers to notify the FDA before marketing a GM food and to provide the agency with data affirming the food's safety. Still, the FDA asserts that under its original procedure it had seen "no evidence that the bioengineered foods now on the market pose any human health concerns or that they are in any way less safe than crops produced through traditional breeding" (Thompson 2000, 3).

As of 2000, the United States had still not imposed separate labeling requirements on GM foods, because the FDA did not consider the rDNA

---

9. New GM food products must be assessed for unexpected genetic effects, toxin levels higher than those for other edible non-GM varieties, nutrients differing from those in traditional varieties, introduced genes from sources associated with human allergies, new composition, marker genes that potentially could transfer antibiotic resistance to clinically significant organisms, plants not originally developed as food products, and nutrients or toxins making the product unacceptable for animal feed (ESCOP 2000).

method used in the development of GM plants to be material information needed by consumers (any more than consumers needed to know if a food plant was a hybrid or not). The FDA has encouraged voluntary labeling but only if it is truthful and not misleading, and it has not required different labeling for GM crops except when the use of biotechnology has resulted in a significant change in the composition of a food product, such that its nutritional content no longer conforms to normal expectations or when a new health or safety risk exists (Korwek 2000). Even then, the label is required to describe only the change in quality of the product not the GM process that produced the change.

A less promotional stance would be to acknowledge consumer anxieties about novel GM foods by imposing a separate screening process on those foods and by imposing distinctive labeling requirements on those foods. If these separate screening processes and label requirements are made lenient enough, they might give consumers a greater sense of informed choice without imposing too costly a burden on GM food producers or food industries.

Many European countries have attempted this permissive approach, albeit with uneven results. European governments initially approved GM foods for human consumption using methodologies not so different from those of the FDA. Yet a number of these governments—led by France, Denmark, and the Netherlands—went on to require labels on GM foods so as to inform consumers of the GM content. In January 1997 the European Union sought to harmonize these emerging national labeling regulations for GM foods by adopting a Novel Foods Regulation (CE 258/97). This required foods to be labeled GMO if the food contained materials not present in its non-GM counterpart that were possibly consequential for the health of certain groups of people. The European Union then tightened this rule in 1998 to require simply that all foods containing detectable rDNA-derived materials above a level of 1 percent per ingredient must be labeled as containing "genetically modified" ingredients, with or without demonstrated connections to human health (European Commission 2000b).

EU officials adopted this "consumer's right to know" approach even while continuing to assert that all GM foods approved for consumption in Europe were as safe as their non-GM counterparts. In 2000 the European Commissioner for Health and Consumer Protection, David Byrne, asserted: "Right around the world, the scientific evidence is that there is no problem with GMOs over and above any other food" (Birchard 2000, 321). Since the 1986 mad cow disease scandal, however, consumers in most European countries have been less willing to trust such pronouncements from official food safety regulators. They have insisted on mandatory labeling of GM foods so they can make up their own minds about what might be safe to consume. In 1999 the European Commission issued a White Paper signaling its intent to address the lack of consumer confidence in food in Europe by creating a European Food

Authority to provide independent scientific advice in the food safety area by the end of 2002; in the meantime it would rely heavily on a "right to know" food labeling approach (Byrne 2000).

The European Union's labeling policy was designed to be affordable to agricultural industries and to permit GM and non-GM foods to be sold in supermarkets side by side. The 1 percent per ingredient content-based standard meant that processed GM foods in which the transformed DNA or the associated proteins were no longer detectable or existed in only trace quantities would not have to be labeled. For foods with detectable GM content, enforcement could be achieved through physical testing[10] rather than through costly identity preservation systems based on an unbroken tracking of specific products all the way through marketing, processing, and retailing channels. To avoid a "may contain GM" label, some more generic segregation of non-GM from GM foods would be needed, but segregation of animal feeds would not be necessary and the relatively high content threshold could make the costs of segregation more affordable. At zero tolerance for GM content, the cost of segregating non-GM soybean protein meal might add 50 percent to the market price, but at a 1 percent tolerance level only a 15 percent increase might be implied (OECD 2000; USDA 2000b).

In practice, this permissive "informed consumer choice" approach has not operated as intended in Europe. Consumer anxieties regarding GM foods became so strong as to induce a voluntary decision by many private food chains to advertise themselves as GM free and to remove labeled GM products from retail shelves completely (in effect removing consumer choice). Also, since most farmers in Europe have decided not to plant any GM crops, the problem of product segregation has mostly been moot. Some GM commodities continue to be imported, but almost entirely for use in processed foods or animal feed. In the case of maize, in 1998 the European Union stopped its purchases of bulk shipments of maize from the United States altogether, even for animal feed use, because the internal halt of new European Union GM crop approvals meant bulk shipments from the United States might begin to contain some new GM maize varieties approved in the United States but not yet in the European Union.

Japan provides another example of an essentially permissive labeling policy toward GM foods. In August 1999 Japan's Ministry of Agriculture,

---

10. Physical tests of samples of unprocessed foods using techniques such as polymerase chain reaction can detect the presence or absence of either the transformed DNA or the protein resulting from that DNA. Such tests can cost US$400–700 per sample and take 3–10 days. Novel proteins can also be detected in GM crops using immunoassays, which are capable of determining GM concentrations quantitatively. One form of immunoassay (the immunochromatographic strip test) has been developed for testing GM crops in the field. The cost is less than US$10 per test, it can be performed truck-side, and it takes only 5–10 minutes (Stave and Durandetta 2000).

Forestry and Fisheries outlined a mandatory set of labeling requirements for roughly 30 food products made from GM corn and soybeans, to go into effect in April 2001. This policy covers only corn and soybeans and imposes no labeling requirements on foods that are sufficiently processed so that genetically modified DNA or proteins no longer exist—such as soy sauce, soybean oil, corn oil, corn syrup, corn flakes, or brewed beer. The market disruptions implied by this regulation could be minimal because GM corn and soy products are not being grown by farmers in Japan, and Japan's corn and soy imports— which do have GM content—are used almost exclusively either for animal feed or for processed foods that will escape labeling requirements (*Inside U.S. Trade* 1999). Yet in Japan, much as in Europe, many private food industries— including even brewing industries—have decided to go well beyond official regulations and impose a GM-free standard on themselves voluntarily.

A still more precautionary food safety approach would be for governments to screen GM foods not just by a separate standard but by a higher standard, one designed to test not only for familiar food safety hazards but also for more speculative or hypothetical hazards. In Europe, in response to consumer anxieties, movement toward this much higher and thoroughly precautionary safety standard—one that would shift the burden of proof even more heavily onto those who wanted a new product approved—was formally recommended by the European Council in June 1999. In terms of labeling policy, a more precautionary approach might require positive labeling for all approved GM foods, including all fresh and processed foods and even meat from animals raised on GM feeds. This system would not be enforceable through physical testing because GM labels would be required even on processed foods that no longer retained any detectable transformed DNA or proteins. The only way to enforce this comprehensive mandatory labeling requirement strictly would be to require totally segregated marketing channels for all GM versus non-GM commodities and animal products, from the farmer's field all the way to the consumer's plate. This would be a costly option for any nation growing, importing, or exporting GM foods, since it would require a massive duplication of equipment and facilities in food (and feed) transport, storage, and processing. Yet it would be the only way to give all consumers at home (or customers abroad) a fully informed choice. In 2001 the European Union began moving toward a labeling policy that would include processed GM foods, plus a separate approval and "traceability" requirement even for GM feeds and feed products.

A comprehensive labeling system based on identity preservation might actually be beneficial for GM crop producers in the long run if a second generation of products with distinct benefits for consumers is permitted to come onto the market. The first generation of GM crops has been easy for some consumers to spurn because they have offered clear benefits to producers, patent holders, and some input suppliers but few tangible benefits for consumers (Falck-Zepeda, Traxler, and Nelson 1999). A second generation of "output trait" GM foods might become sought after by consumers. Some examples of output trait GM foods already developed but not yet on the market include soybeans with increased protein and amino acid content and crops with modified fats, oils, and starches to improve both processing and digestibility (OECD 2000).

GM foods engineered to confer health benefits could be of particular interest to consumers in the developing world. Rice engineered to code for beta carotene, which is used by the body to make Vitamin A, is one possible example. In 1999, researchers in Switzerland inserted genes from a daffodil and a bacterium into rice plants to produce a modified grain with significant beta carotene to help meet vitamin A requirements in a typical Asian diet. This research team has also been able to add a gene from a French bean to double the iron content in rice, potentially useful because 40–50 percent of children under the age of 5 in developing countries are iron deficient. These products are years away from the market, but the International Rice Research Institute (IRRI) is currently working on methods to transfer the genes required for beta carotene biosynthesis into the popular *indica* rice varieties preferred by most Asian consumers.

If a developing country wished to adopt a food safety policy that would be fully preventive toward GM crops, it could either ban the sale of GM foods entirely or require positive labels on all foods derived from GM crops that would include stigmatizing warnings. This ultra-precautionary step to protect domestic consumers against hypothetical or unknown risks could also be embraced as part of a larger effort to remain a GM-free country, so as to be able to seek premiums in export markets for GM-free foods and commodities. A total ban might be cheaper for this export purpose than market segregation, because duplication of storage, transport, and marketing facilities would not be required. Everything exported from the country would be credibly presented as GM free, because everything sold within the country would also be GM free.

Table 2.4 summarizes the policy choice gradient in the food safety policy area. As in the trade policy area, governments in the developing world have considerable freedom to choose among the four different approaches. They have some international obligations in the food safety area within the Codex Alimentarius Commission and the WTO and under the new Biosafety Protocol, but these obligations impose few significant constraints.

The Codex Alimentarius Commission is a voluntary, consensus-based, and traditionally industry-dominated body for setting international food standards. It suggests common food safety standards that tend to be low rather than high, but Codex does not prevent governments from setting higher standards inside their own borders if they wish. Codex has considered calling for manda-

TABLE 2.4 Food safety and consumer choice policies toward GM crops

Promotional policy	Permissive policy	Precautionary policy	Preventive policy
Draw no regulatory distinction between GM and non-GM foods, either when testing or when labeling for food safety	Use a separate but comparable safety standard when screening GM foods; Require labels for some GM products, but based only on detectable GM content	Use a separate and higher standard when screening GM foods, and require comprehensive labeling of all GM foods enforced through fully segregated market channels	Ban sales of GM foods or require warning labels that stigmatize GM foods as unsafe for consumers

tory labeling of GM foods, but objections from the United States and Argentina have blocked this initiative so far. Codex did establish a working group to consider the need for special rules related to GM food; the group held its first meeting in March 2000 and was not scheduled to complete its work until 2003 at the earliest. The chair of this group, a U.S. Department of Agriculture official, has defended the prevailing approach based on scientifically certified risks, whereas European delegates and environmental activists (who are permitted to participate in Codex meetings) call for a more precautionary approach. The Codex is important because its decisions on food safety have traditionally been considered authoritative by the World Trade Organization.

Traditionally, the WTO has also been relatively lenient in the food safety policy area. The WTO is empowered by its parties to scrutinize food labeling policies, but mostly to ensure they are not unwarranted "technical barriers to trade." Labeling standards can be weak or strict, so long as they do not treat imported products differently from home-grown products. The WTO may actually be sympathetic to strict labeling requirements on imports if they are used by regulators as an alternative to outright import restriction (Sykes 1995).

A wide range of food safety policy choices, especially for importers of GM crops, is also preserved under the terms of the new Biosafety Protocol within the CBD. The Protocol gives governments ample room to be precautionary when making import decisions in circumstances of scientific uncertainty, but it imposes no obligation on them in this direction. Exporters of GM crops, seeds, and materials are obliged to share more information with importers under the Protocol, and commodities available for export that may contain GM products are to be labeled as such, but the Protocol stops short of requiring exporters to use segregated market channels and it imposes few new obligations, beyond information sharing, on importers. When selecting food safety policies toward GM crops, then, governments in the developing world are relatively unconstrained by international obligations.

Public Research Investment Policy

Nearly all developing countries make significant public investments in agricultural research, for the good reason that these investments have long tended to generate high rates of economic return in the form of increased farm productivity. During the Green Revolution era, public sector national agricultural research systems emerged as an important key to development progress in many poor countries. Because these national systems were constrained by scarce resources, they often had to make difficult choices about which crops or farming systems they would emphasize. Now, because of the GM crop revolution era, they also face a difficult choice about how much research emphasis to place on genetically engineered crops. Should they use scarce treasury funds or donor funding to make public investments in this new technology?

If the GM crop revolution is ever to reach poor farmers in the developing world, local public research and extension services will almost certainly have to play a large role. The international private biotechnology and seed companies that have led in the commercialization of GM crops in the developed world have paid less attention to the needs of poor farmers in tropical countries, partly because these farmers are a less attractive customer base than wealthy commercial farmers in the industrial world and partly because developing-country governments have traditionally sought to preserve monopolies for local or state-owned companies in national seed markets. From this historical starting point of a heavy reliance on the public sector, if developing-country governments wish to promote a GM crop revolution within their borders they will almost certainly have to engage their own national agricultural research and extension services in the task.

Advocates of modern crop biotechnology have looked for ways to help national agricultural research systems in poor countries play this necessary supporting role. Over the 10-year period 1985–94, prior to the actual commercial release of GM crops in rich countries, various bilateral and multilateral international donor organizations contributed an estimated total of US$260 million in grant funds to international biotechnology initiatives primarily focused on public sector research and capacity building in the developing countries. In addition, the World Bank extended US$150 million to support national agricultural research projects in biotechnology in developing countries during this period (Komen 1997). Much of this early support focused on the least controversial crop biotechnology techniques, such as tissue culture and marker-assisted plant breeding, but work on genetic engineering techniques was initially emphasized as well.

Some of the most effective international support for national systems in the area of GM biotechnology applications has come from the Rockefeller Foundation, which over the period 1985–2000 spent some US$100 million to fund plant research and training for over 400 developing-country scientists working primarily on rice biotechnology in a variety of international locations (Conway 2000). Some of these Rockefeller efforts operated through research institutes in wealthy countries (for example, the Golden Rice project in Switzerland) and some through international institutes in poor countries (for example through the International Rice Research Institute in the Philippines), but Rockefeller's International Rice Biotechnology Program also trained national scientists and helped equip national public sector research laboratories directly, in China, India, and Thailand.

National agricultural research systems in poor countries have also received government-to-government assistance in biotechnology. The United Kingdom's Overseas Development Administration, the French government's Center for International Research on Agronomy for Development, and the Swiss and Swedish governments have all provided bilateral assistance. The U.S. government, through the Agency for International Development, initiated a six-year project in 1992 in Agricultural Biotechnology for Sustainable Productivity (ABSP) with a budget of US$6.7 million, focused primarily on Egypt, Indonesia, and Kenya. The government of the Netherlands, through its Directorate-General for International Cooperation, began to advance agricultural biotechnology in the developing world in 1992 through a Biotechnology and Development Cooperation Special Programme with a five-year budget of US$27 million, although this program was designed to rely on local farmer-led initiatives rather than centralized national agricultural research systems. Public sector international institutions have also supported biotechnology, including the Consultative Group on International Agricultural Research (CGIAR) chaired by the World Bank. Twelve of the CGIAR's international agricultural research centers—including IRRI—have invested in a range of biotechnology research programs, including in some cases genetic engineering. Yet, of the CGIAR's total budget of US$340 million, less than 10 percent goes to any kind of biotechnology, and the links between CGIAR research programs and national programs in the developing world are not always tight (Serageldin 2000). International donor funding is important in the area of crop biotechnology in developing countries, but to date it has not been as important as national funding. For biotechnology research and development in poor countries overall, roughly twice as much funding has come from the resources of national governments as from international bilateral and multilateral donors (Persley 2000).

Operating in this international environment, governments in developing countries seeking either to promote or to block the planting of GM crops might once again take a wide range of policy stances. At a promotional extreme, they might invest not only donor funding but also their own national treasury resources in the local development of their own varieties of GM crops. For this purpose international training and research contacts would be essential, and a minimum of in-country research facilities and capabilities would also have to be established and maintained, including adequately equipped crop transformation laboratory facilities. Unfortunately, international support for laboratory creation and maintenance in the area of modern crop biotechnology tends to be scarce. On average less than 10 percent of donor funding in biotechnology is directed toward the construction of facilities or the acquisition of new equipment (Komen 1997). Some of the specialized laboratory equipment needed for the conduct of modern GM crop research—including fine chemicals or documentation and communication equipment—may not be available for local purchase in many poor countries or may be costly to maintain locally. International support is more often available for the training of local scientists in the key specialties (such as molecular biology) required for GM crop research. To retain these scientists within national institutes, however, governments will have to provide adequate salary compensation and adequate competitive grant funding. For this purpose, only a sustained outlay of significant national treasury resources is likely to suffice.

The specialized knowledge and facilities needed to maintain adequate biosafety are another expense that developing countries must confront if they desire to pursue an ambitious local GM crop development program. Biosafety is one area where the international donor community has been more than willing to provide policy guidance and some technical training, but the implications for poor countries of accepting international assistance in this area can be mixed. Industrial-country donor agencies and international organizations such as the Global Environment Facility within the United Nations Environment Program naturally model their international training and assistance programs on the GM crop biosafety systems already in place in rich countries. Officials in developing countries who agree to operate under these demanding biosafety rules must then confront the high costs of creating a state-of-the-art physical and institutional national biosafety infrastructure for GM crops, including well-trained biosafety committees at each research location and the specialized laboratory and greenhouse facilities needed to develop GM crops under fully contained conditions prior to environmental release. The donor community has been less willing to finance the complete infrastructure needed to implement a strong biosafety program.

Governments pursuing this fully promotional public research investment strategy would not want to refuse international donor assistance or to avoid productive partnerships with the international private sector, particularly for the purpose of gaining access to proprietary GM crop technologies. In some circumstances, national research systems might need to enter into a joint venture or a licensing agreement with patent-holding international seed companies or foreign universities. This reliance on the international private sector can be reduced, however, if sufficient national investments are made at the same time. A strong national GM crop research capacity strengthens the hand of government scientists when negotiating the terms of any international GM crop technology transfer with private foreign companies. It also improves public control over the final research outcome, to ensure benefits to poor subsistence farmers growing "orphan crops" as well as to more advantaged farmers growing commercial crops.

Governments in poor countries that want to be slightly less promotional toward GM crops might opt not to invest significant treasury resources for the task of plant transformation in local laboratories through rDNA genetic engineering techniques. Rather than trying to replace or compete with international companies and international research centers that have already developed potentially useful GM crop applications, national governments in developing countries could use conventional breeding and backcrossing techniques to move the desirable GM traits of crops that have already been transformed into local varieties of those same crops. Governments wishing to pursue this approach would not have to train and equip molecular biologists for local crop transformation efforts, but they may have to make significant new public investments in conventional plant breeding sciences, in greenhouse and field testing facilities, and in the more expensive biosafety containment facilities needed for GM crops.

A more precautionary approach toward public sector research in GM crops would be to allow the transfer of GM traits into local cultivars through conventional breeding if donors wished to pay for that activity, but to spend no significant national treasury resources for such a purpose. If donors or international agricultural research centers wanted to sponsor the backcrossing of desirable transgenes into local germplasm and if they wanted to finance the associated upgrading of facilities and biosafety training, this would be welcomed. But treasury funds would be reserved for more traditional agricultural research activities, including perhaps some non-GM biotechnology research in areas such as tissue culture or molecular marker assisted breeding.

A preventive approach to GM in public research investment would simply be to make no investments at all—either treasury funds or donor funds—in any transgenic technology work.

Table 2.5 presents the gradient of policy choice in GM crop research investment. The implicit choices made do not have to be GM motivated of course. In some cases governments might fail to spend significant treasury funds on GM crop research because they have decided to slight agricultural research overall, both GM and non-GM. The result would be a cautious research investment strategy toward all agricultural technologies, with minimal productivity enhancement gains expected across the board. We would still classify this as a precautionary policy toward GM crops. Nor is the embrace of

TABLE 2.5 Public research investment policies toward GM crops

Promotional policy	Permissive policy	Precautionary policy	Preventive policy
Spend treasury as well as donor resources on crop transformation capacity	Spend treasury resources to breed into local varieties the desirable traits of GM crops already transformed elsewhere	Spend no significant treasury resources on local breeding or transformation of GM crops; allow donor funding of GM trait transfers through conventional breeding	Spend neither treasury nor donor funds on the development of any GM crop technology

a promotional public investment policy toward GM crops any guarantee that useful GM technologies will actually reach farmers. These new technologies might be blocked within the laboratory itself if the transformations attempted are unsuccessful, or they might remain confined to the laboratory if the downstream links between public researchers and private seed marketing institutions or national extension agents are poorly developed. IPR or biosafety constraints could also keep a potentially useful new GM crop technology restricted to the laboratory.

Summary

This chapter has outlined a series of alternative policies toward GM crops for governments in developing countries, ranging from the most promotional to the most preventive. I have sketched out these policy alternatives in five significantly separate settings: IPR, biosafety, trade, food safety and consumer choice, and public research investment. This policy classification scheme is not intended to prescribe any one pattern of choices overall for the developing world. The purpose of this chapter has been classification rather than prescription. Nor does this classification scheme assume that governments will want to make the same kind of policy choice in all five venues. For example, a developing-country government might wish to pursue a promotional public investment policy toward GM crops while at the same time holding on to a less promotional IPR policy, hoping that strong private IPR guarantees will not be needed to induce private investments if sufficient expenditures are being made by the state. Alternatively, a government might decide to pursue a highly promotional IPR policy as an alternative to an expensive public sector investment policy.

Developing countries' policy choices toward GM crops and foods might also differ depending on such things as their size, their research capacity, their trade posture, and the distinctive agricultural development challenges they face. Countries with large commercial seed markets, for example, may be able to attract significant private sector investments and technology transfers even without the lure of a strong IPR policy. Countries with rural environments that contain wild relatives of GM crops may wish to select a more cautious biosafety policy. Countries starting with small internal research capacities have fewer options to pursue a promotional public investment strategy than countries starting with a large or strong capacity. In countries where most foods are sold in rural markets without any packaging or labeling, some of the consumer choice policy options listed here could simply be moot.

Overall, we might expect the actual policy choices made by developing countries to depend most heavily on their differing agricultural development circumstances or their external trade postures. On the one hand, developing countries with significant unsolved agricultural development problems might be expected to take at least a permissive view of GM crop technologies. For example, if farmers in these nations might stand to gain from a GM crop technology already successfully in use in the industrial world (for example, herbicide-resistant soybeans or Bt cotton), we might expect the government, other things being equal, to embrace a permissive or even a promotional set of policies toward that technology. On the other hand, a nation's trade posture could offset such a permissive or promotional policy choice. Developing countries heavily dependent on commodity exports to Europe or Japan might be driven, other things being equal, toward an outright preventive internal policy toward GM crops given the recent backlash against those crops by consumers in Europe and Japan.

In the case-study chapters that follow I explore such possibilities by examining actual GM crop and food policy choices made in 1999–2000 by officials in Kenya, Brazil, India, and China. Each of these countries is individually significant, each is a regional political leader, and each in different ways is heavily dependent on the performance of its agricultural sector. We shall see in chapters 3–5 that in Kenya, Brazil, and India highly cautious biosafety policies have until now blocked the legal planting of any GM crops. This is despite a stated preference by top political leaders in each of these countries that the modern biotechnology revolution in agriculture be allowed to go forward. Chapter 6 shows that only in China, so far, have biosafety policies been permissive enough to support an official release of any GM crops. Chapter 7 explores some reasons for these divergent and partly unexpected choice patterns.

3 Governmental Caution and Weak Capacity in Kenya

The GM crop revolution has not yet spread in any significant way to farming in Africa. As of 2000, transgenic maize and cotton were being grown commercially in small quantities in only one country in the region, South Africa. The rest of Africa was still GM free. This slow uptake of GM technologies is potentially troublesome from a food production standpoint, given the low farm productivity and unmet food needs of the region. One-third of children in Africa under the age of 5 years still suffer from malnutrition, owing in part to the poor performance of agriculture. Over the past two decades the value-added provided by African agriculture has increased at an average annual rate of just 2.5 percent, while population was growing at an average annual rate of 2.7 percent (World Bank 2000).

This chapter examines the case of Kenya, a nation of 30 million people in East Africa where poor farmers face crop disease and pest damage problems potentially treatable with GM crops. Yet as of 2000 the Kenyan government had not yet approved any GM crops for commercial use. Officials in 2000 finally approved field trials for one minor GM crop, a virus-resistant variety of sweet potato, but international plans to develop and introduce GM varieties of maize—a more important food crop in Kenya—were lagging behind. We shall see that this retarded spread of GM crop technologies in Kenya is in part a result of the government's own official policies. Under the policy classification scheme presented in the previous chapter, Kenya's official stance toward GM crops is in most respects highly precautionary.

GM Crop Opportunities in Kenya

Kenya, like so many other countries in Sub-Saharan Africa, has been struggling for decades with unsolved farm productivity problems. Whereas most farmers in Asia and Latin America experienced significant yield gains during the Green Revolution of the 1960s and 1970s, most farmers in Africa did not. Between 1970 and 1983, new high-yielding rice varieties spread to about 50

44

percent of Asia's vast rice lands but to only about 15 percent of Sub-Saharan Africa. Improved wheat varieties spread to more than 90 percent of Asia and Latin America, but to only 59 percent of wheat lands in Sub-Saharan Africa. Partly as a result, average cereal yields in Africa are now less than half those of Asia and Latin America. In some parts of Africa, owing to soil nutrient depletion, yields are actually declining from their already low levels. Farmers have tried to overcome these problems by expanding cropland and grazing areas, which is an environmentally unsustainable option. Roughly 5 million hectares of forest are lost every year in Africa, mostly to crop area expansion. The rate of growth of food production on a per capita basis has nonetheless remained negative in Africa since about 1970, and, despite increased commercial imports and food aid, per capita food consumption in Africa (of cereals, roots and tubers, and pulses) since 1980 has also shown a downward trend (DeVries 1999).

As with Africa in general, so now with Kenya in particular. For a time during the 1970s Kenya was something of an agricultural success story in the region thanks to its embrace of more productive hybrid maize seeds. Even small farmers participated in this technology success. Between 1975 and 1991, the percentage of Kenya's small farmers on high-potential lands that had planted improved varieties of maize—particularly hybrids—increased from 16 percent to 95 percent (Lynam and Hassan 1998). According to data from the Food and Agriculture Organization of the United Nations (FAO), between 1980 and 1990 Kenya's index of total farm production increased by 52 percent.[1] In the 1990s, however, Kenya was not able to sustain this rate of growth. Total agricultural production increased by just 3 percent overall between 1989–91 and 1999, at a time when population was growing far more quickly. On a per capita basis, total farm production in Kenya actually decreased by 18 percent over the course of the 1990s. Because 75 percent of all Kenyans still depend upon farming for income and employment, this low farm productivity implied an expansion of poverty and malnutrition, particularly in rural areas. As of 1996–98, agricultural value-added stood at only US$228 per agricultural worker in Kenya, which is half the average of all low- and middle-income developing countries and actually lower than it was in Kenya 20 years earlier. This is one reason 23 percent of all Kenyans under the age of 5 still suffer from chronic malnutrition (World Bank 2000).

Kenya's farm productivity problems since the 1980s have included a general deterioration in the nation's public institutions and political environment, increasingly difficult soil and water constraints, and continued crop

---

1. These measures are from the FAO's index of agricultural production. This index is based on a sum of price-weighted quantities of different agricultural commodities, except those used for seed or feed. See FAOSTAT Database, item code 2051 (http://apps1.fao.org).

damage from pests and disease. GM technologies cannot address the first of these factors at all, nor are there any transgenic crops yet available that address soil and water constraints, but some of Kenya's pest and disease problems are more clearly suited to a GM technology response. As one example, stem borers are a major pest problem for Kenyan maize farmers, causing estimated losses of 15–45 percent of each maize crop, reducing farm earnings every year in Kenya by an average of 6.3 billion shillings (Obure 2000). Farmer surveys in some districts in Kenya have ranked insect pests—and specifically stem borers—as the preeminent production problem, even ahead of soil fertility problems or labor and land shortages. In Kenya's major mid- and high-altitude maize-growing areas stem borers are farmers' primary concern outside of drought (Mugo 2000). If Kenya's farmers were to gain access to a locally adapted variety of Bt maize, this severe production problem might be more effectively controlled. In South Africa, farmers in KwaZulu-Natal province have used a Bt variety of cotton since 1998 and experienced a 20 percent increase in yield owing to better insect control (Thomson 2000). African farmers in Kenya facing crop pest and disease problems might be expected to gain similar advantages.

Top leaders in Kenya have endorsed the promise of GM crops. In August 2000 the president of Kenya, Daniel T. arap Moi, wrote in a letter to President Bill Clinton of the United States that he saw the new developments in bio-technology as "offering great hope and promise." He pointed out: "While the Green Revolution was a remarkable success in Asia it largely bypassed Africa. Today the international community is on the verge of the biotechnology revolution which Africa cannot afford to miss" (Moi 2000).

Kenya's most prominent agricultural scientists are open to the GM crop revolution. Cyrus G. Ndiritu, then the director general of the Kenya Agricultural Research Institute (KARI), wrote in 1999: "The need for biotechnology in Africa is very clear" (Ndiritu 1999, 7). Dr. John S. Wafula of KARI elaborates: "[A]griculture in Kenya is plagued by a host of pests and diseases such as streak viruses, weevil, leaf blights, animal diseases and pests which work to reduce yields. The methods employed in addressing problems of agricultural development and food production in Kenya are still largely based on traditional approaches. . . . The emergence of biotechnology and its ease of integration with conventional plant and animal breeding provides an opportunity for reducing problems of sustainable productivity" (Wafula 1999, 2).

Whereas agricultural researchers in Kenya have shown an eagerness to develop and exploit potentially useful GM crop technologies, and top political leaders have occasionally endorsed this strategy in principle, the policy choices made by most Kenyan officials have been far more tentative. In vital areas such as intellectual property rights (IPR) policy, biosafety, trade, and public research investment the relevant authorities in Kenya have so far made precautionary choices, rather than promotional or even permissive choices. This official caution by government authorities is one reason farmers in Kenya have not been permitted to grow GM crops.

Intellectual Property Rights Policies

In Kenya, as in much of the rest of Africa, there is no strong tradition of IPR guarantees. Prior to 1989 Kenya had no independent patent system of its own, partly because of its colonial history. Local registration of patents was allowed only for patents already granted in the United Kingdom. In 1989 a National Council for Science and Technology Legal and Patents Committee proposed a new patent law for Kenya, to be based on a world standard set by the model of the World Intellectual Property Organization (WIPO). In the following year a new Industrial Property Act was implemented in Kenya, with registrations to be provided through a new Kenya Industrial Policy Office within the Kenyan Ministry of Trade and Industry. This Industrial Property Act followed the WIPO approach of giving protection only to inanimate inventions, thus generally excluding plant and animal varieties (Juma 1989).

Kenya had also embraced a weak law on plant breeders' rights (PBR) since 1977, but researchers at KARI feared the country would be cut off from conventional international seed exchange if this law was not strengthened. Accordingly, Kenya passed a stronger PBR law in 1991, and subsequently set up a PBR Office within the Kenya Plant Health Inspectorate Service (KEPHIS), a state corporation created in 1996 independent of KARI. KEPHIS is designated to perform a variety of increasingly vital functions in Kenyan agriculture, including not just the granting of PBRs but also plant quarantine, fertilizer and seed quality control, grading and inspection, and final biosafety testing.

With its stronger PBR law in place, Kenya approached the Convention of the International Union for the Protection of New Varieties of Plants (UPOV) in 1993 with a request to accede to the 1978 version of UPOV. Kenya preferred this earlier version to UPOV 1991 because it preserved the traditional farmer's privilege to replicate and replant protected seed varieties on their own farms (Dutfield 1999). Some North African countries—such as Morocco—were passing PBR laws that conformed to the higher 1991 UPOV standard, but Kenya was not ready to take this step (ABSP 1998).

Kenya enacted a new PBR law and sought accession to UPOV in part to facilitate international seed exchange, but also to comply with the nation's new obligations under the 1993 Agreement on Trade-Related Aspects of Intellectual Property Rights (TRIPS) in the World Trade Organization (WTO). Recall that, according to this agreement, Kenya had to embrace either patent protection for plants or some unique alternative *sui generis* system by January 2000. The WTO had given the "least developed countries" until 2006 to comply with TRIPS, but Kenya fell into the cohort that faced the 2000 deadline. Kenyan officials assumed that if the country's PBR laws were strong enough to be judged acceptable under UPOV 1978, it would be credited with meeting this WTO obligation. Kenya's effort to accede to UPOV 1978 was finally success-ful in March 1999, after a lengthy process that included a delay to complete technical corrections to Kenya's own internal 1977 and 1991 PBR laws. With-out this permitted delay Kenya would have missed the deadline for acceding under UPOV 1978 and might have been obliged to accede under the 1991 version instead.

Kenya can thus be classified as having adopted only a precautionary IPR policy for attracting GM crop technologies. The relatively weak UPOV 1978 standard does not provide patent protection and so does not prevent farmers from replicating and replanting seeds on their own farm; nor does it prevent breeders from freely using protected varieties or varieties essentially derived from those that are protected as an initial source of variation for the creation of their own new varieties. Under this relatively weak IPR standard, private companies might have little incentive to engage in GM crop technology re-search in Kenya or bring their own more valuable proprietary GM crop tech-nologies into Kenya, since the research results might not be protected from independent commercial use by other breeders in Kenya and the GM seeds would not be protected from on-farm propagation, exchange, and replanting by farmers.

Given the relative weakness of Kenya's IPR policies, will there be alterna-tive ways to encourage private companies to bring GM crop technologies into the country? One approach might be to offer private foreign companies guaran-tees against commercial piracy through bilateral contractual agreements. For example, Kenya's researchers might contract for permission to use a protected GM seed technology for research purposes only. Kenyan researchers have nonetheless found it difficult to negotiate such contractual bargains because private international seed companies expect IPR piracy in Kenya and tend to drive a hard bargain. When the Rockefeller Foundation attempted at one point to sponsor an agreement between KARI, Monsanto, and the International Maize and Wheat Improvement Center (CIMMYT) to bring a GM variety of herbicide-resistant maize into Kenya, negotiations broke down after Monsanto demanded full ownership of all future research results derived within Kenya, a demand that the Kenyans understandably refused.[2]

Unresolved IPR issues might also slow down a second Rockefeller Foun-dation GM crop project in Kenya, the Insect Resistant Maize for Africa (IRMA) project. Formally presented at a stakeholders' meeting in Nairobi in March 2000, this project is again built around a KARI/CIMMYT partnership,

---

2. This effort then lapsed following an IPR challenge to Monsanto from a rival company and a court ruling that prevented Monsanto from continuing to sell the patented GM maize materials in question.

but this time for the purpose of bringing in insecticidal Bt maize rather than herbicide-resistant maize. The case for Bt maize is compelling from the vantage point of Kenya's farmers, because stem borers have recently infested up to 87 percent of Kenya's maize areas, destroying 15–45 percent of this important food and cash crop. With US$6 million in funding from the Novartis Foundation for Sustainable Development, CIMMYT and KARI scientists plan to identify Bt genes active against Kenyan stem borers (employing various Bt gene constructs already developed by CIMMYT in Mexico), use these constructs to transform maize germplasm (again in Mexico), conduct trials of the transformed germplasm in Kenya initially in biocontainment greenhouses, and then backcross the most successful samples into adapted Kenyan maize germplasm. This research and development phase of the IRMA project could run for three to five years. IRMA's ultimate goal is to help KARI gain a capacity to transform Kenyan germplasm directly in its own laboratories, without such heavy dependence on CIMMYT (Mugo 2000).

Even though this is a concessional rather than a commercial venture,[3] the IPR issues raised by this IRMA project are highly complex and far from fully resolved. CIMMYT has developed its own Bt gene constructs, yet it has also used (so far for research purposes only) GM technologies owned by private companies. KARI and CIMMYT have agreed to share any new intellectual property that emerges from the project but, when the time comes for KARI to commercialize Bt maize in Kenya, probably by licensing the backcrossed GM varieties to local seed companies, it may become necessary to satisfy multiple foreign IPR claims. CIMMYT has had to begin conducting an audit of IPR in the Bt area, simply to learn who owns what.

Private companies expect that commercially significant markets for herbicide-resistant and borer-resistant maize will eventually develop in East Africa, yet without more credible IPR protection they are not especially eager to invest in developing this market. If patented GM materials were to escape a contractual arrangement in Kenya and get into the hands of opportunistic local seed companies, it would be easy enough to identify the desirable traits of those varieties and then use conventional methods to breed those traits into local varieties for commercial sale. Under the relatively weak UPOV 1978 standards that prevail in Kenya, it would be hard to prevent local breeders from doing just that. Even hybrid seeds are not safe from this kind of piracy in Kenya. A fear that local breeders might pirate protected parent lines has so far blocked U.S. hybrid maize seed companies from producing even conventional non-GM hybrid maize seed within Kenya.

These cases notwithstanding, Kenya's relatively weak IPR policies have not been the most salient barrier to a GM crop revolution in that country. The

---

3. The Novartis seed company, which has its own Bt maize varieties, is not directly involved in the IRMA project. It is the separate Novartis Foundation that is providing financing.

earliest and most sustained effort to introduce a GM crop into Kenya involved sweet potato, not maize, and in this case corporate IPRs were never a blocking issue. Kenya's biosafety policy, not its IPR policy, did the most to slow a commercial release of these GM sweet potatoes.

Biosafety Policy

Kenya's IPR policies toward GM crops are precautionary mostly by accident —GM crops were not an issue when those IPR policies were selected. By contrast, Kenya's biosafety policies toward GM crops are precautionary on purpose, in part out of bureaucratic weakness and in part to satisfy the demands and expectations of the donor community. A number of bilateral and multi-lateral donors have advised Kenya to embrace a distinctly precautionary bio-safety policy toward GM crops and have provided assistance in the drafting of such a policy on paper. Unfortunately, these same donors have provided much less assistance to the actual operation of Kenya's biosafety policies, leaving the nation with a strong policy on paper yet with inadequate administrative and technical means to carry it out. Because of this capacity deficit, as well as a fear of being criticized by GM crop opponents and international nongovernmental organizations (NGOs), biosafety regulators in Kenya have hesitated to make timely decisions, thereby slowing the movement of GM crop technologies into the country's farming system.

Kenya's formal biosafety policy toward GM crops emerged slowly during the 1990s and is now spelled out in several official documents. The most important of these was published in 1998 by Kenya's National Council for Science and Technology (NCST); it is titled "Regulations and Guidelines for Biosafety in Biotechnology for Kenya" (NCST 1998). Preparation of this document was heavily funded by the government of the Netherlands and to a lesser extent by the World Bank and the United States Agency for International Development (USAID). These "Regulations and Guidelines" (hereafter the R&G) focus specifically on biotechnology and have emerged as the nation's most often referenced source of operational guidance on GM crop biosafety approval.

The R&G prescribes a standard categorization of different GM organisms (GMOs) based on level of biosafety hazard, and sets out requirements for the design and designation of appropriate laboratory facilities to limit the spread of hazardous GM organisms. It calls for use of containment facilities and other safeguards when carrying out work on GM organisms, procedures to use in the case of an accidental release of GM organisms, and a set of "penal sanctions" to be legislated to give final effect to the guidelines. The biosafety screening processes called for by the R&G are permissive to the extent that they prescribe standard scientific experiments as the best means to classify levels of risk to human health and to the environment from GM crops, yet elsewhere the tone of the R&G is distinctly precautionary. The document singles out GM crops for tighter scrutiny than non-GM crops and calls for attention to potential as well as scientifically documented biosafety risks from GMOs (NCST 1998, 18). The R&G also stresses uncertainty, advising that permissions for commercial release of GM crops should take into account "whether enough is known to evaluate the relative safety or risk of introduction of such organisms" (NCST 1998, 1–2). This cautious tone is in part traceable to the influence of European donor countries in the drafting process. Dutch foreign assistance largely financed the drafting, and the guidance documents used by the drafters included the biosafety regulations in use in the Netherlands, plus those used by the Stockholm Environmental Institute in Sweden. The World Bank also assisted in the R&G drafting process, providing input from several internationally recognized biosafety consultants.

To implement its R&G, NCST put in place a National Biosafety Committee (NBC) composed of persons drawn from both the public and private sectors. The NBC was appointed in 1996 and began its actual implementation of biosafety reviews in 1997. As stated in the R&G, the NBC has a wide operational mandate to review all "relevant" proposals for the importation, field trial, and commercial release of new GM crop and animal varieties, although the initial determination of relevance is made by the Office of the President, to which all formal applications regarding GM crop import, testing, or release initially must go. The NBC also has the task of reviewing the suitability of physical and biological containment and control procedures, establishing a database, maintaining a directory of experts, and keeping a record of biotechnology and biosafety activities in the country.

The NBC is designed to work at the apex of a national system of Institutional Biosafety Committees (IBCs), which must be separately formed within the various institutes conducting biotechnology research in Kenya, including KARI. These IBCs are responsible for assisting their respective institutions in drawing up the applications that must go by way of the president's office to the NBC. Applications to the NBC for the import, field trial, or commercial release of GM animals or crops must come through a relevant Kenyan institution and must first be vetted by the relevant IBC within that institution.

The NBC has been constituted since 1996 yet it still struggles to operate because of limited facilities and budget resources. The committee has 15 members, including representatives from the NCST; the Office of the President; the Ministry of Agriculture and Rural Development; the Ministry of Environment and Natural Resources; the Ministry of Education, Science and Technology; the Kenya National Farmers Union; and the universities, as well as experts from Nairobi's International Livestock Research Institute. However, the NBC's full-time professional support staff has consisted of just one person, it has had no independent facilities, and for its first two years it had no budget of its own, so it had to borrow NCST resources to cover administrative costs.

To help cover its costs, NBC has considered charging fees to its applicants (ISNAR 1999). Lacking its own facilities, a larger staff, and a secure budget sufficient to ensure database development and Internet access, the NBC has been challenged to carry out the more ambitious parts of its biosafety policy mandate, including the careful review of applications.

Given these capacity constraints, Kenya's NBC faces a difficult dilemma. When it approves the import, field testing, or commercial release of GM crops, it risks being accused of not following its own biosafety guidelines strictly enough (because of its known capacity deficits). But if it denies such approvals simply to protect its own institutional reputation, it will have moved Kenya's biosafety policies from being merely cautious to being virtually preventive. As we shall see below, Kenya's NBC has resolved this dilemma thus far by looking for opportunities to delay making decisions.

The R&G is not Kenya's only biosafety document. Elsewhere within the NCST in the 1990s Kenyan officials prepared another guidance document, a "National Biosafety Framework," which was not specific to biotechnology. This second document was also donor financed, through a grant from the Global Environment Facility (GEF) within the United Nations Environment Programme (UNEP). It too sets a cautious tone, having been based in part on UNEP's own guidelines, the December 1995 "UNEP International Technical Guidelines for Safety in Biotechnology" (UNEP 1995). These guidelines warn about the hypothetical biohazards that could result if GM organisms ("organisms with novel traits") are brought into developing countries that have weak biosafety testing and monitoring capabilities, and they go on to promote as a remedy to this problem the "advance informed agreement" (AIA) procedure that was later written into the Protocol on Biosafety of the Convention on Biological Diversity (CBD) in 2000. Since 1997, UNEP, with GEF funding, has attempted to extend these cautious biosafety guidelines to the developing world under a Pilot Biosafety Enabling Activity Project. Kenya's NCST applied to participate in this project (along with 16 other countries) and subsequently received GEF funding to conduct workshops in biosafety policy, to carry out a survey of its existing biosafety laws and capacities, and finally to produce a "framework" document to guide national biosafety policy. The drafting of this document included peer review by international experts so as to promote harmony with international standards. It is not yet clear what final authority this national framework document on biosafety policy will have in Kenya, but it could provide guidance for Kenya's eventual implementation of the AIA procedures in the Protocol on Biosafety.

Kenya's Ministry of Environmental Conservation has also produced a potentially significant document touching on biosafety policy—a Draft Bill on Environmental Management and Protection, recently under debate in Parliament. This draft bill grew out of Kenya's 1994 National Environment Action

Plan and more recently out of a 1999 sessional paper from the Environment Ministry that called for a "comprehensive statute on the environment" to formalize all legal mechanisms for environmental impact assessment, to implement international legal instruments, and also to provide judicial and administrative mechanisms for redress (Kenya, MOEC 1999, 99–101). As an act of Parliament, such a measure would enjoy greater legal status than the R&G, and might move final authority over biosafety policy closer to the preferences of the Environment Ministry rather than the NCST.

Kenya's various efforts to elaborate a national biosafety policy toward GM crops were in part driven by the practical needs of a specific GM crop project, an ongoing internationally sponsored effort to introduce a virus-resistant GM sweet potato into the country. In 1991, the Monsanto company approached USAID with an offer to give away to farmers in the developing world a coat protein gene it had discovered that conferred resistance to the Sweetpotato Feathery Mottle Virus. Monsanto saw little immediate commercial value from this gene, so it offered—through the offices of USAID's new Agricultural Biotechnology for Sustainable Productivity (ABSP) project—to make this discovery available to farmers in the developing world at no charge through a royalty-free license. Monsanto's motive was partly to build good will, but also in part to build useful institutional relationships in emerging-market countries. USAID helped put Monsanto in touch with KARI, but USAID's Biosafety Committee first insisted that the project not go forward until KARI had established a formal set of biosafety guidelines (ABSP 1998, 34). In 1992 KARI thus became the first institution inside Kenya to develop institutional biosafety guidelines, partly with ABSP assistance (Wafula and Falconi 1998, 4).

This USAID sweet potato initiative not only triggered the first writing of biosafety guidelines at the institutional level in Kenya, but also led to some practical biosafety training experience for Kenyan scientists, nine of whom were eventually instructed in gene technology at Monsanto's own labs in the United States. Within Kenya itself, USAID and Monsanto helped Kenyans prepare for the arrival of the GM sweet potato materials by assisting with two years of mock field trials in four regions of the country. The trials used non-GM versions of the plant materials that were being transformed by Monsanto in the United States. Such donor support for actual biosafety policy implementation capacity has otherwise been rare in Kenya. USAID's other agricultural policy efforts in Kenya have tended to emphasize the privatization of state functions rather than enhancement of public sector capacity. Fortunately, the World Bank has supported some actual scientific capacity-building in the area of biotechnology under Phase II (1997–2001) of its National Agricultural Research Project (NARP II). Through NARP II a consortium of donors extended US$0.75 million to KARI for agribiotechnology work, including funding for some improvements to facilities of the kind that will be needed to measure up to biosafety standards.

The other donors supporting agribiotechnology in Kenya have not focused on biosafety implementation capacity. One of the largest donors in Kenya since 1992 has been the Netherlands' Directorate General International Cooperation (DGIS) through its "special programme" for biotechnology development. The first two years of this "special programme" in Kenya consisted of a US$5 million participatory bottom–up priority-setting exercise, subcontracted by the DGIS to a local NGO named ETC-Kenya (Government of the Netherlands, Ministry of Foreign Affairs 1992). This process brought together farmers, researchers, and extensionists, as well as policymakers, but it built very little state capacity because it was intentionally run outside the regular channels of government. To ensure local ownership of the initiative, the "special programme" financed the formation of a 10-person all-Kenyan local committee called the Kenya Agribiotechnology Platform (KABP).[4] This committee—which again included NGOs, academics, and farmers as well as policymakers—eventually advised the "special programme" on the selection, management, and implementation of eight specific agribiotechnology projects in Kenya with a total budget of US$3 million for the years 1997–2001. Yet most of these projects revolved once again around community-based problem identification rather than the delivery to farmers of specific new biotechnologies. The funding was in any case later withdrawn as part of a larger decision by the government of the Netherlands to discontinue assistance policies in developing countries with bad governance such as Kenya.

In the area of biosafety policy, therefore, Kenya has responded to donor concerns by adopting a policy toward GM crops that is precautionary rather than permissive. Yet it has not received capacity-building support from the donor community to be able to implement this demanding new policy with complete confidence. Kenya's biosafety regulators have compensated by becoming still more cautious when reviewing GM crop applications, including applications for the import of GM crop materials into the country.

Trade Policy

Kenya's trade policy toward GM crops has also been highly precautionary, using import restrictions to keep most GM commodities and plant materials out of the country. These import restrictions have been imposed largely through the National Biosafety Committee, as an extension of Kenya's cautious internal biosafety policies. Under the R&G, Kenya's NBC must give separate approval

---

4. Beginning in 1994, the KABP also used "special programme" funding to create a taskforce of seven Kenyans (including a lawyer and scientists in agriculture, environment, biochemistry, and medicine), which drafted the document that eventually was approved by NCST as Kenya's R&G in 1998.

for imports of GM crop and plant materials into the country; to date the NBC has been slow to do so, primarily on biosafety grounds.

Kenya's restrictions on GM commodity imports are part of a larger policy pattern of farm trade protectionism. Historically, Kenya's commercial farmers and its parastatal agricultural industries have both sought protection at the border from international competitors. For example, Kenya's important market for (non-GM) hybrid maize seed was protected for years against foreign competitors and it remains partly closed even today. A superficially privatized government parastatal, the Kenya Seed Company, continues to enjoy 90 percent of the market, and Cargill's seed company, which was recently acquired in the United States by Monsanto, has not been given a license to sell hybrid maize seed directly into Kenya. In 1998, all of Kenya's food and animal product imports totaled only US$350 million in value.

On top of this traditional aversion to all agricultural imports, Kenya has pursued an especially restrictive policy toward imports of GM commodities and plant materials. One reason is that Kenya's GM import policies have been made and managed more by the nation's environmental and biosafety authorities than by its traditional food or agricultural policy authorities. Overall policy on GM imports has been made by Kenya's ministry of the environment as a by-product of its lead role representing the country in negotiation of the 2000 Biosafety Protocol. In the CBD Conference of Parties meetings leading up to the negotiation of the new Protocol, Kenya participated as a member of the Like Minded Group and endorsed the highly precautionary trade policy lead of that group's spokesperson, Tewolde Behran Gebre Egzhiaber of Ethiopia.[5] Kenya has thus fought for the right to restrict imports of GMOs on precautionary biosafety grounds even when the scientific evidence of risk is uncertain. The Kenyan delegation to the Protocol negotiations was drawn mostly from the Environmental and Natural Resources Ministry and from the Foreign Ministry, rather than from either the Agricultural Ministry or the Ministry of Tourism, Trade and Industry. Because the Protocol has not yet come into full effect, it remains to be seen how much it will influence import decisions in practice. Kenya's Environment Ministry may continue to favor a precautionary import policy linked to the Protocol, whereas other ministries may seek something closer to a permissive import policy following from Kenya's obligations under the WTO's Sanitary and Phytosanitary Agreement.

Whatever Kenya's general policy toward imports of GM crop or plant materials, case-by-case import approvals on biosafety grounds still must be given under the 1998 R&G by the NBC. Legally, the NBC shares this authority with KEPHIS, which has traditionally exercised authority over the issuing

---

5. Tewolde has led the Like Minded Group into a highly precautionary trade policy stance toward GM commodities, based partly on his view that poverty in Africa is "structurally rooted in prevalent North–South relationships" including trade (Tewolde 2000).

of Plant Import Permits; these legally enable the movement of all plant materials—GM and non-GM—into Kenya. But if the NBC holds back, KEPHIS cannot go ahead on its own.[6]

These cumbersome import permit procedures can be set aside quickly in an emergency. In 2000, Kenya imported maize from the United States and Canada to help feed 5 million of its citizens suddenly at risk of starvation because of severe drought. Bulk shipments of maize from these countries were likely to carry significant GM content, but one senior government official justified the decision as follows: "The government and Kenyans did not have time and the necessary scientific capacity to undertake risk assessment. Our confidence was established in the fact that if Americans are eating it, it should be safe for our starving people" (Mugabe et al. 2000).

In less urgent cases, however, the import approval process can slow nearly to a stop, particularly if biosafety risks are seen to be at issue. Consider the long delays encountered, primarily on biosafety grounds, when the NBC was asked by KARI, in 1998, for permission to bring GM sweet potato materials into the country.

Delays of one kind or another had plagued this GM sweet potato project from the start. KARI and Monsanto originally formed their partnership to bring virus-resistant GM sweet potato materials into Kenya in 1991. However, when Kenyan cultivars were taken to Monsanto's lab in the United States to be transformed, technical problems were encountered (the construct being used was old and crude by modern standards), and in the end a sweet potato variety from Papua New Guinea had to be used in place of a Kenyan variety. Delay was also encountered prior to 1998 because Kenya did not yet have its national biosafety guidelines formally in place. These guidelines were finally published in February 1998, and six months later KARI made formal application to the NBC for permission to import the materials, initially for research purposes only.

It should have been relatively easy for the NBC, on biosafety grounds, to grant this request since the possible biohazards presented were either remote or non-existent. Virus-resistant GM potato varieties were not a new technology; they had been field tested in other countries for eight years and produced commercially for two years without any evidence of biohazard. The possibility of unintended geneflow was slight because sweet potato is propagated vegetatively and hardly flowers, and when it does flower the pollen is infertile. Moreover, the sweet potato originated in Ecuador, so there are no wild relatives

---

6. It is less clear what would happen if the NBC approved an import request but KEPHIS attempted to hold back. KEPHIS believes it could block an NBC decision to import by claiming that NCST's current R&G document has not yet been drafted into a formal act of parliament. One more possible veto point over imports of GM crop materials into Kenya is the Standing Technical Committee on Imports and Exports (KSTCIE), which is empowered to review all plant material import decisions with pest and disease issues in mind.

anywhere in Africa to which the virus resistance trait could accidentally flow (Wambugu 2000). The NBC should also have been reassured that the import request came from KARI, a respected government institute, and it knew KARI would have to come back with an additional request if it wanted to proceed to large-scale field trials of the GM sweet potato, and then again if it wanted to get a final commercial release. The NBC nonetheless waited more than a year before it eventually approved KARI's application to bring these GM plant materials into the country.

Some of the delays were entirely procedural. The NBC first responded by asking KARI to vet its proposal through the Standing Technical Committee on Imports and Exports. The Standing Committee took its time but raised no serious questions and eventually gave approval. KARI then sent its proposal back to the NBC in mid-1999, again hoping for a quick positive response. When the NBC met on the matter in September 1999, however, new questions were asked, including some linked more to producer acceptance than to bio-safety. KARI was questioned about the actual benefits Kenyan farmers might get from a virus-resistant potato variety, given that weevils are actually a bigger threat in Kenya, and also about how an exotic variety from New Guinea could be bred to function properly under Kenya's specific growing conditions. These further delays were demoralizing not only to KARI but also to Mon-santo, which had been keeping the transgenic sweet potato materials ready for export in growing chambers in its own labs in the United States at a significant cost since May 1999.

The NBC finally gave its approval for KARI to bring Monsanto's trans-formed sweet potato materials into the country in January 2000, and the trans-formed materials arrived in Kenya in March 2000. Small-scale field trials were scheduled to begin at four different KARI locations later in the year, to be followed by larger trials and a commercial release some time thereafter, with further applications required to NBC in the meantime.

NBC's caution in allowing GM crop materials into the country does not appear to reflect any great concern, yet, about the export risks Kenyan farmers might face if the nation begins producing GM commodities. The sweet potato delay cannot be linked directly to fear about commercial export loss, since Kenya does not export any sweet potatoes. The impending decision to go ahead with Bt maize in Kenya has so far also been significantly decoupled from national farm export policy choices; for Kenya, maize is increasingly an import crop rather than an export crop. Total maize exports in 1998 were valued at just US$2.5 million, or less than 0.25 percent of the nation's total food and animal exports. Products from GM soybeans and oilseeds are resisted by importers in some countries, but once again this has not so far had much influence on Kenya because soybean and oilseed exports from Kenya are even smaller than maize exports. The crops that Kenya does export most heavily to Europe, such as coffee and tea, are not yet a focus of consumer GM anxieties in Europe because transformed varieties are not yet in commercial use in Kenya, or anywhere else. Consumer resistance to GM crops in Europe could nonetheless begin to reinforce Kenya's cautious import policies, as has already happened elsewhere on the continent. In 1999, in light of refusals by some European importers to accept Namibian beef from animals fed with GM maize, Namibia asked the government of South Africa to guarantee that none of the maize it was shipping for feed purposes to Namibia was GM (Van Der Walt 2000).

Food Safety and Consumer Choice Policy

Farmers in Kenya are not yet growing any GM foods and only a small part of Kenya's food supply is supplied through imports. The government has therefore not yet felt significant pressure to develop a food safety or consumer choice policy specifically addressing GM crops. Public health officials in Kenya would be unlikely in any case to target the GM issue for priority given the far more pressing concerns Kenya's food consumers routinely face. The 1998 R&G document for the regulation of GMOs makes no reference to consumer food safety issues. Because Kenya does not yet have a separate food safety or labeling policy toward GM products, by default in this one policy area its stance is nominally promotional rather than precautionary.

In Kenya, food safety policy is still governed by the 1980 Food, Drugs and Chemical Substances Act of the Laws of Kenya (Chapter 254), which is administered by the Ministry of Health. This food safety law predates the development of GM foods and is designed to protect against more conventional concerns such as the sale of unwholesome, poisonous, or adulterated food or food sold deceptively or prepared under unsanitary conditions. Because this law predates the GM crop revolution, it refers only to chemical substances, ingredients, and additives in food, not to GM content or the GM process (Laws of Kenya 1980). The Minister of Health, in consultation with a Public Health Board, can make regulations under this law about the labeling and packaging of foods being offered for sale or the use of any substance as an ingredient in any food, and can declare any food (or drug or chemical substance) to be "adulterated" according to the standards of the country. The Ministry of Health can also inspect and report to Kenya's Customs Office the import of unsafe foods into the country.

Under subsidiary legislation in Chapter 254 the Ministry of Health also has jurisdiction over food labeling policy in Kenya. The law specifies that no person shall sell a manufactured, processed, or prepackaged food unless a label has been affixed or applied to that food. The label must carry the common name of the food, the brand name if any, the contents in terms of volume, number, or weight, the name of any preservatives used, food coloring or artificial or imitation flavoring added, and "any other statement required under the provisions of the regulations" (Laws of Kenya 1980, 254). Again, the language of this labeling law predates the GM crop revolution, so it makes no reference to GM foods. When the language refers to food additives, it is only to "chemical" additives.

Kenya's Ministry of Health has many problems other than food safety to worry about, including large-scale outbreaks of deadly or crippling diseases such as polio, malaria, and HIV/AIDS. To the extent that food safety is an issue in Kenya, official concerns focus more on sanitary storage and preparation, refrigeration, and adulteration than on genetic modification. This reflects a low level of consumer protection awareness overall in Kenya and the more obvious severity of non-GM food safety concerns, as well as the fact that GM crops are not yet being grown in the country.

If Kenya were to begin growing GM crops—such as the virus-resistant sweet potato—and if Ministry of Health officials in Kenya were then to decide that consumers deserved a right to make an "informed choice" about consuming GM foods, practical problems of various kinds would arise. A truly comprehensive labeling policy would be difficult to devise because a large share of the food sold and consumed in Kenya today is not "manufactured, processed, or prepackaged" and consequently has not fallen under any labeling requirement at all. Most food sales in rural Kenya are still made by individuals who bring unprocessed or unpackaged foods to market directly from their own farms. If smallholding farmers in Kenya eventually begin growing transgenic varieties of maize or sweet potato, they will offer these items for sale unpackaged and unlabeled in hundreds of different tiny rural market settings, beyond the easy reach or control of public health officials.

These issues are just now beginning to confront Kenyan officials. Except in the earlier case mentioned of food aid shipments of maize from the United States and Canada, the government has been able to avoid choice by asserting that GM foods are not yet on the market in Kenya. Imported GM foods (especially imported GM maize starch, and also GM soy) are in fact being sold in the country in small quantities but until recently there has been no need to admit this officially. This could change under the terms of the Biosafety Protocol, which will oblige exporters to give official notice to importers when commodity shipments might contain GM varieties. It remains to be seen whether at this point Kenya might choose to move toward an internal GM labeling requirement of either a permissive or a precautionary variety.

Public Investments in GM Crop Research

If Kenya wants to be an early participant in the GM crop revolution, it will have to make substantial public resource commitments. Private international seed companies are not likely to create and deliver to Kenya the GM technologies that low-resource farmers most need, if only because of the weak purchasing power of these farmers. Private foundations such as Rockefeller and the international public sector, including the research centers of the Consultative Group on International Agricultural Research system (for example, CIMMYT), can partly fill the gap but donor support for GM crop research, as noted in the previous chapter, is generally not strong. The international public sector is doing far less to promote today's gene revolution than it did earlier to promote the non-GM Green Revolution. In these circumstances, significant contributions from Kenya's own public sector will be essential.

Kenya's historical record in the area of public agricultural research has been relatively strong. When it gained independence early in the 1960s, Kenya had 37 researchers per 1 million farmers, or more than twice the African average at that time. Further investments were then made, and by 1981–85 Kenya's research institutes and universities had 89 researchers per 1 million farmers, still more than twice the regional average. Measuring farm research expenditures as a percentage of agricultural GDP, Kenya was able to maintain a ratio well above 1.0 percent through the 1980s, compared with less than 0.5 percent for the Sub-Saharan African region as a whole (Roseboom and Pardey 1993, 10).

This traditionally strong public research investment performance in Kenya has lagged more recently. When international donor support for agricultural research stalled in the 1990s, the Kenyan government failed to pick up the slack. Total research spending remained relatively constant as a percentage of agricultural GDP in Kenya between 1989 and 1996, but this was only because agricultural production itself was faltering in Kenya, in part owing to inadequate research outlays. Kenya also saw a significant decline in its total expenditures per researcher in the 1990s—from US$30,000 in 1989 to just US$18,000 by 1996.[7]

Agribiotechnology research in Kenya (lumping together both conventional and transgenic agribiotechnology) has historically been only one small part of this lagging agricultural research total. Agribiotechnology was just 3.3 percent of the total in 1989, and then it fell to just 2.8 percent of the total in 1996. In nominal U.S. dollar terms, Kenya's total spending on all forms of agribiotechnology research in 1996 was just US$1.18 million. Most of this scant spending was donor financed. Kenya's public research institutes (such as KARI) spend roughly 71 percent of the nation's agribiotechnology research total, and 84 percent of KARI's total agricultural biotechnology funding comes from donors rather than from the Kenyan government itself. Two-thirds of donor assistance to KARI for agribiotechnology has actually gone for infrastructure; this is valuable but it implies that actual research operations have been less well funded (Wafula and Falconi 1998, 11–14).

How much of this small amount of agribiotechnology spending went specifically for GM research? This can be estimated roughly by counting the

---

7. This measurement is in nominal U.S. dollars; see Wafula and Falconi 1998, 16.

number of researchers at KARI focused on either genetic engineering of crops or biotechnology vaccines for animals. In 1996 these numbers were 2 and 5, respectively, out of a total of 28 researchers at KARI (Wafula and Falconi 1998, 15). Transgenic work is therefore hardly a dominant focus even within KARI's small annual budget for biotechnology.

Kenyan scientists have built a commendable record in conventional non-GM agribiotechnology work. Through tissue culture techniques they have produced pyrethrum since 1979, citrus since 1983, sugarcane since 1991, bananas since 1995, and also sweet potatoes, Irish potatoes, coffee, and tea. The application of molecular marker-assisted technology has been an important activity at KARI since 1995, with a special focus on the development of Kenyan maize varieties with improved resistance to stem borer and maize streak virus and also with tolerance for drought (Wafula and Falconi 1998, 3–4). Commercial applications of these non-GM biotech approaches to food crops are still in the early stages of development, but disease-free potato planting material is now being supplied to farmers in various parts of the country (ISNAR 1999). KARI has conducted both on-station and on-farm field trials of tissue culture bananas, yet here Kenya is still a bit behind South Africa, where the use of in vitro banana plantlets as a source of disease-free planting material is already common practice (Qaim 1999).

In the area of genetic engineering, KARI has to date done much less. KARI's crop scientists have worked at Monsanto's labs in the United States to develop the transgenic sweet potato described earlier; KARI's negotiations with Monsanto to collaborate on herbicide-resistant maize did not progress however. The recent collaboration with CIMMYT on Bt maize is promising, but still new. Although KARI's livestock scientists have worked on bio-engineered recombinant animal disease virus vaccines, the commercial attraction of this approach is unproven. With more resources, KARI's scientists could be doing much more GM crop and livestock work. Thanks in part to the transgenic sweet potato partnership with Monsanto, nine Kenyan scientists at KARI have been trained in gene technology. Additional training may take place soon with help from the Swedish International Development Cooperation Agency through its BIO-EARN Programme (the East African Regional Programme and Research Network for Biotechnology, Biosafety and Biotechnology Development). In 1999, funding was approved through this program to train several Kenyan Ph.D. biotech scientists in Sweden, then send them back to KARI. Possible projects for these scientists will include transgenic cassava, sorghum, and barley with modified starch content, and genetic manipulation of oil quality in sesame (ISNAR 1999). Yet this donor support is inadequate to cover the operating costs that will have to be incurred at KARI, such as the purchase of expensive chemicals. Without a larger budget to support ongoing GM research, the scientific talent that has been brought together at KARI risks being lost either to private companies or to universities abroad.

GM advocates inside KARI lament that only a small share of the institute's annual US$40 million budget goes on agribiotechnology operating costs.[8]

Kenya's current public investment policies toward GM crops must therefore be rated as highly precautionary. The government does not yet spend significant treasury resources either for the development of new GM crop technologies or for the backcrossing into local germplasm of GM varieties developed elsewhere. Kenya does allow donors to finance projects designed to transfer GM traits into local crop varieties through conventional breeding and propagation methods but, even with donor assistance, less than 3 percent of the total public agricultural research and development budget goes to any kind of agribiotechnology, and only a small portion of that total goes specifically to GM crop research.

Explaining Kenya's Precaution

I began by observing that Kenya's agricultural sector suffers from severe farm productivity constraints, some of which are linked to highly specific pest and disease problems that GM crop technologies are seemingly well suited to address. From such a starting point, one might have expected Kenya to embrace policies toward GM crops that were either promotional or highly permissive. Yet this chapter has shown that, in all four of the policy venues most relevant in Kenya, a highly precautionary policy approach has instead been taken. In the area of intellectual property rights Kenya has a PBR system that meets only the relatively weak UPOV 1978 standard (and this only recently); in the area of biosafety Kenya's National Biosafety Committee had not yet approved any GM crops for use by farmers in Kenya and had slowed the approval process at the research stage in a precautionary manner even when scientific evidence of biohazards had been lacking; in the area of trade policy Kenya has not yet explicitly approved the regular import of any GM commodities for commercial planting or human consumption and was slow to approve the import of GM sweet potato materials for research purposes only; and in the area of public investment the government of Kenya has invested very little of its own treasury resources in agricultural biotechnology research, and only a small portion of that has gone for work specifically in the area of GM. The only policy area in which Kenya has not been precautionary is food

---

8. Prospects for increasing Kenya's public funding of agricultural research (including biotechnology) may have been improved somewhat late in 1999 when, as part of a major bureaucratic restructuring, KARI was placed directly under Kenya's Ministry of Agriculture. This move seemed likely to enhance KARI's cabinet-level visibility and strengthen its ability to secure treasury resources, while also linking researchers more closely to extension workers. This bureaucratic restructuring also brought new leadership into the Ministry of Agriculture, including a Deputy Permanent Secretary previously posted to CIMMYT with a strong interest in Bt maize as a means to control stem borer damage in Kenya.

safety, but this is mostly explained by the fact that no GM foods were yet being grown in the country for any Kenyans to consume. These policy choices are summarized in Table 3.1.

The reason for Kenya's cautious pattern of policy choices toward GM crops is not at first obvious. Fear that Kenyan farmers will become dependent on expensive new GM seeds sold by private international corporations does not seem to be the explanation, since the NBC went slowly in approving the GM sweet potato even though it was being offered to KARI by Monsanto on a royalty-free basis. The possibility that Kenyan officials are being cautious toward GM crops because of genuine biosafety concerns is also somewhat suspect. Although hypothetical biosafety worries do feature strongly in Kenya's official rhetoric toward GM crops, particularly within the Environment Ministry, the government normally has only a weak record in the biosafety area. When it comes to the manifestly severe biosafety hazards that have long been posed by some non-GM farming technologies in Kenya, such as chemical pesticides, or to the problem of non-GM bio-invasions such as the water hyacinth, the government has not shown much concern. The thought that Kenya has been slowing its move into GM crops for fear of losing commercial export markets in Europe can also mostly be set aside, since Kenya's farm exports to Europe do not include the crops—such as maize or soy—that are currently at the leading edge of the GM revolution. Nor can internal food safety within Kenya be offered as the reason for policy caution, since food safety policies in Kenya are not only underdeveloped in general but silent so far toward GM foods in particular.

A more plausible explanation for Kenya's caution can be found in its weak governmental capacity and its high dependence on the donor community. Given Kenya's large need for sustained donor financing, it should not be surprising to find that some of its policies are donor driven. Especially in the area of biosafety, key bilateral donors have made precautionary policies a precondition for assistance. It was the Biosafety Committee at USAID that prompted KARI to put in place its original institutional biosafety guidelines as a condition for receiving any GM materials from Monsanto. And it was "special programme" funding through the DGIS that prompted Kenya to draft its 1998 national R&G document, a precautionary document inspired by Dutch and Swedish standards.

These donor efforts in the area of biosafety policy are well meaning but they leave the government of Kenya in an awkward position. Kenya has been willing to assume strict biosafety obligations regarding GM crop technologies on paper, but it still lacks the full capacity (in terms of financial, technical, institutional, and human resources) to implement those policies confidently and carefully on a case-by-case basis. Kenya's biosafety policy officials, who know that their every move in the area of GM crops is being watched closely by the international media and by some international and European-based

TABLE 3.1 Policies toward GM crops in Kenya, 1999–2000

Policy	Promotional	Permissive	Precautionary	Preventive
IPR			Kenya's law on plant breeders' rights was strengthened slightly in 1991, and in 1999 Kenya finally acceded to the 1978 version of UPOV	
Biosafety			Kenya's National Biosafety Committee screens GM crops according to a separate and higher biosafety standard, and when in doubt opts for delay	
Trade			National Biosafety Committee has not yet explicitly approved GM commodity imports and has been slow to approve imports of GM plant materials for research purposes	
Food safety and consumer choice	Kenya's food safety laws and labeling laws make no distinction between GM and non-GM foods			
Public research investment			Small public sector investments in GM are mostly donor financed, and used mostly for conventional transfer into local varieties of GM traits developed by others	

NOTE: UPOV = International Convention for the Protection of New Varieties of Plants.

environmental NGOs such as Greenpeace, have become doubly cautious. To avoid being accused of falling short of their own announced policy standards by failing to implement biosafe GM crop field testing or commercial release policies properly within Kenya, these officials have so far erred on the side of slowing down official approvals for such activities.

This projection of Europe's anti-GM anxieties into the policy debate in Kenya has been frustrating to Kenya's agricultural scientists, many of whom are eager for their country to move ahead more quickly with GM crops. Cyrus G. Ndiritu, former director of KARI, spoke to donors about these matters at an international gathering in Washington, D.C., in 1999:

> There is overwhelming evidence and knowledge that the needs and drive for biotechnology in Africa are quite different from those of industrial countries. Africa's agenda is based on the urgent needs for technological change to enhance food production and to alter the course of widespread poverty, hunger, and starvation. Industrial countries are driven by market and profit. These distinctions must be understood and appreciated at the national, regional, and global levels. The ongoing debate creates fear, mistrust, and general confusion to the public, and has failed to seek the views of African policymakers and stakeholders. . . . The need for biotechnology in Africa should not be confused with the marketing/food surplus-driven forces of the industrial countries. (Ndiritu 2000, 112–113)

Some biotechnology researchers in Kenya have been even more blunt. In 1999 Kenya's African Biotechnology Stakeholders Forum (ABSF) published an open letter accusing anti-GM Europeans of trying to block the technology at Africa's expense:

> Already the industrialized nations have perfected their biotechnology skills while Africa on the other hand has been made to be a mere observer and discussant of the issues generated by nations in the North, some of whose agenda is to stifle the continent's acquisition and utilization of appropriate biotechnology, especially that which aims to enhance food production, forestry, health and environment conservation. . . . There are signs that global transfer of crucial biotechnology skills and products to developing countries may soon slow down considerably if those in the industrialized world continue to assume they know what is best for Kenya and other African countries. (ABSF 1999)

It is Kenya's misfortune to be so dependent on donor community preferences and support in the area of agricultural research. If the government of Kenya had been willing to spend more of its own treasury resources on agri-biotechnology research and if it had been willing to open its own economy more decisively to private sector trade and investment (in part by offering private investors stronger IPR guarantees) some valuable GM technologies might have been induced to move into the country more quickly. KARI's frustrated researchers might then also have exercised a greater influence over biosafety policy, and specifically over the terms under which they could conduct research on GM crops and then ultimately get those crops into the hands of farmers.

4 The Courts Intervene in Brazil

In the global contest over GM crops, Brazil has emerged as an important battleground. Whereas a majority of industrial states—including the United States, Canada, Argentina, Japan, and most countries in Europe—had approved several GM crop applications by 1996, the approval process in Brazil was originally on a slower time schedule. This seemed at first a commercial disadvantage for Brazil's export-oriented agricultural sector, because soybean farmers in the United States and Argentina were able to cut their production costs by growing GM varieties at a time when farmers in Brazil were not. However, when a consumer backlash against GM crops began to gain strength in Europe and Japan after 1997, Brazil's status as a country that was still nominally GM free took on interesting new significance. Some agricultural interests in Brazil began to see the country's official GM-free status as a possible advantage in export markets vis-à-vis Argentina and the United States. European-based consumer and environmental advocacy nongovernmental organizations (NGOs) also began fighting hard to keep Brazil GM free. They were worried that, if Brazil joined other major exporters in planting GM crops, the new technology might become pervasive in global commodity markets, and hence more difficult and more costly for importing regions such as Europe or East Asia to resist.

Altered international trade calculations and new international NGO pressures such as these began in 1997–98 to push against the official plan of Brazil's federal government to go ahead and release GM seeds. When an official release effort was made for herbicide-resistant GM soybeans in 1998, Brazilian opponents of GM countered with legal actions to block the release. A federal court sustained this legal action, and as of 2000 a successful commercial release of GM seeds had not yet taken place in Brazil. This blockage persisted despite the clear desire of farmers in Brazil to begin planting GM seeds (many were doing so illegally) and despite the desire of Brazil's federal government to have those seeds planted.

Some of Brazil's policies toward GM seeds are therefore not easily classified. The federal government has sought in most cases to be permissive or even promotional toward GM crops, yet important actors at the state level in Brazil's political system, in civil society, and in the federal court system have frustrated this intent. At this writing the political battle over whether to keep Brazil GM free or to go ahead and release GM seeds for commercial planting is still under way. The highly contested nature of Brazil's still evolving policy toward GM crops—particularly in areas of biosafety, trade, and food safety— reflects the intensity of this battle.

Policies toward GM crops in Brazil are highly contested in part because of Brazil's commercial significance in international commodity markets. Brazil is the world's third-largest exporter of agricultural products after the United States and France. In international soybean markets, Brazil is the world's second-largest exporter after the United States. Agricultural value-added per worker in Brazil increased at a strong 3 percent annual rate in the 1990s, and has doubled since 1980 (World Bank 2000). Inside the country, Brazil's expanding farm and agribusiness sector still accounts for some 40 percent of total GNP, and agricultural products such as coffee, soybeans, and oranges make up roughly one-third of Brazil's total exports (Brazil, Ministry of Environment 1998). In Brazil, agricultural policy is therefore always high politics. But politics in Brazil has also become more participatory and more democratic of late. The number of organized groups participating in the making of agricultural policy has increased. In particular, stronger consumer rights and environmental protection movements have emerged within civil society and have learned to use Brazil's strengthened opposition parties, the media, and the more independent judiciary system to make their views heard. In some of the wealthier areas of southern Brazil, "green" party leaders, consumer advocacy organizations, and environmental NGOs are nearly as influential as in Europe. These groups have been mobilizing against GM crops and foods since 1996, in much the same way as their counterparts in Europe.

The GM crop policy struggle in Brazil thus pits research scientists and commercial farm and agribusiness interests on the political right against organized advocates for urban consumers and environmentalists on the left. Somewhat overlooked in this struggle, unfortunately, have been Brazil's millions of low-resource farmers, many of whom are not producing the crops such as soybeans, maize, or cotton for which GM applications are currently available. These farmers are producing crops such as cassava, beans, rice, or banana, which have not traditionally received much attention either from the private companies or from the government research institutes that have been working to bring GM technologies to Brazil. Even if the federal government eventually wins its battle to commercialize GM soybean seeds in Brazil, additional policy actions will thus be needed to extend useful transgenic crop varieties to resource-poor farmers in the tropical regions of Brazil, to ensure a realization of social as well as purely commercial benefits from the GM crop revolution.

Because Brazil's policies toward GM crops have been rapidly shifting and highly contested, the best I can do here is to provide a snapshot of what those policies looked like in 1999–2000 in each of the five areas under consideration in this study.

Intellectual Property Rights Policies

Policies to protect intellectual property rights (IPRs) in Brazil were strengthened in the 1990s. Just as in Kenya, this IPR strengthening took place for reasons mostly unrelated to GM crop technologies. Yet Brazil's policies were strengthened to a greater degree, making them permissive rather than precautionary toward GM crops. These stronger government guarantees of IPR protection in the end helped stimulate international private sector interest in moving new GM crop technologies into the country. Strengthened IPR guarantees have also helped encourage research on GM crop technologies by Brazil's own agricultural scientists working inside state-funded institutes. If Brazil fails in the end to participate in the GM crop revolution, weak IPR policies will not have been the reason.

Brazil's IPR policies toward GM crops are contained in two separate statutes, a patent law and a Cultivar Protection Law. The current patent law (officially titled the Industrial Property Code) was approved in May 1996, and for the first time gave legal protection to inventions related to pharmaceuticals, food processes, and biotechnology. Prior to 1996, Brazil had used an Industrial Property Code that did not recognize property rights for pharmaceutical or food products, including biotechnologically derived ones. Brazil introduced this new patent law partly to support a more general opening of the Brazilian economy to private foreign investments, but partly also in response to the new requirements in the World Trade Organization's Agreement on Trade-Related Aspects of Intellectual Property Rights (TRIPS). This new Industrial Property Code is not fully promotional toward GM crops, because it explicitly excludes the patentability of plant varieties, animals, or natural biological processes. It gives patent recognition to transgenic micro-organisms (as required by TRIPS) if they meet the patentability requirements of novelty, inventiveness, and industrial application, but not to whole plants or parts of plants (Sampaio 2000).

The IPR standard to be applied to whole plants in Brazil is spelled out in the separate Cultivar Protection Law, also known as the Plant Variety Protection (PVP) Law, which became fully active in December 1997. The PVP Law is implemented not by Brazil's National Industrial Property Institute in the Ministry of Industry, but rather by a National Plant Variety Protection Service within the Ministry of Agriculture. Brazil's PVP Law was prepared in accordance with the International Convention for the Protection of New Varieties of Plants (UPOV) and it provided the basis for Brazil's accession in May 1999 to the 1978 version of UPOV. Since Brazil's PVP Law goes beyond the UPOV 1978 standard in some respects, it is strong enough here to be classified as permissive toward GM crops rather than just precautionary. As an incentive to innovate or introduce valuable GM traits into plants, it is important for breeders with IPRs to be able to exercise control over the minor modifications that some competing "cosmetic breeders" might subsequently undertake with those varieties. Brazil's new PVP Law assures breeders protection for these "essentially derived varieties," in conformity with the stronger UPOV 1991 standard. The PVP Law also specifies that the free exchange (but not selling) of protected seeds is permitted among small farmers' communities involved in government-supported programs. This restriction on the traditional farmer's privilege is also in conformity with UPOV 1991 (Sampaio 2000).

Private international seed companies with GM technologies were among those that welcomed these new Brazilian IPR protection guarantees. Monsanto, Novartis, AgrEvo, Mycogen, Dupont, and other large life science companies saw these stronger protections as one more inducement, after 1997, to begin investing hundreds of millions of dollars in the purchase of local Brazilian plant breeding, seed multiplication, and distribution firms. Monsanto alone purchased five different national seed companies in Brazil and, with stunning speed, some of Brazil's best-established national seed companies (including Agroceres) passed into international corporate hands. In one year Brazil's previously domestic hybrid maize seed industry became 82 percent owned by Monsanto.

Brazil's permissive IPR policies have encouraged foreign investors, but they have been no less encouraging toward Brazil's own scientific innovators at home. Conventional plant breeders working within Brazil's formidable public sector agricultural research system Embrapa (Empresa Brasileira de Pesquisa Agropecuaria) have developed many of the local plant varieties of soybean, maize, and cotton that are best suited to Brazilian conditions, and Embrapa has eagerly used Brazil's new IPR system to establish legal ownership of this extremely valuable collection of locally improved germplasm. Embrapa has roughly two-thirds (and the best two-thirds) of all soybean germplasm in Brazil, and roughly half of Brazil's soybean area is currently under Embrapa cultivars. International companies wishing to use these local varieties as carriers of the transgenic traits they wish to sell to Brazil's farmers will thus have to negotiate access agreements with Embrapa.

It went somewhat against Embrapa's traditional culture to begin using Brazil's plant variety protection laws in this fashion. It meant developing a "protect before you publish" attitude and, in some cases, keeping visitors away from laboratories and maintaining the confidentiality of data sets. Most of all it meant institutionalized instruction in IPR rules and procedures, a task accomplished through the creation at Embrapa in 1997 of an Intellectual Property Committee and separate "local" IPR committees at each of Embrapa's research units. The cost to Embrapa of providing this kind of internal IPR literacy was roughly US$300,000 and the commitment of human resources was considerable.

Brazilian scientists developing GM crops can discover that foreign companies or universities hold IPRs not only to the specific transgene in question but also to some of the basic biotechnology tools to be used in the project, including the promoters, markers, or transformation processes. International companies have offered Brazilian laboratories relatively easy terms when entering into a GM crop materials transfer agreement for research purposes only, but, when the Brazilian partner then begins negotiating for a license to commercialize the research result, the companies have tried to drive a harder bargain. The resulting negotiations are also difficult because of the multiple IPR holders and the multiple institutions that are frequently involved. As one example, researchers at Embrapa developed a transgenic papaya cultivar carrying virus disease resistance, but they then realized it would be necessary to negotiate separate commercial license agreements with each of the seven different companies with property rights claims incorporated in the product. A package agreement negotiated through the Cornell Research Foundation was used to solve this problem. Embrapa has also found it may have to negotiate separate licenses, first for commercial use of the company-owned gene and second with a local Brazilian seed company to permit use of Embrapa-owned germplasm in seed production. The international company then might have to issue the seed-producing company its own separate license for use of the gene.

Embrapa's IPRs over locally improved germplasm are fortunately not its only card to play in these commercial contract negotiations. When Embrapa bargains for permission to use protected GM technologies commercially it also points to the readiness of its own traditional plant breeders to move traits from transformed varieties into local germplasm and to its well-developed working relations with the local companies that may be useful in producing and distributing the transformed seed. These relationships of mutual trust between Embrapa and local seed producers provide extra reassurance to international companies that might otherwise worry about piracy of transgenic seeds. Embrapa can also present itself as an essential partner for any international venture seeking to operate nationwide in Brazil, because its 39 far-flung separate research units guarantee institutionalized access to every part of the country. Embrapa's hand is further strengthened because its scientists have already developed their own independent capacity to perform genetic transformations on plants, implying less dependence on international partnerships in the long run.

Private international companies such as Monsanto are nonetheless being careful in Brazil, partly because of their earlier experience in neighboring Argentina. In 1995 Monsanto was refused IPR protection for its herbicide-resistant (Roundup Ready, or RR) GM soybean seeds in Argentina. Yet Argentina's biggest seed company, NIDERA, had purchased a former partner company of Monsanto (Asgrow Argentina) and by this means had gained access to the seeds. NIDERA then began selling the seeds in Argentina without any IPRs, which meant NIDERA lacked control over on-farm replication and selling of saved seed. Also, NIDERA could not charge Argentine farmers the "technology fee" that Monsanto has been able to charge farmers in the United States (DePalma and Romero 2000). Meanwhile, Monsanto gained nothing directly from the sale of its transformed seeds by NIDERA in Argentina. The seeds are designed to work with Monsanto's glyphosate herbicide product Roundup, so the company does profit from some chemical sales in Argentina, but Roundup itself is out of patent and more than 20 other companies in Argentina are also producing and selling glyphosate. Monsanto views this experience in Argentina as one it should try to avoid in Brazil, and this is one reason it has sought to drive a hard bargain in its IPR negotiations with Embrapa.

As of 2000, Embrapa had successfully used research contracts with various private companies to develop transformed varieties of soybeans, corn, cotton, papaya, black beans, and potato, but it had not yet completed any of the more difficult commercial contract negotiations that will be needed if farmers are ever to gain access to these varieties. Some important sticking points in these negotiations have been the rights of companies in Brazil to collect technology fees or to sign contracts with farmers to prevent on-farm replication and replanting of GM crops. Since Monsanto continues to ask farmers in the United States to sign contracts, it worries about being criticized by its U.S. customers if it allows farmers in Brazil to buy its technologies without these contracts.

In sum, Brazil's IPR policies toward GM crops are not fully promotional because the nation's patent law excludes whole plants and parts of plants. The terms of Brazil's PVP Law are strong enough, however, to mark the nation's IPR stance toward GM crops as permissive rather than precautionary. Although Brazil has acceded internationally only to the 1978 version of UPOV, its PVP Law nonetheless incorporates significant features of the stronger 1991 version of UPOV. Private holders of GM crop technologies might want more than this in Brazil, but IPR disputes are not the central reason Brazil has been slow to commercialize GM seeds. The GM crop revolution has been slowed down in Brazil more by biosafety policy, trade policy, and food safety policy than by IPR policy.

Biosafety Policy

Policymakers in Brazil originally intended to pursue a permissive approach toward GM crops in the area of biosafety policy, screening commercial GM applications for biological safety on a case-by-case basis and looking only for scientific evidence of demonstrated risk. In 1995–96 Brazil set in place the formal institutions and procedures it thought would suffice to implement this approach. Yet these institutions and procedures subsequently came under strong challenge from environmental advocates, consumer advocates, and other GM crop critics in Brazil, and the original intent of the federal government to be permissive toward GM crops was thus frustrated. In place of a permissive biosafety policy, a federal court injunction placed all commercial releases of GM crops temporarily on hold. Although there were multiple motives behind this challenge to GM crops in Brazil—including jurisdictional disputes within the federal government, food consumer fears, partisanship, economic nationalism, and perhaps also a partial recalculation of trade interests given international consumer doubts about GM crops—the challenge was first launched primarily in the name of biosafety.

This strong challenge was not anticipated in 1995 when Brazil's federal government first set in place the legal and institutional system it hoped to use for governing the biosafety aspect of GM technologies. This Biosafety Law (Law Number 8974) set broad standards for the use of genetic engineering techniques and for the environmental release of genetically modified organisms (GMOs).[1] To provide more specific judgments regarding the safety of GM technologies on a case-by-case basis it created a new institution, the National Technical Commission on Biosafety (CTNBio). With this new legal and institutional system in place, Brazil should have been ready to go ahead with individual approvals for GM crops only a few years behind the United States and Argentina. Partly because of CTNBio's obvious permissive bias, however, a backlash quickly emerged against biosafety approvals of GM crops in Brazil and this led by 1998 to paralysis. The ambiguous constitutional standing of CTNBio, plus the fact that it contained representatives from the very companies applying for biosafety approvals, weakened its ability to break out of this paralysis.

The 1995 Biosafety Law covered GM pharmaceuticals as well as GM crops and was intended to govern the safe use of GMOs in all areas of Brazilian life (including environmental protection, human health, animal health, and plant health). The CTNBio therefore had to be structured broadly—almost like a government within the government. Representation was given to academics (in the four areas of environmental, human, animal, and plant health), to virtually every interested government ministry, including Science and Technology, Health, Environment, Education, External Affairs, and Agriculture

---

1. This Biosafety Law specifically outlaws a few GM practices, such as genetic manipulation of human cells (except for the treatment of genetic defects) and in vivo intervention in the genetic material of animals (except when it constitutes a significant scientific advance). It also establishes two abstract categories of GMOs: those that are non-pathogenic, free of known harmful effects, with limited survival and/or multiplication, and with no negative effects on the environment (Group I), and all others (Group II). But the law itself makes few technical judgments about how to classify specific GM crops or products.

(with separate representatives for plant and animal safety), and to organizations from three areas in civil society—consumer protection, worker safety, and the private biotechnology industry (CTNBio 1998). CTNBio was given the task of operating like a technical commission, so its members and staff were selected for their professional credentials as well as for the constituencies they represented: 25 of the 36 members were Ph.D. scientists, and the staff included 5 M.A. scientists. Brazil's CTNBio was not held back by the weak institutional and technical capacity that slowed the operation of Kenya's National Biosafety Committee.

The CTNBio began operating in June 1996, just as GM crops were being planted in significant quantity for the first time in the United States. Since Brazil had not yet even conducted field trials for transgenics, it knew it was behind. Brazil was even behind Argentina, where the process of field trials and commercial release had earlier been expedited, partly because biosafety screening for plants in Argentina was done by an agency under the Ministry of Agriculture rather than by a broadly based commission such as CTNBio attached to the Ministry of Science and Technology.

International companies with GM varieties to sell in Brazil came to CTNBio immediately in 1996, requesting field trials to get the long approval process started. In February 1997, only six months after becoming operational, CTNBio gave Monsanto its first approval to field-test Roundup Ready herbicide-tolerant GM soybeans in Brazil. As many as three years of field trials can ordinarily be required to screen a new crop variety for such things as performance, food safety, safety to other crops, and insect or weed problems, but CTNBio was determined to move quickly. CTNBio's record of approving field trials for GM crops was at first uniformly permissive: between February 1997 and December 1999, CTNBio approved 687 field trials, and 43 more requests were not yet approved but under consideration. This review process was expeditious, but at the same time procedurally careful and substantially transparent. Both the initial field trial requests and the eventual approvals, when given, were openly published by law in Brazil's Official Daily Register.

CTNBio also tried to take a permissive approach to commercial release. In September 1998, only 18 months after its first approval of field trials, CTNBio offered a technical opinion giving approval to five varieties of Monsanto's RR soybeans for commercial release.[2] As something of a precaution, CTNBio initially limited commercial release of these GM soybean varieties to only some parts of Brazil and required biosafety monitoring on this commercial acreage for five years. The monitoring requirement was an interesting innovation: herbicide use and weed resistance were to be measured, and soil samples were to be collected so as to compare populations of nitrogen-fixing

---

2. Several other commercial release applications, for Bt maize, herbicide-tolerant maize, and Bt cotton, were under review by the Commission but not yet approved.

micro-organisms in GM versus non-GM fields. Greater precaution than this seemed unnecessary; there were no close wild relatives to soybeans in Brazil, or anywhere else in the Western hemisphere for that matter, so the danger of geneflow and outcrossing was remote. On the question of food safety, CTNBio took reassurance from knowing that RR soybeans had been grown and consumed extensively—and to all appearances safely—in the United States since 1996.

CTNBio's commercial release opinion in September 1998 for Monsanto's RR soybeans nonetheless triggered a political and legal backlash, one that indefinitely delayed the commercial release of any GM crops in Brazil and called CTNBio's authority to permit such a release into question on constitutional grounds. The organized energy behind this backlash came from within Brazil's own consumer protection movement, from environmental NGOs with close connections to Europe, from opposition party and state government leaders seeking to discredit federal government decisions in Brasilia, and even from some agencies of the federal government itself, seeking to take the initiative on GM biosafety policy away from CTNBio.

First to challenge the commercial release of RR soybeans was Brazil's respected Institute for Consumer Defense (IDEC). A representative from IDEC had originally been a member of CTNBio but resigned from the commission within its first year of operation after discovering that most other commission members preferred a permissive rather than a precautionary biosafety approach. This was not just true of the commission members who represented the private biotechnology industry (whose presence on the committee was enough by itself to suggest a strong conflict of interest). It was also true of most of the scientists on the commission who were trained in biotechnology, and it was certainly true of the chair of the commission, who by most accounts failed to play a neutral role. Rather than fight for a more precautionary approach on the inside, IDEC decided to oppose GM crops from the outside. Even before CTNBio had issued its favorable technical judgment on RR soybeans for commercial release, IDEC had gone to a federal court judge seeking a restraining order against any such release. IDEC's argument was that CTNBio had failed to seek a full environmental impact assessment (EIA) before giving technical approval to RR soybeans. The Brazilian Constitution and various environmental laws predating the 1995 Biosafety Law seemed to require an EIA any time an action is taken that might do environmental harm. IDEC also pointed to CTNBio's alleged failure to conduct a sufficiently independent assessment of the food safety implications of RR soybeans.

IDEC is a low-budget NGO but it has some 40,000 dues-paying associates in Brazil and it has often used both media contacts (including its own widely read magazine) and court actions to give consumers in Brazil better information about the products they buy. Its lawsuit was enough in 1998 to incline a sympathetic federal judge to issue an immediate temporary restraining order against any commercial release of RR soybeans, pending an investigation of the EIA and consumer food safety issues raised by the suit. It was at this point that an activist environmental NGO—Brazil's office of the Europe-based international NGO Greenpeace—joined the IDEC lawsuit against CTNBio. Earlier in 1997, Brazil's Greenpeace office had taken legal action of its own against the import of GM commodities into the country, and was cultivating a special hostility toward Monsanto. As a giant U.S.-based multinational company prominently engaged in buying up large parts of Brazil's national seed industry, Monsanto emerged as an easy target for IDEC and Greenpeace in Brazil. Monsanto was easy to impugn on environmental grounds because it had earlier manufactured Agent Orange and it still made most of its money selling herbicides. When it became known in 1998 that Monsanto had acquired a company with patent rights to a so-called "terminator gene," the NGO community in Brazil found it that much easier to rally public resistance against the company.[3]

What helped guarantee the power of IDEC's lawsuit within Brazil's court system was a subsequent decision by the Brazilian Institute for the Environment and Renewable Natural Resources (IBAMA) within the federal government's own Environment Ministry to join IDEC and Greenpeace as a formal plaintiff. IBAMA is responsible for carrying out EIAs and it joined the suit to assert that it did not want CTNBio to infringe its EIA prerogatives in the area of GM crops. Brazil's Environment Ministry had not objected when CTNBio made its RR soybean release judgment (the Environment Ministry had a seat on CTNBio), but IBAMA joined the lawsuit for a time after the fact anyway.

In response to the lawsuit, CTNBio claimed it was only exercising the responsibilities it had been given in the 1995 Biosafety Law. It said it had taken adequate precautions in the case of RR soybeans by doing an environmental risk assessment in accordance with its own GM-specific protocol, known as CTNBio Instruction No. 3. This assessment had included scrutiny of Monsanto's reports on field trial results in Brazil, plus re-examination of the data on food safety and environmental safety that Monsanto had used earlier to secure commercial release of RR soybeans both in Europe and in the United States. CTNBio observed that IBAMA did not yet have any GM-specific protocols to work with and argued that IBAMA was technically unprepared to understand the biosafety issues associated with transgenic crops, let alone take over final technical jurisdiction on such issues. Finally, CTNBio pointed to a federal decree stipulating that EIAs were legally required for GM crops only when CTNBio itself "deemed necessary."[4] Monsanto and its Brazilian subsidiary

---

3. This gene use restriction technology existed on paper but was never engineered into an actual plant. Under heavy criticism for even entertaining the idea of engineering a sterility trait into its GM plants, in 1999 Monsanto pledged not to commercialize the technology.

4. Decree No. 1752, December 20, 1995, Chapter II, Article 2.XIV.

(Monsoy) at this point joined the legal case on CTNBio's side, with the thought that since most of the evidence on biosafety came from the company it should be an integral part of the legal process.

IBAMA, IDEC, and Greenpeace argued in response that a full EIA by IBAMA was necessary not only for RR soybeans but for any other GM crop that might be released in the future. They argued that Brazil's pre-1995 constitutional and statutory requirements trumped a mere decree linked to the 1995 Biosafety Law. CTNBio's procedures, moreover, were not close enough to a genuine EIA because not all of the data examined on RR soybeans had been collected from Brazil's environment, and the information provided on pest and weed issues was linked more to the safety of other agricultural plants than to the larger environment. CTNBio also had not done the "socioeconomic" assessment that is a routine part of EIAs in Brazil.[5]

The top leadership of Brazil's federal government has attempted, fitfully, to overcome the court injunction against RR soybeans. Parts of the original restraining order against planting RR soybeans were briefly reversed by a federal judge in Brasilia in November 1998, but other parts of the original decision (including some requiring labeling and market segregation of GM from non-GM soy) were maintained, which was enough to keep RR soybeans from being planted in Brazil that year. In May 1999, when Brazil's Agriculture Ministry tried to authorize formal registration of RR soybeans for the next crop year, they were blocked by another court injunction, this time at the request of both IDEC and IBAMA. Brazil's opposition Workers' Party (PT) joined as well, by filing an action of unconstitutionality. Monsanto had expected all this, but was surprised in August 1999 when the federal judge overseeing the case turned the second temporary injunction into a final court decision. RR soybeans were not to be commercially released in Brazil pending completion of an EIA among other things.[6] CTNBio and Monsanto appealed this decision.

In July 2000, senior Brazilian officials and scientists favoring GM crops launched a stronger campaign to move public opinion in their favor. Hoping to dispel the impression of divisions within the federal government, President Cardoso persuaded six senior cabinet members—including even the Environment and Health ministers—to sign a "manifesto" supporting GM crops and the lead role of CTNBio. Brazil's National Academy of Science then joined a prestigious gathering of scientists from other countries[7] in issuing a ringing endorsement of GM crops, and the Brazilian Genetics Society posted a strong

---

5. When IBAMA does an EIA for the construction of a new factory or a new shopping mall, for example, it is not unusual to call for actions to "mitigate" any expected socioeconomic damage to those whose livelihoods might be adversely affected.

6. For the complete 59-page text of this decision, see Poder Judiciario, Justica federal, secao Judiciaria do Distrito federal, Sentenca No. 753/99, Brasilia, August 10, 1999.

7. China, India, Mexico, the United States, the Third World Academy of Sciences in Trieste, and Britain's Royal Society.

declaration in favor of transgenics on the Internet and received 80 percent approval. The courts were unmoved, however, and kept the de facto ban on commercial release in place.

Late in December 2000, President Cardoso took another strategy by signing a provisional law that redefined the role of CTNBio, making it clear that the agency had exclusive authority to authorize the production and sale of GM crops. According to the Brazilian system, such provisional laws can have full legal power if they are reissued by the president every month—pending congressional passage. The president's new law took effect immediately. Monsanto claimed that this measure might make possible its sale of RR seeds in time for the next planting season, but even if eventually passed by Congress this new law could still face court challenges on constitutional grounds. The president's action faced immediate challenge from activist GM crop opponents in any case. In January 2001, as part of a larger anti-globalization action organized by an international NGO network, more than 1,000 Brazilian workers from the radical Landless Workers Movement invaded a Monsanto biotechnology plant in Rio Grande do Sul and threatened to camp out indefinitely to protest against genetically modified food.

The commercial stakes in this case were high for Monsanto, in terms of both lost seed sales and also lost sales of the herbicide designed for use with RR soybeans. Monsanto had invested US$550 million in an industrial plant located in the northeastern state of Bahia to make the inputs used in Roundup herbicide; this plant was scheduled to begin operation in mid-2001 and would be Monsanto's largest industrial plant outside of the United States. Overall, Monsanto can lose perhaps as much as US$100 million for each year the GM ban in Brazil continues. As one way around the full effects of the ban, Monsanto has sought permission from the court to plant RR soybeans in restricted areas for the purpose of seed propagation, pending the outcome of the court case, so the company will be ready to meet commercial seed demands if the court eventually finds in its favor. Meanwhile, Monsanto is also reviewing the data it might need to provide if full EIAs are in the end deemed necessary. The company believes it could have provided this data in a timely fashion on the RR soybean case if it had known from the start that an EIA was going to be required. Yet it is hardly eager at this point to see technical jurisdiction for GM crop biosafety pass from CTNBio to IBAMA. As of 2000, protocols for testing the biosafety of GM crops still had not been developed by IBAMA, leaving Monsanto unsure about what information might eventually be requested. In these circumstances a shift in jurisdiction from CTNBio to IBAMA could add more to the delay of Monsanto's launch of RR soybeans.

The stakes in this case are in some ways highest for CTNBio itself. If the IDEC suit is ultimately successful or if the president's December 2000 law is not approved by Congress, CTNBio's technical jurisdiction to rule on GM crop biosafety will in effect have been given to IBAMA. Sensing a need to improve its reputation with Brazilian consumers and environmentalists in order to protect this jurisdiction, in 1999 CTNBio gave itself a new chair (from the Health Ministry) and began seeking broader support for its actions through more extensive prior consultations with non-biotechnologists from Brazil's National Academy of Science, which now has a seat on CTNBio. Unfortunately, CTNBio is still required by the 1995 law to include representatives from the private biotechnology companies, so the corporate conflict of interest issue remains. Because CTNBio retains its reputation as a cheerleader for GM crops, it has had trouble finding independent representatives from Brazil's consumer protection movement to replace IDEC on the commission. A government-associated body of jurists called PROCOM still sits on the commission in IDEC's place. IDEC is meanwhile using the leverage gained from its lawsuit to pursue consumers' rights goals in several other areas, including labeling policies for GM foods (as discussed below).

Trade Policies

All of Brazil's policies regarding GM crops and foods are significantly conditioned by the importance of farm exports to Brazil's economy. The farm and agribusiness sector overall accounts for about 40 percent of the nation's GNP, and Brazil exports roughly US$15 billion worth of agricultural products every year, an amount equal to one-third of all national exports. Trade policy concerns in Brazil initially worked in favor of planting GM crops as a means to boost the nation's export competitiveness. More recently, as international markets have turned against GM crops, trade concerns have emerged as a source of caution.

The debate in Brazil over the commercial release of GM soybeans links directly to trade issues. Brazil produces roughly 31 million tons of soybeans a year and almost one-third of that production is exported. This makes Brazil the second-largest exporter of soybeans in the world after the United States. Competitiveness issues arose in 1996 when Brazil's two largest competitors in the soybean export market—the United States and Argentina—began growing GM soybeans engineered for resistance to glyphosate, which helped producers in those countries reduce input and labor costs. There seemed to be no disadvantage associated with planting GM soybeans for export to Europe and Japan at the time: the European Union had authorized commercial planting of transgenic tomato, canola, and soybean by 1996 and Japan had authorized commercial planting of soybean, canola, potato, and maize (CTNBio 1998). Trade interests therefore pushed Brazilian agriculture toward the planting of transgenics at this point. Exporters in Brazil had estimated in 1995 that there would eventually be a US$30 billion international market for GM commodities, including a US$7 billion potential market for GM seeds alone (CENARGEN 1995).

After 1998, the trade advantage that might come from promoting GM crops in Brazil became less certain. At roughly the same time IDEC and Greenpeace began challenging GM crop technologies on biosafety grounds within Brazil, a consumer and environmentalist backlash was gaining momentum in Europe and Japan. The European Union began to espouse mandatory labeling for GM soy products in 1997–98, Japan announced in 1999 that mandatory labeling of roughly 30 products made from GM corn and soybeans would come into effect in 2001, and South Korea embraced mandatory labeling as well. In April 2000 South Korea's Agricultural & Fishery Marketing Corporation announced that beginning in 2001 the only food-grade soybeans it would buy from abroad would have to be GMO free. As these demands for GM-free soybeans increased among some of Brazil's most important foreign customers, export-minded Brazilians began to consider that blocking the planting of GM crops, rather than promoting those crops, might be the wiser national trade policy.

When the IDEC/Greenpeace lawsuit temporarily blocked the official release of GM soybeans in Brazil in 1998, some state-level opponents of GM crops sought to exploit the possible trade advantage of being GM free as an excuse to make the blockage permanent. In Brazil's southern state of Rio Grande do Sul, a soybean-producing region, an opposition party governor followed the lead of IDEC and Greenpeace and sought to block the production of GM crops in his state. Elected narrowly in 1998, Governor Olivo Dutra was from the Workers' Party (PT), a left-leaning party that instinctively opposes the more centrist positions of the Social Democratic Party controlling the federal government in Brasilia. The PT is mistrustful on ideological grounds of all foreign multinational corporations (such as Monsanto) and is eager to be seen taking a protective approach toward consumer interests and the environment. With this motivation, Governor Dutra took a regional lead in what became a growing campaign to keep GM crops out of Brazil. He tried to sell this policy to farmers in his state by arguing that the consumer backlash against GM foods in Europe and Japan would soon lead to a price premium in export markets for any Brazilian grower able to certify that his product was GM free.[8] Early in 1999 Governor Dutra issued a decree to make his state a GM-free zone.

Constitutionally, the Rio Grande do Sul governor was acting within his rights. States cannot approve GM crops on their own, but they can dissent from a federal approval by banning them on their own. And since the federal approval process had been blocked in the courts, Governor Dutra's state-level ban was not technically at odds with national policy. Yet his policy ran into strong opposition from his own farmers, many of whom wanted the option to plant GM soybeans. These farmers also doubted that the declaration of a GM-free

---

8. For a clear statement of these views by Jose Hermeto Hoffmann, secretary of state for agriculture in Rio Grande do Sul, see Hoffman 1999.

zone would be enough to generate significant price premiums in international markets. In the hopes of persuading them otherwise, the governor sent a trade mission to Europe in search of price premiums, and this mission did make one deal with a French cooperative to sell 150,000 tons of soybeans from two Rio Grande do Sul cooperatives at a 5 percent premium, but this was not enough to offset the higher production costs associated with growing conventional as opposed to GM soybeans. Foreign buyers were not willing to offer significant price premiums for large-scale bulk soybean shipments from Rio Grande do Sul for several reasons.

First, Rio Grande do Sul was anything but a GM-free source of supply; a number of farmers in the state had for several years been smuggling GM soybean seeds in from neighboring Argentina. Since the harvested seeds from these GM varieties can themselves be saved by farmers and then planted successfully, unauthorized planting of GM soybeans in Rio Grande do Sul spread quickly. Sources in Brazil's seed industry estimated in 1999, based mostly on a fall-off in sales of conventional seeds, that of the 2 million hectares currently planted to soybeans in Rio Grande do Sul, perhaps 400,000–750,000 hectares were already transgenic.[9] This widespread illegal embrace of transgenic varieties by soybean farmers in southern Brazil was easy to explain, given the significant reductions in production costs that GM seeds made possible. With GM seeds, producers can control weeds with less tillage and limit their herbicide applications to just one spray over the top of the plants within a wide time window, rather than following the complicated and more costly sequence of pre-emergent and post-emergent sprays used with conventional soybeans. Seed industry sources estimate that GM soybeans are about 17 percent less expensive, per hectare, for farmers in Brazil to produce.

With the illicit planting of GM soybeans so widespread in Brazil, attempts to capture price premiums in international markets have mostly met frustration. For bulk commodities such as soybeans, where supplies from many different farms are routinely amalgamated, only a few farms producing GM beans illicitly in a region can be enough to discourage foreign customers from offering GM-free price premiums on bulk shipments. Rio Grande do Sul authorities seeking to make the state GM free were thus forced, beginning in 1999, to engage in a virtual war against their own farmers to halt illicit plantings (Hoffmann 1999; Sampaio 1999). To this end they warned farmers with GM crops in the field not to harvest those crops, threatening to jail those who dared to disobey. The state government purchased GM crop identification test-kits and went onto farms looking for storage bins containing GM seeds. Some

---

9. The secretary of state for agriculture in Rio Grande do Sul tried to deny widespread planting of GM soybeans in the state, and blamed what GM planting there was on an intentional failure by the predecessor state government (in league with the current federal government) to alert farmers to the fact that GM soybeans were still illegal.

farmers resisted with violence, causing legal actions against them to be initiated. The farmers were supported, however, by some local municipal authorities, which indicated that they would not discipline those replicating and replanting GM seeds. In December 1999 the state legislature voted 28 to 13 in favor of a bill that took power away from the governor to determine GM crop policy in the state. The governor vetoed this bill in January 2000, but three months later 29 deputies voted to overturn the veto, a move that placed state policy on GM crops more directly under federal legislation (CE 2000).

A second reason export price premiums did not emerge was the relatively small quantity of Brazil's exported soybeans that went for direct human consumption (in Japan for tofu, as one example). Exported soybeans and soybean products are most heavily consumed in Europe and Japan as livestock feed, and consumer anxieties had not yet grown sufficiently acute to create price premiums there. One European poultry and animal feed maker, Carrefour in France, did pay a price premium of about 12 percent to purchase small quantities of GM-free soybeans from Brazil, but the beans they purchased came from the central state of Goias rather than from Rio Grande do Sul, and Carrefour in any case hired local companies to certify the GM-free nature of the product. Only this kind of hands-on certification, not Brazil's state or national policy stance, is capable of generating a price premium for non-GM beans.[10]

Critics of GM crops in Brazil worked hard to make the breakaway policy in Rio Grande do Sul succeed. Greenpeace sent volunteers into the streets in 1999 and collected 45,000 signatures in favor of the governor's decree. The Rio Grande do Sul secretary of state for agriculture attempted to enlist other states in the campaign. At a national forum in Recife in May 1999, Rio Grande do Sul managed to get 17 state ministers of agriculture (out of 27 in the country) to at least sign a motion for continuing the federal-level suspension of commercial planting of RR soybeans. Other states in Brazil also showed an interest in the GM-free option. In June 2000, the state parliament of Para unanimously approved a bill (not at first signed by the governor) to retain at the state level final power to release GM crops and to require labeling of GM crops. This bill sought at least a five-year moratorium on commercial cultivation of transgenics in Para, no matter what the outcome of the federal court case.

It is telling that Brazil's export interests have been invoked by both the supporters and the critics of GM crops. Resolution of the debate may have to await clarification of the consumer acceptance issue among Brazil's leading

---

10. Japanese buyers going to Brazil in search of GM-free soybeans have found unacceptably large quantities of illicit GM varieties mixed in with the legal conventional varieties. In 1999, accordingly, Japan announced plans to source GM-free soybeans mostly from the United States through separate contracts with certified GM-free producers.

export market customers. If significant price premiums develop in the world market for large quantities of GM-free commodities, then the export promotion imperative might push even some internal GM crop enthusiasts into the GM-free policy camp. On the other hand, if price premiums fail to develop or if the illicit spread of GM soybean seed planting continues in Brazil, trade competitiveness imperatives could swing official policy back in a pro-GM direction.

Trade policies toward GM commodities in Brazil have also become highly contested on the import side. Federal officials at first expected they would have no trouble managing a permissive import policy—one that welcomed GM plant or seed imports for research purposes and did not hold GM commodity imports (such as maize or soy from Argentina or the United States) to a higher standard than non-GM imports. The foundation for this permissive import policy was laid in Brazil's 1995 Biosafety Law, which gave CTNBio the authority to offer a technical opinion on imports of "any product containing GMOs or derived from GMOs" and then gave the Ministry of Agriculture the final authority to issue authorization for such imports (Brazil 1995).

Official efforts to operate this permissive import policy toward GM commodities eventually faltered, however. As in the case of biosafety policy, jurisdictional competition with other agencies and activist NGO protests pushed what was to have been a permissive policy in a precautionary direction. While CTNBio thought its jurisdiction over import policy was unambiguous, Brazil's Environment Ministry was staking out its own claim to policy leadership in this area as leader of Brazil's delegation to the Biosafety Protocol negotiations within the Convention on Biological Diversity (CBD). During the formative period of these negotiations, Brazil's Environment Ministry joined the counterpart ministries of other developing countries (such as Kenya) caucusing as part of the so-called Like Minded Group (LMG). Within the CBD context, accordingly, Brazil fell into a habit of endorsing a more precautionary import policy, one that favored import restrictions on GM commodities based on scientific uncertainty alone. Brazil's Environment Ministry naturally favored this cautious approach, given its primary mandate of biodiversity protection and given that Brazil is a country of great diversity, ranking first in the world in terms of numbers of species of mammals, freshwater fish, and vascular plants, second in terms of amphibians, and third in terms of birds (Brazil, Ministry of Environment 1998).

Not all the members of Brazil's delegation to the Biosafety Protocol negotiations agreed with this cautious approach, however. As the LMG's restrictive trade policy preferences toward living modified organisms (LMOs) grew more apparent, the agriculturists on Brazil's delegation, who hoped their country would soon be a producer and exporter GM crops, worried that the LMG's precautionary import procedures for LMO commodity shipments would eventually compromise Brazilian export interests. Accordingly, at the

1999 Biosafety Protocol meetings in Vienna, Brazil's delegation moved toward a more neutral and permissive position on GM trade issues, more in line with the so-called "Compromise Group" of non-EU industrial countries such as Switzerland and Japan.

Amid these abstract debates over import policy, GM crop critics in Brazil have tried to force the question in a more focused way since 1997, by seeking to block specific shipments of GM soybeans and maize arriving from Argentina and the United States. In 1997, the Brazilian office of Greenpeace took legal action through the Ministry of Justice in a effort to block any further bulk shipments of soybeans from the United States, using the argument that no labeling law for GM products was yet in place within the country to protect consumers. This first challenge was eventually resolved with a drawback arrangement that ensured the re-export of any imported GM soybeans after processing. But the controversy led to mandatory testing of imports for GM content (at the importer's expense), and for a time significant GM imports from the United States and Argentina were avoided to minimize controversy. In 2000, however, a drought in Brazil's southern grain belt brought a need to import corn from Argentina as animal feed to support Brazil's important hog and poultry industries. A public debate developed when boats filled with GM Argentine corn arrived at Brazilian ports but were then turned away and held offshore or quarantined, pending a decision on whether or not to bring GM commodities into the country. To protest this de facto import ban, poultry producers in Recife gave away 20,000 free chickens that they said they could no longer afford to feed because of the drought. On this occasion it was CTNBio that was able to find a local judge willing, despite anti-GM protesters, to declare that the feed shipments from Argentina should be unloaded.

Brazilian authorities have thus been able to import some GM commodities, but only for animal feed and only in a drought emergency. This is not the permissive import policy the federal government had originally planned. A highly precautionary import policy has taken hold in Brazil, once again in response to initiatives from local and internationally connected NGOs. Food safety and consumer choice concerns, in addition to biosafety concerns, have helped motivate these NGO initiatives.

Food Safety and Consumer Choice Policies

In the food safety area, Brazilian officials originally intended to adopt a promotional policy toward GM foods, one that held these foods to no greater safety standard than other foods and imposed no separate mandatory labeling. Internal consumer advocacy pressures in 1998–99 forced these officials to move toward a permissive policy instead, one that imposed at least partial labeling in the name of informed consumer choice. This move was not enough to satisfy Brazil's more intense consumer advocacy organizations, which wanted a precautionary comprehensive labeling policy and perhaps even a ban on GM food sales.

No positive evidence existed in 1998–99 that GM foods were less safe than non-GM foods; consumer advocates in Brazil nonetheless began making strong demands that any foods sold with GM content should be separately labeled in order to give consumers an "informed choice." The federal government of Brazil finally acknowledged the political force of these demands in 1999 by taking steps to put a GM labeling policy in place. An early draft of the government's proposed policy was released for public discussion in December 1999. The labeling standard established in this draft policy was essentially permissive rather than precautionary, since it stopped short of requiring a complete segregation of GM from non-GM food marketing channels within Brazil.

Brazil's Ministry of Health had traditionally exercised jurisdiction over the nation's general food labeling policies, but this changed early in the 1990s with the maturation of a strong consumer rights movement in Brazil dominated by lawyers and jurists. Concerns for truth in labeling and the consumer's right to know came to the fore, so policy jurisdiction on the labeling of retail foods in Brazil passed to the Department of Consumer Protection inside the Ministry of Justice.[11] Anti-GM activist organizations in Brazil were comfortable with this change because it played to their precautionary preferences. If informed consumer choice is the issue, tight labeling requirements can be promoted even without any positive evidence of specific new risks to human health.

Public demand for GM food labeling in Brazil was a direct outgrowth of the 1998 lawsuit against the commercial release of RR soybeans. As noted above, it was the Brazilian consumer advocacy organization IDEC that initiated the lawsuit, and one of IDEC's key arguments was Brazil's lack of any GM-specific food labeling policy. All subsequent court rulings on the case consistently mentioned labeling as an essential condition for lifting the court-ordered suspension. A public hearing was held on this issue in Congress in November 1998, after which representatives from all parties signed a statement demanding mandatory labeling of all GM foods in Brazil. In June 1999 the federal government finally succumbed to these pressures, announcing that it would soon devise a mandatory labeling policy for GM foods. The president of Brazil, acting through the Ministry of Justice, instructed that a special commission be formed for this purpose, with representation from the ministries of Justice, Health, Agriculture, and Science and Technology and with technical support from CTNBio.

The supporting role given to CTNBio is noteworthy here. Although CTNBio was already under a cloud of suspicion with consumer advocates for

---

11. Consumer Protection Law Number 8078 of 1990 is currently the primary reference point governing GM food labeling policies in Brazil.

its decision to approve the release of RR soybeans, under Brazil's 1995 Biosafety Law it nonetheless retained technical jurisdiction over the new risks that might be posed by GM crops and foods to human health. Only after CTNBio judges a GM product fit for human consumption does jurisdiction pass to the Ministry of Justice, or any other ministry, to establish labeling standards.

Brazil's special commission proceeded by reviewing the GM food labeling rules recently imposed by the European Union and also by consulting evolving standards within the Codex Alimentarius Commission. In December 1999 it finally released for 90 days of public discussion the draft labeling policy it had devised.[12] The draft policy was designed as a minor supplement to rather than a comprehensive replacement for food labeling laws already in place. It covered only packaged GM foods and GM food ingredients destined for final consumers. It did not cover unpackaged fresh foods currently sold without labels or food additives, food preparations, or processed foods. Thus it required no new labels, only that some existing labels be slightly changed. Labels on packaged GM foods would now include an easy to read phrase (located close to the price), for example "GM soya" or "meal from GM soya."[13]

This draft policy was written carefully so as not to require costly steps to segregate GM from non-GM foods in all of Brazil's internal markets. By excluding processed foods and food preparations (such as soybean oil or tomato catsup), the law covers only GM foods retaining enough identifiable transformed DNA or protein to be detected as GM through physical testing. This could allow the law to be enforced through testing alone without market segregation, depending in part upon the percentage threshold for protein at which an ingredient is considered to be GM. The lower the percentage threshold, the more likely that some form of market segregation could be required. The draft policy was also carefully written not to frighten consumers. It prohibits any label that might attribute to GM foods effects that cannot be proven and, although it provides a voluntary option for labeling products as "GM free," those using such labels must be able to prove the claim to competent authorities either through a chain of certification or through complete market segregation.

It remains to be seen whether this or any other comparably "permissive" labeling policy will be enough to satisfy Brazil's more aggressive consumer advocacy organizations. IDEC responded by demanding through the court system a more precautionary labeling policy based on mandatory market seg-

---

12. After public discussion, the Consumer Protection Department of the Ministry of Justice would be empowered to make any changes in this draft it saw fit, then put the new policy into effect after giving food packagers a 180-day grace period to adjust (Brazil, Ministry of Justice 1999).

13. Packages of mixed products containing one or more ingredients derived from GMOs would have to have an asterisk after each such ingredient (it is already required that ingredients be listed) and a phrase at the bottom next to a similar asterisk such as "produced partly with GMOs."

regation. This approach would be costly to Brazil's farm and agribusiness sector because it would require separate storage, transport, and processing facilities for GM and non-GM commodities, all the way from farm to market. Some farm and agribusiness organizations in Brazil might actually prefer to remain entirely GM free (if this were possible) rather than have to pay the costs of full market segregation. Knowing this, anti-GM activist groups in Brazil are all the more comfortable demanding market segregation.

Public Investment Policy

The government of Brazil has a strong record of public investment in agricultural research. Among the national agricultural research systems of Latin America, Brazil's Embrapa has traditionally been second to none. Modern agribiotechnology formally became a significant part of Embrapa's research agenda as early as 1974, with the creation of a separate Center for National Genetic Resources (CENARGEN). The development of transgenic crops was not an original mission at CENARGEN and it has still not developed into a dominating central mission. Yet Brazil has invested enough of its own treasury funds in crop transformation, through Embrapa and CENARGEN and other national institutes, to mark its policies in this area as promotional toward GM crops.

Embrapa has a significant annual budget of approximately R$550 million (about US$320 million at 1999 exchange rates). Yet roughly 80 percent of this budget goes to pay the routine salary expenses of the organization's 8,000 employees (many of whom are nearing retirement and command high salaries), so Embrapa's annual expenditures for actual research activities may total only R$100 million annually. Within Embrapa, CENARGEN's treasury-funded budget has recently been stable in local currency terms, despite severe fiscal austerity pressures in Brazil since the financial crisis of 1998. CENARGEN's total budget within Embrapa in 1999—including salaries—stood at roughly R$30 million, or about US$18 million, so only about 5 percent of Embrapa's total budget has recently gone to agribiotechnology and genetic resources.

Within the category of agribiotechnology and genetic resources, CENARGEN's programs in the narrower area of molecular and transgenic applications are smaller still. If only Embrapa's direct treasury funding is considered, GM work has recently received only about R$1.8 million per year (about US$1 million). This underestimates total public spending on GM, however, because Embrapa's own funds tend to be roughly matched by treasury funds from CNPq, a funding agency in the Ministry of Science and Technology, and still other moneys are available through ad hoc links to private or bilateral international sources and through PADCT, a World Bank lending facility for research administered by the Ministry of Science and Technology. Brazil's total current annual public sector research effort in the area of GM crops is frequently estimated at about US$2.5 million (at 1999 exchange rates). This figure measures genuine research funding and does not count salaries, facilities, overheads, or equipment. This annual public investment by the Brazilian federal government funds separate molecular or GM projects on a range of crops including soybeans, cotton, maize, potato, papaya, common black bean, banana, cassava, and rice. In some cases, as noted above, these federal treasury funds are augmented by contributions from international companies (which may also be lending the transgenes essential to the research) and from bilateral donors, including the European Union, which has supported Brazil's work on transformed potatoes.

Significant results in the area of GM crop development have been achieved with these public investments. Embrapa/CENARGEN has even developed and patented its own system for crop transformation (applicable to more than one species of crop) and, as noted above, it has field-tested its own transformed herbicide-resistant soybeans and virus-resistant potatoes. Further progress toward commercialization of these Brazilian transgenic varieties will await more complete field trial results, then successful negotiation of commercial contracts with the international companies holding key patents, and finally approval on biosafety grounds by CTNBio. Publicly financed work on transformed cassava and rice is also under way, but is less far along.

The government of Brazil has thus embraced a promotional public investment policy toward transgenic crops. It does not want to depend entirely on foreign companies to bring in foreign-owned GM technologies. Research policy leaders also want the nation to be able to develop its own GM crop technologies independently. The goal is not so much to try to outspend or outperform the international private sector as it is to learn enough about the new technology to be able to partner with foreign firms on more even terms. For example, Brazil's alternative transformation protocol (for Dicotyledonae plants) developed independently by CENARGEN gives the nation a useful "bargaining chip" to strengthen its hand in research and commercial contract negotiations (Sampaio 2000).

Brazil's promotional public investment policy has remained in place despite uncertainty regarding future consumer acceptance of transgenics in international markets. President Fernando Henrique Cardoso's most recent four-year Pluri-Annual Plan (PPA) presented to the Brazilian Congress established biotechnology (including pharmaceuticals as well as agribiotechnology) as one of five basic foundation programs to guide Brazil into the new millennium. The projected budget for this new GENOMA program, as endorsed by the Ministry of Science and Technology and presented to the Congress late in 1999, also suggested significant near-term growth in total state funds available to Embrapa/CENARGEN. One preliminary version of the PPA requested a 45 percent increase in state funding from all sources for Embrapa's agribiotechnology research (of all kinds) between 2000 and 2003. Within this total, a

55 percent increase in funding for Embrapa/CENARGEN work on molecular and transgenic applications of agribiotech was indicated.[14]

Although Brazil's public investment policies have qualified as promotional toward GM crops overall, they have not always been well balanced among crops. In particular, most public investment efforts have not gone toward the crops produced by the nation's poorest farmers (for example, cassava, beans, rice, potato, papaya, or banana). Struggling small farmers in Brazil might enjoy large benefits if public investments focused more heavily on developing disease-resistant transgenic varieties of the crops they produce. Some potato varieties in Brazil, when affected by PVX virus in conjunction with PVY, can suffer synergistic losses of up to 70 percent of yield. Losses from bean tree mosaic virus can range from 40 percent to 100 percent (CENARGEN 1995). Papaya is severely affected by ring spot virus, for which genetically engineered resistance might provide cost-effective control (Burnquist 1996). GM technologies can address such problems, but the greatest efforts are still being made instead on the key commercial crops—especially soybeans and maize—grown by larger and more prosperous farmers in Brazil. It is easy to understand and to justify this focus on commercial grounds, but it represents something of a missed opportunity on social grounds.

One way to compare the commercial against the social focus of public sector GM crop development in Brazil is to count the number of field trials for transgenics approved between 1997 and 1999 by CTNBio. During this period, CTNBio approved 687 separate field trials for GM crops. Of this total, 631 were for maize alone and 36 were for soybeans. These two commercial crops together thus made up 97 percent of the field trial total. Cane sugar—an industrial crop in Brazil—was next on the list with 11 field trials, followed by cotton with 3 and eucalyptus and tobacco with 2. Rice and potato—among the more traditional crops of small farmers— each had just one field trial approved (CTNBio 1999).

Transgenic crop research investments do tend to be somewhat transferable across crops, more so than conventional plant breeding investments. Investments in training Brazilian scientists to work on GM commercial or industrial crops could therefore help to build the nation's capacity to work on GM varieties of "social" and "family" crops as well. For example, Brazil's major private sugarcane institute has helped to fund a multi-year genomics (expressed sequence tag sequencing) project for sugarcane, and participation in this project has provided valuable training in genomics for a significant number of Brazilian graduate students working in 38 university-based research groups. This development of scientific capacity could eventually help support follow-on efforts in Brazil to transform poor farmers' crops.

---

14. Source: interviews at Embrapa/CENARGEN, December 1999.

Researchers at Embrapa know that they have a legal mandate to work on social crops, and they have at times attempted when negotiating research contracts to secure technologies from international companies that are especially suited for "orphan crops" and hence unlikely to be used by the companies themselves. Yet the strongest political pressures for research breakthroughs in Brazil naturally come from more prosperous growers, processors, and exporters of commercial crops. In Brazil, political pressures constantly push public sector research away from poor people's crops. Long a problem in non-GM agriculture research in Brazil, this pattern is now emerging in the GM era as well.

When Brazilian agricultural policy leaders dream, it is often of combining their nation's nearly limitless natural resource capacity with the most modern of agricultural technologies, such as genetic engineering, to "feed the world." They see the nation positioned to become, in the twenty-first century, one of the world's most important breadbaskets for basic farm commodities. The space for agricultural expansion in Brazil is unmatched. The Cerrados region, with a potential agricultural area of 127 million hectares, has been only 37 percent exploited to date (Embrapa 1998). Brazil's public investments in GM technologies may some day help give substance to this dream but, unless the focus of those investments can somehow be spread more toward coverage of poor people's crops, the task of providing adequate income and nutrition to all Brazilian farmers will remain elusive.

Conclusion

Summarizing the above discussion, Table 4.1 maps out Brazil's recent policies toward GM crops. The complexity of this summary reminds us that Brazil's policies toward GM crops and foods in most areas are far from settled. In the area of biosafety policy, CTNBio tried at first to follow a permissive policy but was blocked from doing so by an NGO lawsuit and a federal court injunction. Brazil's policies are likewise contested and confused in the area of trade. At the federal level, officials tried to be promotional or permissive toward imports of GM products to keep their own future export options open, yet they were forced by GM critics into a precautionary import posture that screens GM commodities more closely than non-GM ones. Federal officials also tried to be promotional in the food safety area, but were forced in 1999 under NGO pressure to retreat toward a permissive policy.

Only in the two areas of intellectual property rights and public research investment has it been possible for Brazil's federal government to persist with essentially the same policies it originally adopted in the mid-1990s to promote the GM crop revolution. In the IPR area the federal government moved further than its WTO obligations alone would have required to put in place a permissive set of policies; it was rewarded with a surge of investments by interna-

TABLE 4.1 Policies toward GM crops in Brazil, 1999–2000

Policy	Promotional	Permissive	Precautionary	Preventive
IPR		Plant Variety Protection Law has elements of UPOV 1991, and a restricted definition of farmer's privilege to save and replant seed		
Biosafety			In 1998/99, the Institute for Consumer Defense, Greenpeace, and IBAMA secured federal court rulings requiring a highly precautionary biosafety approach	
Trade			GM commodity imports screened and partially blocked; some states (not the federal government) attempt to preserve GM-free status to promote exports	
Food safety and consumer choice		Draft labeling law distinguishes between GM and non-GM on some existing labels, but does not require full market segregation		
Public research investment	Significant treasury resources are spent on building capacity to develop independent national crop transformation capabilities			

NOTE: UPOV = International Convention for the Protection of New Varieties of Plants; IBAMA = Brazilian Institute for the Environment and Renewable Natural Resources.

tional companies eager to bring GM seeds into the country. In the area of public research investment, Brazil's determination to spend at least some treasury resources to advance its own independent national GM crop transformation capacity has also continued. If the Brazilian federal government were free to operate without having to confront resistance from adversarial NGOs, media critics, independent judges, opposition party leaders, or defiant state governors, its policies toward GM crops would probably have remained permissive or promotional across the board. Yet under this mix of pressures the federal government was forced after 1998 to shift its food safety policies from promotional to permissive and its biosafety and trade policies from permissive to precautionary. Because of the resulting freeze on biosafety approvals in particular, as late as mid-2001 farmers in Brazil were still not officially permitted to grow any GM crops.

5 NGOs Stir Anxieties in India

India's GM Crop Opportunity

The Indian people are far better fed today on average than in the past. Nevertheless, 2.7 million children still die in India every year, 60 percent of them from diseases linked to malnutrition (Sharma 1999). A leading cause of malnutrition in India is poverty, and in rural areas a leading cause of poverty is low productivity in agriculture. Of the nation's 1 billion people, two-thirds still gain their livelihood from farming; 75 percent of India's farmers are disadvantaged, with 1 hectare of land or less (Swaminathan 1999). Meanwhile, population growth makes larger demands on Indian agriculture year after year.

The productivity of Indian agriculture has recently improved overall. The annual rate of growth of value-added in farming increased from 3.1 percent in the 1980s to 3.8 percent in the 1990s, at a time when population growth rates were falling (World Bank 2000). Amid these productivity gains, poorly managed government marketing policies occasionally generated embarrassing public stocks of food, including 27 million tons of surplus wheat at the end of 2000. Yet this recent impression of national food abundance in India is misleading. During the 1990s total food grain production in India did not increase at all on a per capita basis, and 230 million Indians remained food insecure owing to persistent poverty, linked most often to the low productivity of their agricultural resources.

Solving India's poverty and hunger problems will require more than just a further boost in overall farm productivity. A number of other issues will also have to be addressed, including persistent rural illiteracy, social marginalization, landlessness, and caste or gender discrimination. And, even where low farm productivity is the problem, GM crop technologies might not be the solution. On India's drylands, where farm productivity is low in part because of poor soil fertility or scant rainfall, the GM technologies currently available provide few new options. India's poorest farmers are those who live in dryland areas with less than 750 mm of rainfall a year and therefore lack the ability to irrigate their crops. Non-irrigated farming in India still accounts for 67 percent

93

of the total cultivated area and supports 40 percent of the population, plus two-thirds of the nation's livestock. Average grain yields on non-irrigated land in India are only 0.7–0.8 tons per hectare, which is one-third the yield on irrigated land (Singh and Venkateswarlu 1999). With yields on irrigated land now leveling off, India has little choice but to seek new technical solutions for its low-production farmers in dry, rainfed areas, as 80 percent of millets and pulse crops are grown under rainfed conditions, and roughly 50 percent of rice is rainfed.

GM crops might seem an unlikely solution for farmers in hot drought-prone regions, since it has been far easier so far to engineer crops for specific resistances to pests or disease than to engineer the multigene traits needed to provide greater resistance to drought or heat. Yet India's producers of dryland crops (such as sorghum, groundnut, or pigeon pea) also face severe pest and disease problems. For groundnuts and pigeon pea, crop losses to biotic stress are actually greater than losses to abiotic stress (ICRISAT 1992). Pigeon pea farmers can sometimes lose their entire crop through damage from a single insect. Pod borers attack all pulses and viral diseases are a widespread blight on India's dryland crops. Small dryland cotton farmers in India are devastated by bollworm infestations. Together with conventional breeding programs and improved training in integrated pest management, genetic engineering might help provide solutions to these biotic stress problems facing India's poorest farmers.

Environmental protection imperatives also argue for a GM crop revolution in India. The current practices of India's poor dryland crop farmers are damaging to rural ecosystems. If use of GM varieties could produce yield gains for these farmers, there would be less need to clear new lands in rural India, plow fragile sloping lands, or destroy still more habitat. If farmers had insecticidal GM crops they also might escape having to risk their own health, pollute the environment, and kill so many non-target species as they do now with conventional chemical sprays. Farm chemical use has even become a rural economic welfare issue in India: cotton farmers currently spend Rs 16 billion annually on insecticide sprays; vegetable producers in India currently suffer a US$2.5 billion loss annually to insect damage, even while spending (on tomatoes, for example) US$100–200 per hectare on insecticides (Padmanabhan 2000).

Somewhat further into the technological future, GM crops could eventually help address more directly some of India's severe nutritional problems. Roughly 50,000 children in India go blind every year from vitamin A deficiency, and iron deficiency is a major threat to the health of women. The possibility of engineering rice rich in iron, or rapeseed oil rich in vitamin A, would become interesting in this context. Some traditional food crops in India that currently contain dangerous substances (neurotoxins in kesar dal, cyanide in tapioca, aflatoxins in groundnut) might also be rendered safer if genetic engineering could be used to "silence" these undesirable traits (Prakash 1999).

And in a nation where refrigeration facilities are not yet abundant it might at some point be attractive to engineer fruits and vegetables less prone to spoilage. Tomato producers in India today lose 20–30 percent of their crop through postharvest spoilage.

Political leaders as well as scientists and technocrats in India have noticed these opportunities, and they now routinely endorse the potential contributions that biotechnology—including transgenic crops—might make to agricultural productivity growth and poverty reduction in the years ahead. In 1999, Dr. R. K. Pachauri, director of India's Tata Energy Research Institute, stated that India's future increases in food production "would necessarily have to come from the application of biotechnology" (Pachauri 1999, 10). At India's 87th Science Congress in January 2000, Prime Minister Atal Bihari Vajpayee singled out information technology and biotechnology, plus "other knowledge-based sectors," as the propellers that would move India's economy ahead in the new century. At this same meeting Dr. R. A. Mashelkar, director general of India's Council of Scientific and Industrial Research specifically endorsed biotechnology in agriculture as a means to turn farmers into high-productivity "knowledge workers" (BGE 2000).

Although many top leaders in India have endorsed the value of agri-biotechnology in general and scarce treasury resources have even been allocated to promote GM crop research within India's national agricultural research system, India's policies toward GM crops have hardly been promotional, or even permissive, across the board. Biotechnology policy leaders in India originally intended to pursue at least a permissive approach toward GM crops, yet this aim has recently been frustrated. Critics of GM crops were able to work within India's open and democratic political system to push for a precautionary or even a preventive approach toward GM crops instead, especially in the area of biosafety policy. Indian biosafety authorities, somewhat like their counterparts in Brazil, ran up against forceful public criticism when they attempted to pursue a permissive approach toward the testing and release of GM crops. As of mid-2001 this meant that farmers in India, like their counterparts in Brazil and Kenya, had not yet been given official permission to plant any GM crops.

Intellectual Property Rights Policies

Although GM crop critics in India have focused most on possible biosafety risks, they have also attempted to block the technology by voicing strong objections to what they describe as the disadvantageous IPR implications of GM crops. To the extent that GM crops come with stronger IPR conditions attached, it is not surprising to hear voices of objection raised in India, a nation without a strong IPR policy tradition, least of all in the area of animals and plants. And to the extent that private multinational seed companies are the holders of the IPRs, India's misgivings are that much easier to understand, given the culture of mistrust toward international companies that has long pervaded both India's government and its civil society. India's IPR policies toward GM crops, in part for these larger social and cultural reasons, have been extremely weak. As of 2000, India's parliament still had not enacted even a basic plant variety protection law.

For decades India was able to get along without a strong IPR policy in the area of farm crops because it relied on its own public sector scientists and government extension agents, rather than private investors or international private companies, to stimulate innovation in agriculture. During the 1960s and 1970s, agricultural research and development (R&D) in India were almost exclusively the business of the Indian Council of Agricultural Research (ICAR), a vast network of government institutes, directorates, research centers, and public universities. The private sector was in effect excluded through tight controls over germplasm exchange, technology imports, seed trade regulations, and restrictions on investment (Selvarajan, Joshi, and O'Toole 1999). In this environment, innovation was stimulated through public expenditure rather than by offering IPRs to plant breeders. India operated without a plant variety protection law and its 1970 Patent Act specifically excluded the patenting of life forms such as plants (Mishra 1999).

This system served India well enough in the early years of the Green Revolution, and in some respects it continues to work well, as marginal economic rates of return to agricultural research in the state-dominated Indian system have remained high (Evenson, Pray, and Rosegrant 1999). By its own count during the 1992–96 Eighth Plan period, ICAR developed and released more than 2,300 high-yielding varieties and hybrids, including 452 new varieties of field crops ready for general cultivation. Yet by the 1980s overall state support for agricultural research in India had begun to falter and scientists in India began looking for greater rewards through the private sector. Government attitudes toward the private sector also became less hostile. Starting in the early 1980s the government decided to provide its own breeder seed to private companies for multiplication and duplication. Foreign investment rules were relaxed and in 1988 a New Seed Policy liberalized industrial licensing options. As a result, multinational seed companies began making significant investments through India's own private sector companies. From the mid-1980s to the mid-1990s, 24 companies representing roughly 17 percent of all private seed concerns in India initiated technical or financial collaboration with foreign companies.

These liberalizations brought pressures in India to enact a basic plant variety protection law. Officials in the agricultural research establishment had concluded by 1991 it was necessary and prudent to move India's IPR policies closer to international standards. By 1993 a draft plant variety protection act (PVPA) was ready for submission to parliament. It measured up to the 1978 standard of the International Convention for the Protection of New Varieties of Plants (UPOV) by creating minimal plant breeders' rights (PBRs), which preserved the farmer's privilege to replant and exchange saved seed. The drafting of this basic PVPA preceded final negotiation of the Agreement on Trade-Related Aspects of Intellectual Property Rights (TRIPS) in the World Trade Organization (WTO), but when India formally ratified TRIPS in 1994 these issues became linked because India now had an international obligation to have basic IPR protections in place for plant varieties by January 2000.

This decision to move toward a conventional plant variety protection law in the context of TRIPS triggered a surprisingly emotional debate in India's parliament. The first draft of the PVPA was criticized by the private seed industry for being too weak, but nongovernmental organizations (NGOs) claiming to represent farmers' groups warned it was far too strong and would lead to a private expropriation of farmers' rights in the area of crop variety development. Revised drafts were produced in 1996–97 in order to address the farmers' rights issue, and cabinet approval for a revised draft was secured in October 1997. However, under still more NGO criticism, parliament continued to stall and more redrafting was initiated. The version of the PVPA that was working its way through parliament in 2000 was a version produced in December 1999.

These PVPA debates in India would have been contentious even if GM crop technologies had never been invented. Colonization was an especially bitter experience for India and sensitivities about foreign corporate ownership of any part of the national economy remain high. Foreign ownership of genetic resources in India—GM or otherwise—is an especially emotional issue. Advocates of the PVPA argue that IPR guarantees for plant breeders will stimulate useful new innovations in India, bring in foreign capital and technology, and at the same time provide improved protection for the 150,000 accessions and samples of crop germplasm in the hands of India's own National Gene Bank. Yet critics highlight what they describe as the danger of a foreign corporate takeover of India's own national seed industry or the private use of IPR options to gain controlling ownership of the plant genetic resources on which India's farmers depend. An Indian NGO calling itself the Gene Campaign argues prominently that foreign multinational companies might appropriate and exploit India's genetic material without adequate compensation if Western-style IPRs in this area were ever to be permitted (Sahai 1999).

Fueling these fears after 1991 was an increased presence of international companies staking ownership claims within India's food economy. Between 1987 and 1995, even though the PVPA had not yet passed parliament, the share of private seed sales in India made by firms with foreign ownership increased from 10 percent to 33 percent (Pray 1999). Several IPR actions taken outside of India were also represented as threats to national genetic sovereignty. In 1992 the W. R. Grace company secured a patent in the United States for a distinctive chemical formulation of a naturally occurring pesticide from neem trees. Anti-corporate activists in India began asserting that international companies such as Grace were planning to use such patent protections to monopolize the locally developed folk knowledge that had long been available to India's farmers and rural communities for free. Grace argued that this charge was unfounded because the patent was on a new chemical formulation and did not prevent traditional farmers all over the world from continuing to use neem extract as they always had. Nonetheless, the neem case enflamed popular anxieties about the foreign appropriation of local knowledge and led to an international struggle by environmental NGOs to remove the patent. In May 2000, the European Patent Office did revoke Grace's 1995 patent in Europe for the neem oil extraction process, but litigation against the patent in the United States was sure to prove more difficult.[1]

Some of India's most respected leaders in the area of agricultural research have shared the concern that patent protections for plants, or even a national move toward a conventional PBR system, might leave the nation's poor farmers at a disadvantage. Rural communities in India have for thousands of years employed their own on-farm seed selection practices to breed a highly diverse stock of plant varieties nicely attuned to local conditions. Under a PBR system, why should IPR protection go only to the professional breeders (working within either international companies or national institutes) who routinely use these already improved local varieties as the basis for their breeding programs? Arguing that indigenous knowledge systems are similar to general scientific information, Dr. M. S. Swaminathan, India's most acclaimed agricultural scientist and the first winner of the World Food Prize, has helped popularize the notion that communities of farmers are as entitled to IPR protection for their efforts as are professional breeders. Largely in response to his leadership, as early as 1989 the Conference of the Food and Agriculture Organization (FAO) in Rome adopted his concept of farmers' rights.

Swaminathan argued that India's own draft PVPA law should incorporate a farmers' rights provision in the form of an institutional mechanism designed to ensure the rights of farming communities to financial compensation for any earlier contributions they might have made to the plant varieties that will finally be protected under the act. The 1999 draft of India's PVPA (in Chapters X and XII) does so by certifying the rights of villages and local communities to claim contributions to the evolution of plant varieties, and then to receive appropriate financial compensation from a centrally managed National Gene Fund (Government of India 1999). In anticipation of this provision coming into

---

1. A second case of alleged biopiracy is the 1997 patent granted in the United States to a Texas-based firm, RiceTech Inc., for basmati rice grains and lines and their breeding and cooking methods. Since March 1998 the Indian government has taken steps to challenge this patent (APBN 2000c, 200).

effect, the government of India began compiling a formal register of the geographic origins of all plant genetic resources that have been or might be used by professional breeders. Registering this indigenous germplasm also puts it in the public domain, thus preempting private bioprospectors from subsequently using the PVPA to take commercial advantage of this germplasm without compensating local communities.

These provisions for financial compensation to farmers have not gone far enough, however, to satisfy India's most determined critics of UPOV-style plant variety protection. In 1998, India's activist Research Foundation for Science, Technology and Ecology (RFSTE) headed by Vandana Shiva—an internationally known opponent of GM crops, the Green Revolution, and virtually all other market-led scientific advances in Indian agriculture—proposed an alternative biodiversity rights and protection bill that would give local farming communities not just financial compensation but actual property rights over the crop varieties to which their traditional on-farm breeding efforts had contributed. The bill specifies that local communities would share these property rights with the central government of India, so private companies seeking to pirate valuable genetic materials would not be able to approach local communities separately to gain access to these materials on unequal terms (Cullet 1999). The aim of this proposal was to reject any movement in India toward a Western-style IPR system in the area of plant genetic resources. When the government persisted with its PVPA approach, the RFSTE initiated a public interest litigation action against the government.

The issue of GM crops only complicates this already intense internal debate in India over plant variety IPRs. In 1998, when the Monsanto company of the United States purchased a 26 percent share of India's Maharashtra Hybrid Seeds Company Limited (Mahyco), a Monsanto executive was quoted in the Indian press as saying: "We propose to penetrate the Indian agriculture sector in a big way. Mahyco is a good vehicle" (*Economic Times,* New Delhi, April 26, 1998). Opponents of transnational corporations within India took this as a direct challenge and began harshly criticizing all of Monsanto's GM crop technologies, especially the "terminator gene" patent it had recently acquired, which was represented as a direct threat to the tradition of seed saving in India. It was Monsanto's misfortune that word of this new gene use restriction technology (GURT) reached India just when limited field trials of Mahyco's Bt cotton were being authorized for the first time. Gene use restriction technologies had not yet been inserted into GM crops anywhere, let alone the Bt cotton being tried out in India, but this issue made Monsanto and Mahyco easy targets for NGO and opposition party criticism. When a Canadian-based NGO, the Rural Advancement Foundation International, spread the alarm that Monsanto's terminator gene might be turned loose in India, local NGOs opposed to international companies and non-traditional farm technologies mobilized against Mahyco's Bt cotton field trials. In November 1998, a local political leader in Karnataka state who had previously gained attention by attacking both the Cargill seed company and a Kentucky Fried Chicken restaurant in Bangalore, staged a brief attack for the media on some of the trial plots. Soon thereafter local communist party leaders in Andra Pradesh pressured the chief minister into calling for an end to the Mahyco Bt cotton field trials under way there.

The mere existence of a terminator gene patent seemed to confirm suspicions that international seed companies were seeking to take away from India's farmers their traditional right to replicate seed on their own farms. In India, 92 percent of all wheat seed and 88 percent of paddy rice seed planted is home grown. NGOs and globalization critics feared that India's small farmers would be pressured by Monsanto or Mahyco into purchasing expensive GURT seeds, only to discover too late that they had to keep purchasing them year after year. The same argument could have been made against conventional non-GM hybrid seeds, which are currently used and repurchased routinely by small as well as large farmers in India growing maize, sorghum (jowar), millet (bajra), sunflower, cotton, and vegetables, but the terminator technology was far more inviting as a proxy for criticizing profit-making foreign companies. Although Monsanto announced in the fall of 1999 that it was not going to commercialize the technology, by then the damage to IPR policy advocates was already done.

Enactment of the PVPA in India was also made more difficult by links to the TRIPS Agreement. Many of the groups that saw IPRs for plants as the opening wedge for external corporate domination also feared the WTO, which is often criticized in India as an instrument used by rich countries to bully poor countries. Under the TRIPS Agreement India was technically obliged to change its patenting system from processes to products and to have a plant variety protection law in place by January 2000, but this deadline came and went without parliamentary action.

The prospects for eventual parliamentary passage of some version—probably a weakened version—of the government's PVPA bill were nonetheless strong in 2000. The National Democratic Alliance government sent its most recent version of the bill to parliament for approval in December 1999, just before its January 2000 WTO deadline for TRIPS compliance. The bill was then referred to a 30-member joint committee of both houses, which redrafted the bill so as to strengthen its farmers' rights provisions by recommending that appeals be heard not by the high courts but by a specially formed tribunal. The delays continued, but the WTO was unlikely to criticize India for not having a PVPA in place so long as the delay stemmed only from the slow movement of democratic procedures.

This failure by India through 2000 to put in place any formal IPR protections for plants was not, however, the principal reason that GM crop technologies were not yet in use by farmers. Because of the size of India's commercial seed market, private international companies have been eager to bring GM technologies into the country even in the absence of IPR guarantees. Their preferred means for doing this has been to seek to introduce hybrid varieties, which carry their own inherent biological protections against seed saving and replanting. India's weak IPR policies do, however, place some limits on what international private companies are willing to do, as well as on what India's own breeders have an incentive to do. Because of weak IPRs, private companies do not like to conduct advanced research in Indian labs. In its Bt cotton venture Monsanto conducted no plant transformations within India itself; instead it brought in hybrid cotton seeds that had already been transformed abroad. Nor did it begin field trials until it owned a secure share of a local corporate partner that had been entrusted with the backcrossing. A Belgian biotechnology firm, Plant Genetic Systems, was almost as cautious when it decided to bring its transgenic "seedlink" technology into India to develop an improved brassica (mustard). It invested an initial US$1 million in a joint venture with a trustworthy local private sector partner, Pro Agro, then limited its work to hybrids.

If India wishes to go into partnership with foreign companies to secure access to GM technologies for plants other than hybrids (for example, glyphosate-resistant soybeans), passage of a credible plant variety protection law may be critical. Up to a point, bilateral contracts can be used to compensate for a weak internal IPR law, yet without at least a UPOV 1978 plant breeders' rights system in place, India's public sector researchers risk being passed over as unsafe technology development partners by the more dynamic international private sector. Guarding India's own nationally managed germplasm accessions from private appropriation could also become more difficult, public registration strategies notwithstanding. For these reasons India's Council for Scientific and Industrial Research has been campaigning for a stronger IPR and patenting system in India, in agriculture as well as in other sectors.

In the longer run, IPR guarantees even stronger than those contained in the current draft PVPA may be necessary if India wishes to keep pace in GM science. The draft PVPA has been criticized by the private seed companies as unattractive for their purposes because it lays a basis (in Chapter X) for compulsory licensing after three years to meet "the reasonable requirements of the public for seeds." It also creates a registration process open to delay and challenge, which could add another three years to the already long period (currently six to seven years) required in India to get a new seed variety completely deregulated and eligible for commercial release. And by embracing the UPOV 1978 standard the PVPA does not provide scientists with sufficient incentive to innovate at the molecular level, because protection of GM varieties may not be extended to include essential derivations from those varieties. The president of India's private Seed Association, although a supporter of the PVPA, has stated that it "does not provide sufficient protection for bioengineered plants" (Selvarajan, Joshi, and O'Toole 1999, v). Private seed companies of course prefer product patents as the best means to encourage innovations in biotechnology, but even Indian scientists working at the molecular level inside the national research system want stronger standards; they would prefer the UPOV 1991 standard over the weaker UPOV 1978 standard contained in the current draft PVPA.

Without any plant variety protection law formally in place, India as of 2000 must be classified as taking a preventive stance toward GM crops in the IPR area. Even after the draft PVPA is eventually enacted, India's posture in this area will be no more than precautionary. Still, it has been India's biosafety policies, not its IPR policies, that have most conspicuously slowed down the nation's GM crop revolution.

Biosafety Policies

Biological safety has not been, historically, a strong public policy thrust in Indian agriculture. Rural biological systems have long been threatened by low-resource farmers who clear new lands and destroy natural habitat in order to graze animals or plant crops. Mismanagement of irrigation water has left once fertile croplands poisoned with salt. Careless application of chemical nutrients has contaminated rivers, streams, and ponds, making water unsafe for human consumption and poisoning fish and amphibian species. Improper use of insecticides has killed non-target species while making target pests increasingly resistant to the poisons. Even after the enactment of India's powerful 1986 Environmental Protection Act (EPA), such conventional biohazards from farming were seldom effectively regulated. It is thus somewhat surprising to see Indian officials paying so much attention to the biological safety of GM crops. Official interest in genetic resource IPRs would have been strong in India even without GM crops as an issue, but government attention to rural biological safety is partly a product of the GM crop revolution itself.

India's first embrace of a formal national biosafety policy dates from the emergence of recombinant DNA (rDNA) technologies in agricultural and human health in the 1980s. Given India's strong development aspirations and its prior history of low attention to rural biohazards, one might have expected its biosafety policies toward GM crops to be permissive or even promotional. Instead, from the start the Indian government adopted a set of procedures that ensured significant precaution, and the implementation of these procedures has become more cautious still in the context of a growing global controversy over GM crops. As of mid-2001, farmers in India were not yet permitted to grow any GM crops because none had received final approval from the nation's biosafety regulators.

The Indian government first issued rules and procedures for handling GM organisms in December 1989, and the Department of Biotechnology (DBT) inside the Ministry of Science and Technology published these rules and procedures in January 1990 (India, DBT 1990). These "Recombinant DNA Safety Guidelines" were revised slightly and republished as "Revised Guidelines for Safety in Biotechnology" in 1994 (India, DBT 1994). They describe the biosafety measures that must be undertaken in India both for contained research activities and also for large-scale open environmental release of genetically altered agricultural and pharmaceutical materials. A subsequent 1998 revision of the guidelines elaborated procedures for screening transgenic plants and seeds for toxicity and allergenicity (India, DBT 1998).

Borrowing heavily from the demonstrated-risk approach employed by the United States Department of Agriculture's Animal and Plant Health Inspection Service (APHIS), India's crop biosafety guidelines require a screening of GM crop technologies for scientifically demonstrated risks, which is compatible with a U.S.-style permissive approach. Yet the implementation of the guidelines is shared with India's Ministry of Environment, a procedure that inclines India's policy somewhat more toward precaution. The guidelines create two separate review committees: a Review Committee on Genetic Manipulation (RCGM), which is empowered to approve (or not approve) applications for all small-scale research activities in India designed to generate information on transgenic organisms, and a Genetic Engineering Approval Committee (GEAC), empowered to approve (or not) large-scale research activities and actual industrial use or environmental release of all GM organisms.[2]

Because the RCGM mostly screens research activities for biosafety, it is composed of representatives from India's leading public universities and research institutes, including the Indian Council of Agricultural Research (ICAR), the Indian Council of Medical Research (ICMR), and the Council of Scientific & Industrial Research (CSIR). It is constituted by the Department of Biotechnology and its member-secretary is adviser to the DBT. It has 13 members and operates by majority vote. The GEAC, in contrast, is a statutory body under the Ministry of Environment and Forests (MoEF) and is empowered to approve or disapprove all large-scale use and environmental release of GM organisms. The GEAC is thus India's most powerful biosafety policy gatekeeper. It is chaired by the additional secretary of MoEF and co-chaired by an expert nominee from the DBT, and it includes representatives from the DBT, the Ministry of Industrial Development, the Ministry of Science and Technology, and the Department of Ocean Development.[3] The GEAC

---

2. Four additional institutional mechanisms are created by the guidelines, but these perform mostly advisory or implementing functions. These are the Recombinant DNA Advisory Committee, the Institutional Biosafety Committees, the State Biotechnology Coordination Committees, and the District Level Committees.

3. It also has as expert members the directors general from ICAR, ICMR, CSIR, and Health Services within the Ministry of Health, the plant protection adviser from the Ministry of Agriculture, and the chair of the Central Pollution Control Board, plus a member-secretary from MoEF and three individual outside experts.

is designed to perform more than a technical function. It is the lead inter-ministerial body empowered to shape by consensus the government's final disposition toward the large-scale use and environmental release of GM organisms. The GEAC can authorize or prohibit, conditionally or unconditionally, the import, export, transport, manufacture, processing, use, or sale of any GM organism (Ghosh and Ramanaiah 2000).

This Indian biosafety system was intended to be permissive at the research stage, where RCGM was given the final word. Since RCGM is constituted by the DBT—the agency explicitly given the task of promoting biotechnology in India—its membership comes from the very research institutes (in some cases the very individuals) that conduct public biotech research and rely on the DBT for funding.[4] When the RCGM hands the regulatory process over to the GEAC after the research stage, a precautionary bias takes over because the GEAC is chaired by the Ministry of Environment and Forests. This built-in tension between permissive research and precautionary release might have some advantages in theory. By allowing research to go forward, India's process is capable of generating the empirical data (for example from field trials) needed to make sound final release decisions (Ghosh 1997). India's system also has the potential to avoid last-minute jurisdictional disputes between biotechnology commissions and environmental ministries of the kind seen in Brazil between CTNBio and IBAMA. In India, biosafety regulation stays legally under the EPA and within the jurisdiction of the GEAC from start to finish. Being dominated by the public sector, the Indian system also excludes representatives of private industry from direct participation (another contrast to Brazil), and it requires that the RCGM send a Monitoring Committee to visit the experimental sites used by applicants to generate biosafety data (India, DBT 1998).[5]

India's guidelines are quite thorough regarding the biosafety questions that must be answered prior to the commercial release of GM technologies. In the area of transgenic plants, basic information must be provided on the characteristics of the donor organisms, the vectors used, and the transgenic inserts, and then on the resulting transgenic plants themselves. Through lab, growth chamber, greenhouse, and field trials, applicants must generate evaluations of

---

4. Private companies, on the other hand, see too much of a public sector bias in the RCGM. Companies suspect the RCGM of going slow on private approvals so as to give ICAR scientists more time to catch up (Jayaraman 2001).

5. These screening procedures for GM crop biosafety in India were set in place after the passage of a comprehensive national environmental protection law (the EPA of 1986) but were based firmly on that law. India's parliament has considered a new cabinet-approved Biodiversity Act, to provide formal legal backing for implementation of the 1992 Convention on Biological Diversity, but the sections of this act touching on the biosafety of GM crops were written to be compatible with the existing guidelines, so the DBT expects no jurisdictional challenge to develop. Brazil's CTNBio and Kenya's National Biosafety Committee are not comparably protected.

toxicity and pathogenicity, of the possibility and extent of transgenic pollen escape and transfer to wild relatives, and of the consequences for both the environment and human and animal health. The data may be generated in India or anywhere else (Ghosh 1997). Guidance is provided on proper (biosafe) procedures for conducting these experiments, along with the proper format for presenting this information as a formal registration document. Some of the data required by India's procedures go well beyond biosafety. In the latest version of the guidelines the RCGM is required to solicit from applicants and assemble information "on the comparative agronomic advantages of the transgenic plants" to assure the GEAC that the technologies under review are "economically viable" as well as environmentally safe (India, DBT 1998, 6). This might seem an added barrier to approval, but it can also favor approvals in some cases by allowing evidence of social benefits to be presented to counterbalance possible environmental risks.

How has India's biosafety review system for GM organisms operated in practice? In the area of health care, a number of GM products have been reviewed successfully with little controversy. As of March 2000, 10 different transgenic healthcare products in India (2 locally produced, 8 imported) had moved all the way through the system and been cleared for biosafety deregulation by the GEAC. Social confidence about the biosafety of GM healthcare products has been consistently high in India. In the area of transgenic plants, however, the system has not moved so smoothly. Under criticism from NGOs, even the RCGM has been forced into a highly cautious posture and, as of mid-2001, the GEAC had yet to grant a commercial release for any GM crops.

India's biosafety review system for GM plants was pushed into this cautious posture in 1998, when the RCGM was accused by NGOs in India of having exceeded its mandate by giving approval to limited field trials for Mahyco/Monsanto's Bt cotton plants. The original guidelines had been ambiguous about where the RCGM's authority to manage small-scale research activities would end and where the GEAC's authority to manage large-scale activities and "environmental release" would begin. When Mahyco applied to conduct contained field trials of its Bt cotton in 1998, the RCGM assumed it had the authority to approve such trials, in part because it had earlier approved contained field trials of transgenic mustard in 1995 without incident. Yet the Bt cotton field trials approved for 40 locations in 9 states in India in 1998–99 soon became a focus of intense national controversy, as earlier noted. NGOs in India, led by the Research Foundation for Science, Technology and Ecology, claimed that only the GEAC had the authority to approve field trials of GM crops because even contained and limited trials constituted an environmental release. In February 1999, the RFSTE filed a public interest litigation against the DBT for the manner in which it had authorized the trials (and also against Mahyco and several other ministries), asking that further field trials be blocked.

The RFSTE's challenge to the Bt cotton field trials was not motivated by any specific biosafety worry. The "Bollgard" Bt cotton seeds that Monsanto had brought in to cross with local Indian varieties had previously undergone extensive testing and monitoring in the United States to meet the biosafety standards set by APHIS and the Environmental Protection Agency. Bt cotton had been grown successfully in the United States on a commercial scale since 1996, and by 1998 it covered 40 percent of the total U.S. cotton area. By 1998 it was also being grown successfully and without incident in Australia, South Africa, and China. Bt cotton was potentially attractive in India as a solution to the bollworm infestations that farmers could no longer control with chemical sprays owing to resistance in the pest population. This emergence of a real pest resistance problem from using non-GM technologies made it harder to invoke possible pest resistance as a reason not to plant GM cotton. Food safety risks were also hard to invoke for Bt cotton, since cotton is an industrial crop rather than a food. The RFSTE was using biosafety rules and procedures to try to block Bt cotton, but the core of its argument against this GM crop was that it was being introduced from abroad by the Monsanto company, which owned rights to the dreaded "terminator" technology.

Yet the RFSTE also sought to make its case by pointing to procedural irregularities in the RCGM's approval of the field trials. First, the RCGM was faulted for having given field trial authority directly to a private company applicant and for then allowing that applicant to launch the trials directly on leased farmers' fields rather than on government research farms under direct public sector management. Although this would seem a logical way to handle an application filed by a private company, the RCGM might have known this would be seen in India as trusting the private sector too much. Second, the RCGM had not secured advance approval from government authorities in several of the states where trials were located, and in at least one of those states the trials even began before a local biosafety committee had been fully constituted. These several irregularities were exploited by RFSTE, and left the RCGM and the DBT politically isolated when fears regarding the terminator gene subsequently broke. Nor did it help that the RCGM's procedures in this case had been largely non-transparent. The RCGM could point out that there was no formal obligation to publish deliberations or invite public comment prior to approving the limited trials, but when the trials became controversial the RCGM and the DBT were criticized all the more heavily for having operated behind closed doors (Raj 1999). In the midst of this controversy in 1999 the DBT's biosafety guidelines were amended to make it clear that the GEAC's approval would be required for all field trials larger than 1 acre per location or larger than 20 acres per year nationally. The DBT also directed that the 1999 field trials for Mahyco's Bt cotton would take place either on university research farms or under closer national institute supervision. This, plus a DBT-led public awareness campaign in 1999 and ministerial promises that the terminator gene would not be allowed into India, helped calm the public mood somewhat.

Although India's Bt cotton trials went forward under protest and criticism, they did manage to generate important evidence of this GM plant's effectiveness against bollworm infestations. These pest attacks on cotton in India had emerged as a visible social issue because of the growing resistance of the pests to chemicals and the resulting desperation of some small farmers. Excessive spraying of diluted and adulterated chemical insecticides—in some parts of India as many as 14 sprayings a season—had brought on a pest resistance problem, and some poorer cotton farmers in India were falling deeply into debt as a result of borrowing heavily at a high rate of interest to buy chemicals that no longer worked. Their plight came to public attention when bad weather worsened the pest crisis in 1998 and as many as 500 farmers resorted to suicide as the only way out (Sharma 2000). The first 1998 field trials of Bt cotton in India had seemed to confirm, meantime, that Bt varieties could provide at least a short-term solution to the bollworm problem. The DBT reported in 1998 that on average (in controlled field trials planted in eight states in India) Bt cotton was able to reduce insect damage dramatically: yields for Bt cotton were 40 percent higher than for the non-Bt controls, and with an average of five fewer chemical sprays (Ghosh and Ramanaiah 2000; James 2000a). For a small Indian farmer with 5 hectares of cotton such a reduction in chemical use from switching to Bt cotton might by itself represent savings of roughly Rs 2,000 per crop (about US$50).

The RCGM was pleased and reassured by the 1998 field trial data, but nonetheless asked Mahyco in 1999 for 10 more field trials, seeking more data on the commercial advantages to farmers and also on at least one hypothetical geneflow concern, the possibility that insects could take Bt cotton pollen far enough away from the plant to result in unwanted gene transfer to other plants. Only after these additional trials had been completed did the RCGM formally express its technical confidence in Bt cotton in April 2000. The RCGM noted that its latest evidence showed that farmers growing Bt cotton obtained 25–75 percent higher yields and used six fewer chemical sprays, with no evidence of harm to crops in adjacent plots.

Having received this approval at the research stage from the RCGM, Mahyco promptly applied to the GEAC for permission to begin large-scale trials. In response to this application the GEAC did approve large-scale field trials for Bt cotton (up to 85 total hectares) in July 2000. Additional acreage was also permitted for seed production, in anticipation of a possible commercial release as early as 2001. To appease protesters, the GEAC made large-scale field trials conditional on obtaining an independent Indian laboratory certification that the cotton plants did not contain the "terminator" gene. Even so, the RFSTE was antagonized and submitted an additional petition against the trials. The GEAC's prompt field trial approval increased somewhat the likelihood of an eventual commercial release for Bt cotton in India, although the first release may be only within a tight acreage restriction.

Has the Indian system been precautionary in this case only because the Bt cotton is a Monsanto variety? A second application working its way through India's system from another company (ProAgro-PGS), to develop transgenic hybrid mustard, also met a cautious response from the RCGM. Contained field trials of GM mustard began in 15 different locations in 1995, followed by open field trials. None of these trials was disrupted by anti-GM activists, yet the process of bioscreening was highly precautionary just the same. In 1999, India's regulators asked ProAgro-PGS for one more year of field trials to screen for effects on soil micronutrients, an issue that had never been high-lighted before. ProAgro-PGS hoped for eventual approval and deregulation from the GEAC, but recognized that it might be only a conditional release, perhaps with a requirement (which would be hard to enforce) that farmers planting the GM mustard seeds separate themselves by at least 40–50 meters from non-GM fields as an extra precaution against unwanted geneflow. India's anti-GM NGOs may be focused almost exclusively on keeping Monsanto's products out of the country, but biosafety regulators in India have been highly precautionary toward all GM crop applications, whether from Monsanto or not.

Trade Policy

Because GM crops are politically controversial in India, the government is under pressure from NGOs to impose a GM-free trade policy requirement on the nation's commodity imports and exports. So long as no GM crops are being planted within India on biosafety grounds, an official GM-free trade policy is relatively easy for the government to embrace and implement. A policy of standing aloof from international GM commodity trade is also relatively easy to embrace because India has, for decades, tended to stand somewhat aloof from all international food commodity trade in its official pursuit of "national food self-sufficiency." Ever since India's bad experience with excessive dependence on international food aid in the 1960s, political leaders have sought to avoid not only renewed concessional dependence on world markets but commercial dependence as well.

India's policy aversion to international food trade of all kinds is reflected in the fact that the nation has recently accounted for roughly 10 percent of total world agricultural production but less than 1 percent of world commodity trade (Sharma 2000). With continued income growth in India, demand for imported grains is likely to grow, yet actual imports will continue to be slowed by significant trade barriers at the border. As one example, India recently imposed an 80 percent duty on rice to curb the influx of what it called "cheap grain." India occasionally imports small quantities of corn but it strictly controls these imports with a tariff rate quota, imposing a 60 percent duty on imports larger than the quota. In the case of wheat, India allows imports only in rare cases to offset specific internal transport cost problems, for example to allow less expensive imported wheat to reach some coastal flour mills in the southern part of the country. India also exports very little wheat, despite its occasionally large internal surplus stocks.[6]

These larger aversions in India to free international food commodity trade and the absence so far of any GM crop production within India itself have made it easy for the Indian government to impose an effective ban on the import and export of GM commodities. Under India's official GM guidelines it is the GEAC that must approve any large-scale import of GM commodities, so long as the GEAC has not approved the commercial planting of GM crops at home, it naturally will go slow on approving commercial imports from abroad. Politicians now resist GM crop imports as well. Ever since the 1998 controversy over field trials for Monsanto's Bt cotton, government ministers have routinely retreated to a statement that GM foods are not being grown or imported into India and will not be imported without proper safeguards.

India's unofficial GM crop import ban was tested in unusual circumstances in the summer of 1998 when the nation experienced a highly publicized food safety emergency unrelated to GM crops. More than 50 people in Delhi died after eating a contaminated locally grown (and non-GM) mustard oil, the most popular cooking oil in northern India. The government responded by banning sales of mustard oil pending safer packaging, then to make up the shortage it had to authorize temporary imports of soybeans and lower its import duties on soybean oil (*Wall Street Journal,* December 8, 1998, A10). Anti-trade and anti-GM NGO leaders responded with a letter to the prime minister, alerting him to the fact that some of the soybeans about to be imported might be genetically modified. The government sought to handle the issue on this occasion by arranging to import soybeans that were already split and hence suited only for oil production and not for planting. Because the soybeans were not intended for environmental release and were not explicitly labeled GM, the government on this occasion managed to avoid seeking formal import approval from the GEAC.

In the future it may be more difficult for the government to avoid engaging the GEAC in approval of bulk commodity imports. The January 2000 Biosafety Protocol obliges exporters (under Article 18) when shipping living modified organisms (LMOs) internationally to label those shipments as "may contain LMOs" and "not intended for intentional introduction into the environment." Identifications of this kind are more likely to trigger a mandatory

---

6. In 2000, when India's excess wheat stocks reached 27 million tons, efforts were finally made to clear the stocks through export. However, these efforts were frustrated in part by the known presence of a wheat crop disease—"Karnal Bunt" fungus—in some parts of India, which has put wheat from India on the import ban list of some 30 countries (APBN 2000a).

review in India by the GEAC, or at least more vigorous complaints by NGOs if the GEAC is again avoided. NGOs in India opposed to GM crops and foods are prepared to take extreme positions on the import question. In June 2000, RFSTE reacted with outrage when it learned that some of the corn–soya blend food aid that was being imported via CARE and Catholic Relief Services (to provide relief to Indian victims of a super cyclone in the eastern coastal state of Orissa) had come from the United States and was thus likely to be "genetically contaminated." The RFSTE castigated the United States for "using the Orissa victims as guinea pigs for GE products" and called on the government of India to explore alternative sources of food aid (RFSTE 2000).

India's policy on imports of GM germplasm for research purposes has so far been permissive rather than preventive. Some extra steps are required when importing GM materials for research and some bureaucratic delays are encountered, but the imports themselves have never been held back. This partly reflects the fact that the RCGM rather than the GEAC has final authority to clear transgenic imports for research purposes (India, DBT 1998). Technically, any importer of GM germplasm must also get phyto-sanitary clearance from India's relevant quarantine authority, the National Bureau of Plant Genetic Resources (NBPGR). However, the NBPGR typically acts on the recommendation of the RCGM and conducts a phyto-sanitary evaluation as a routine precaution against the importation of diseased or infested materials.[7] The RCGM is dominated by representatives from the government institutes doing some of the research, so its permissive stance on imports is not surprising, yet private companies too have had little trouble bringing GM materials into the country if the purpose is research only.

The import decision process in India is prone to a jurisdictional dispute between the RCGM and the GEAC similar to that discussed earlier in the case of field trials. The RCGM is authorized to approve small-scale imports only, and the GEAC alone can approve large-scale imports, but there is not yet a clear definition of the dividing line between the two. Tiny quantities of 10 kg or less have until now fallen clearly under the RCGM's jurisdiction, but a potential for conflict over larger shipments remains. India's official guidelines empower the GEAC to approve or disapprove (from an environmental vantage point) all large-scale "import, export, transport, manufacture, process, [or] selling of any microorganisms or genetically engineered substances or cells including food stuffs" (India, DBT 1990, 17). The encompassing language of this provision again suggests how little the government of India has been willing to entrust this new technology to private sector market forces, let alone international market forces.

---

7. The NBPGR has been responsible for developing testing procedures to detect the presence or absence of GM materials in imports, and India's Ministry of Commerce is now partially responsible as well for monitoring imports for GM content.

In export markets, India has on occasion faced a temptation to use its GM-free status to seek price premiums. India is a small exporter of soybean meal (1.5–2.2 million tons per year in recent years) and it has recently promoted these meal exports (as well as sunflower meal and rapeseed meal) as "GM free" for sale to overseas markets such as Japan, Indonesia, Thailand, the Philippines, the Gulf countries, and the Middle East (APBN 2000b). Yet most of these sales are for animal feed purposes, so price premiums have been difficult to secure. Indian meal exporters have nonetheless begun hoping that Asian countries such as Thailand, because they export chickens to the GM-conscious European market, will soon see the advantage of taking feed imports from a GM-free supplier such as India rather than from nations that plant GM crops such as the United States.

India can thus be classified as embracing a trade policy toward GM crops that is fully "preventive" by the definition in use here: a de facto blockage on GM commodity imports coupled with occasional efforts to use the nation's GM-free status to seek premiums in export markets. The strength of this policy will be tested if and when GM crops—particularly food crops (not just cotton)—are finally given biosafety approval for planting by Indian farmers. At this point the nation's overall GM-free status will disappear, so costly internal market segregation and labeling procedures will be required in order to offer GM-free guarantees to foreign customers. Avoiding this costly trade-linked inconvenience could become an additional reason for India's GEAC to go slow on the final approval of internationally traded GM food crops for planting by India's farmers.

Food Safety and Consumer Choice Policies

As of 2000, India had not yet developed an explicit consumer food safety policy toward GM crops. This partly reflected India's status as a low-income developing country where poor consumers tend to be concerned more about the availability or the price of food than about its exact characteristics or ingredients. It also reflected India's official claim that GM foods were not yet being sold in the country. In this regard, India was in a similar position to Kenya. If the government of India begins approving GM food crops (not just cotton) for commercial production, it may need to develop a more explicit food safety and consumer policy as an accompaniment.

Consumer protection laws have been slow to emerge overall in India. This is partly because of the nation's poverty and partly the result of the large role played by the state itself in providing consumer goods through state-owned industries. The state has historically been reluctant to sponsor a strong consumer protection movement, partly for fear of liabilities to its own public industries. The notion of protecting consumers by giving them an "informed choice" has also been slow to develop in India, in part because India's citizens and its government officials have historically been comfortable with a more direct regulatory approach. Consumer advocates in India tend to focus more on issues of state regulatory failure rather than on informed choice. In the food safety area, for example, the state is routinely held accountable by opposition parties or the media for occasional failures to prevent the contamination or adulteration of processed and packaged foods. As noted above, a 1998 dropsy outbreak in Delhi linked to contamination of edible oils prompted a quick tightening of packaging rules. Because so much food consumption in India has traditionally been satisfied from unpackaged natural ingredients, consumer fears regarding adulteration of packaged foods understandably remain widespread. According to one survey, 60 percent of Delhi's population fears that branded milk could be adulterated and hence unsafe to drink (Rao 1999).

Because India does not yet officially grow or import any GM foods, it has been able to continue operating within food safety policies that draw little or no distinction between GM and non-GM food ingredients. India's 1954 Prevention of Food Adulteration Act predates the GM crop revolution and does not mention transgenic entities. In 1998, however, India made at least one adjustment to the GM crop revolution when it revised its biosafety approval guidelines to require that GM seeds, plants, and plant parts be separately screened for toxicity and allergenicity (India, DBT 1998). By introducing a separate regulatory procedure for GM crops, this more recent RCGM guideline gave India a permissive rather than a fully promotional safety policy toward GM foods. Yet the protocols published in the revised guidelines do not set a higher food safety standard because of the GM nature of the products; they were developed by the RCGM through consultation with conventional industrial toxicologists and scarcely go beyond the testing that might be appropriate for judging the safety of pesticide residues.[8] Also, the new procedures allow for test results generated in other countries to be used in India, on the grounds that food safety testing does not have to be site specific. This means the data used by the U.S. Food and Drug Administration to give approval to a GM food in the United States could presumably be re-used for the same purpose in India. The process thus can be a quick one, and RCGM officials have already indicated informally that in the GM mustard application (the first food crop application going through India's approval system) their review of the information submitted thus far found no new food safety risks (Ghosh and Ramanaiah 2000).

Labeling policies in India have also been a moot question until now, partly because of the nation's nominal GM-free status and also because most food consumption continues to be satisfied through home or street preparations of

---

8. The tests required for toxicity now include in vitro receptor binding assays and animal model testing, and those for allergenicity include in vitro sero-panel assays, animal model testing, and comparisons with known allergens, plus quantitative estimates of transgenic proteins as a percentage of total proteins in different plant parts at different ages (Ghosh and Ramanaiah 2000).

natural foods that are never packaged at all, let alone carefully labeled. Although foods grown in India for export purposes must be labeled according to the policies of the importing countries, the nation's GM-free status has transformed this requirement into something of a competitive advantage for the country rather than a burden. Without any costly market segregation, all of India's soy or castor oil seed cake destined for Europe and Japan can be labeled "GM free."

Labeling requirements are likely to be imposed as soon as GM food crops (as opposed to fiber crops such as cotton) are released by the GEAC for commercial planting by India's own farmers. Transgenic pharmaceutical products in India that have been deregulated for sale by the GEAC already must be labeled GM. Anticipating the GM labeling problem for foods, India's Ministry of Food Processing Industries has sought advice from the DBT, and India's Ministry of Health and Family Welfare has approached both the DBT and the Codex Alimentarius in Rome to ask how the nation's 1954 Prevention of Food Adulteration Act can be adjusted to take GM ingredients into account. If and when GM foods do officially come onto the market in India, the DBT can be expected to advocate labeling requirements that are permissive rather than precautionary so as to avoid a need for full market segregation.

Public Research Investment Policies

The government of India, principally through its Department of Biotechnology, has for more than a decade directed a small but steady stream of treasury resources toward the development of its own GM crop varieties, as well as toward the simple backcrossing of foreign-developed GM traits into local germplasm. Between 1989 and 1997, the DBT spent a total of nearly Rs 270 million from the treasury (roughly US$6 million) on plant and molecular biology research, with projects focused primarily on development of transgenic plants (Ghosh 1999). India's public research investment policies toward GM crops thus deserve to be classified here as promotional. Tangible scientific payoffs from these investments have been slow to develop, however, reflecting both the modest total size of the investment plus some longstanding limitations within India's public sector research establishment. Without greater public spending on research and without significant institutional reforms and policy adjustments, including some to help public researchers enter into more effective partnerships with the domestic and international private sector, India's goal of developing its own commercially useful GM crop technologies could remain elusive.

As noted earlier, India has a long and distinguished history of making effective public investments in agricultural research through national institutes and universities that operate under the Indian Council of Agricultural Research. Public research by state-level governments in India has also grown since the mid-1970s, even rivaling total ICAR spending at one point in the mid-1980s. India's public sector investments in agricultural research, together with its formidable extension system, have been the source of roughly three-fourths of all agricultural productivity growth in India in recent decades (Evenson, Pray, and Rosegrant 1999). By some estimates these impacts from research and extension have been larger even than those from government investment in rural infrastructure, education, irrigation, or power (Fan, Hazell, and Thorat 1999).

Not all agricultural research in India has been public sector led. After the mid-1980s, India's more liberal international investment policies helped attract more private agricultural R&D spending into the country. Between 1987 and 1995, private seed company R&D expenditures in the country increased from Rs 41.7 million to Rs 154.9 million. Still, total public sector agricultural R&D in India continued to exceed private sector R&D by a wide margin of roughly 6 to 1 (Pray 1999).

Modern biotechnology was first introduced into the Indian research community in the 1970s when large numbers of Indian scientists trained in the United States and Europe returned to take up work in India (Balasubramanian 2000). Significant government investments began quite early as well, with the establishment in 1982 of a National Biotechnology Board. In 1986 this board was established formally as India's Department of Biotechnology inside the Ministry of Science and Technology (Sharma 1999). A major part of the DBT's mission has always been to distribute and finance specific research contracts. In the area of agriculture the DBT set up six centers for plant molecular biology in different regions of the country and has provided research funding to those centers—primarily through the ICAR—for the improvement of specific priority crops such as rice, mustard, chickpea, pigeon pea, and wheat (India, DBT 1999). The DBT must secure its budget every year from the Planning Commission and the Ministry of Finance, and the resources it receives are quite modest despite the fact that senior political leaders frequently list biotechnology as among the keys to India's future economic growth and prosperity. In 1998/99, the total research budget of the DBT across all agricultural and non-agricultural areas was Rs 1,040 million (roughly US$26 million). About 15 percent of this total (US$3.8 million) was for all plant biotechnology, including medicinal and aromatic plants, tree and woody species, and pilot plants for tissue culture. The DBT's investments in transgenic plant biotechnology in 1998/99 totaled only about US$1.3 million.[9]

With these modest treasury investments, the DBT has been attempting to fund a significant spread of GM crop research activities, including not only

9. India's DBT has a far larger budget for non-GM research in areas such as genomics. The DBT expects to spend Rs 3 billion (US$65 million) on genomics research over the upcoming five-year period.

basic transformation work but also research in extremely challenging areas such as abiotic stress (for example, drought tolerance) and improved nutritional quality (for example, protein quality, oil quantity and quality, or higher starch content). The ICAR is even making efforts at Jawaharlal Nehru University in New Delhi to engineer potato and rice with improved protein content, and elsewhere it is using GM to modify the starch content of potato and the vitamin E activity of mustard and groundnut (Paroda 1999). A number of more standard GM applications are also being researched, including Bt varieties of rice, cotton, pigeon pea, potato, and mustard. National researchers have also worked with transformed eggplant, cabbage, cauliflower, and tomato.

Ambitious as this GM research agenda is, the budget is spread thinly and most of the work so far is at an early stage or confined to laboratory or greenhouse trials (Ghosh 1999, Table 1). As of 2000, of all the ICAR GM varieties under development the DBT had approved field trials only for GM eggplant and mustard. The Indian Agricultural Research Institute and the Central Institute for Cotton Research have produced their own transformed Bt cotton, but as of 2000 just 100 plants had been grown in the laboratory; several years of backcrossing with local varieties may have to take place before any full-scale field trials can be undertaken.

Over time, there is little doubt that India's national researchers will be able to develop and field-test their own GM crop varieties suitable and ready for farmers to use. Prior to commercial release, however, some significant IPR impediments are likely to be encountered. Many of the transgenes that India's researchers have been inserting are owned by foreign companies and have been made available by private companies for research purposes only. In the case of India's GM rice, the transgenes come from the International Rice Research Institute (IRRI) free of charge, but IRRI in turn has them for research purposes only through materials transfer agreements with the private patent holders. When the time comes to consider a commercial release in India, negotiations with these international patent holders will be necessary. The ICAR has not yet spelled out a clear strategy to break through such looming IPR bottlenecks, and it has yet to undertake the kind of IPR literacy program for its researchers that Embrapa earlier undertook in Brazil.[10]

In several other respects the ICAR may face difficulties pursuing its independent course toward GM crop technology development. The ICAR continues to be dominated by conventional plant breeders, many of whom were trained years ago, before the latest advances in GM technologies (Murthyunjaya and Ranjitha 1998). Younger scientists have been trained to do GM work

_____
10. At the ICAR the culture is still to publish any significant finding as quickly as possible, without first considering the option of patenting. In contrast, Indian scientists at the CSIR are far more comfortable with the new world of IPR protection; the CSIR has had a special IPR coordinator working at its headquarters for two decades.

for the ICAR through the Rockefeller Foundation's rice biotechnology program, but often these people are hired away by the private sector, which can pay more than twice the public sector salary. Younger scientists with good ideas can get support from the DBT via the ICAR, but excessive paperwork and long delays are routine. Not only is the DBT's budget small; it also tends to be spread too thinly because each separate institute in the national system lays claim to at least some financing. For example, India's rice transformation budget is divided between at least five different locations within the national system, which weakens the impact at any one location.

India's national system takes pride in its independence yet some of its best work in the area of agribiotechnology has resulted from international donor support. Beginning in 1988 the Rockefeller Foundation became an important catalyst, helping India's national institutes and universities to build infrastructure and train younger scientists, although this important source of external support has recently been phased out. The United States Agency for International Development (USAID) is also providing assistance: since December 2000 a new joint research project run by Michigan State University and India's Tata Energy Research Institute in Delhi has been working to enhance the beta carotene content of mustard oil to fight blindness caused by vitamin A deficiencies. In February 2001, a preliminary agreement was reached through ICAR and DBT to transfer vitamin A–enriched Gold Rice seeds from Switzerland into the hands of five different public sector rice research institutes in India, on a royalty-free basis. Indian scientists would then take the lead in crossing the trait into local rice varieties.

As one further externally supported project, the Ministry of Foreign Affairs of the Netherlands has funded an Andhra Pradesh–Netherlands Biotechnology Programme for Dryland Agriculture since 1996, engaging several ICAR institutes in a fruitful partnership to bring biotechnology applications to non-irrigated low-resource farmers producing sorghum, castor, groundnut, and pigeon pea. This project, supported with Rs 180 million over its first six years, has been more successful than the parallel biotechnology program funded by the Dutch in Kenya (discussed in Chapter 3), so it is now scheduled to be extended for another 10–15 years. The program focuses on low-end village-level biotechnology applications, such as biopesticides and biofertilizers, but it has also given some financial support to ICAR researchers working on insecticidal GM varieties of sorghum and castor (IPE 2000). The ICAR also has benefited from a substantial National Agricultural Technology Project loan from the World Bank to upgrade its scientific skills, infrastructure, and management procedures and to facilitate better links between the component parts of the fragmented system. However, little of this money seems to have reached the labs of younger researchers in the biotechnology area. Links between the ICAR and the private sector also remain difficult to establish (Hall et al. 1998).

Partnerships with the international private sector should be an attractive option in India, where national researchers could offer international companies not only their rapidly improving transformation skills and their long-established conventional breeding skills but also access to Indian germplasm from the 150,000 accessions and samples in India's National Gene Bank (established by the ICAR as a part of India's National Bureau of Plant Genetic Resources). Yet, when private companies show interest in working with the ICAR or the DBT, the response is often muted. The Monsanto company at one point offered to share its Bt technologies with the ICAR free of charge for the transformation and production of orphan crops such as chickpea and pigeon pea within India, but the ICAR showed little interest. And just as the ICAR is leery of partnerships with the private sector, most international companies are cautious about depending too heavily upon the ICAR, which has a reputation for a slow movement of scientific results from the lab to the marketplace. The international private sector has preferred to work not with the ICAR but with local private sector joint venture partners. In 2000, when Monsanto agreed to share its GM technology for high beta carotene mustard with Indian scientists, it agreed to work through the private Tata Energy Research Institute not through the ICAR. Private seed companies in India have not only been ahead of the ICAR in commercializing improved varieties such as hybrid rice; they are also known to have control over the highest-quality hybrid germplasm. The international private sector will also be shy of working with the ICAR on GM crops so long as the other policies of the government of India—especially in the areas of IPRs, biosafety, and trade—remain highly precautionary or preventive rather than permissive. This is a loss, since the chances of getting a new GM crop variety through India's cautious biosafety screening process would probably be higher if the application for deregulation came through the ICAR rather than from a purely private applicant such as Mahyco/Monsanto.

The desire of the government of India to promote GM crop technologies primarily through public sector research investments is in some respects commendable, given that private sector companies are unlikely to make the GM crop research investments needed to enhance nutritional traits for the malnourished or to address the abiotic stress problems encountered in semi-arid regions by low-resource farmers. Yet the success of this strategy will remain in doubt so long as the treasury resources being invested are so small, so long as the public sector institutions in question retain their current limitations, and so long as the policies of the government in other critical areas—biosafety in particular—remain preventive or highly precautionary.

Conclusion

Table 5.1 summarizes current policies in India toward GM crops and foods. It reveals a seeming contradiction between India's public research policy toward

TABLE 5.1 Policies toward GM crops in India, 1999–2000

Policy	Promotional	Permissive	Precautionary	Preventive
IPR				Until India enacts its draft plant variety protection law and joins UPOV it will not be in a position to protect IPRs
Biosafety			Both the RCGM and the GEAC have moved slowly on biosafety approvals, fearing criticism from NGOs	
Trade				The GEAC has not yet formally approved GM commodity imports; efforts made to seek GM-free premiums in export markets
Food safety and consumer choice		Separate safety testing of GM foods now required, but not by a higher standard than for non-GM; no separate labeling policy yet for GM foods		
Public research investment	Modest treasury funds are spent on independent GM crop transformation research			

NOTE: GEAC = Genetic Engineering Approval Committee; RCGM = Review Committee on Genetic Manipulation; UPOV = International Convention for the Protection of New Varieties of Plants.

GM crops, which is promotional, and its IPR, biosafety, and trade policies, which are precautionary or even preventive. Is there an explanation for this apparently inconsistent mix of policies? Given India's unmet farm productivity needs and given the endorsement of GM crops by its own research community, why the extreme precaution in these other areas? India's sluggishness in developing a plant variety protection law is perhaps understandable because it links to so many issues other than GM crops, and this has not been the highest barrier to getting GM crops into the country in any case. But how can we explain India's strongly precautionary stance toward GM crops in the two areas of biosafety and trade policy?

A comparison with some of India's policies at the outset of the Green Revolution in the middle years of the 1960s can shed some light here. In 1965, when the International Maize and Wheat Improvement Center in Mexico and the International Rice Research Institute in the Philippines first made high-yielding varieties (HYVs) of wheat and rice available to India, a political debate ensued within the country that was not so different from the current debate over GM crops. Indian groups on the political left and those claiming to speak for the interests of small farmers were highly skeptical toward the Green Revolution HYVs, just as today they tend to be highly skeptical toward GM crops. The new Mexican wheat varieties had not yet been widely tested in India itself, so critics argued it might be dangerous to begin planting them on a large scale without more information on their local performance and impact. The new varieties also called for more sophisticated management practices that small or poor farmers might not be able to master, and the use of purchased inputs that some might not be able to afford, so fears arose that only big commercial farmers would gain and India's rural poor might be made poorer still. The new varieties also required more fertilizer than India itself could produce at the time, so critics feared an implied dependence on fertilizer sales by private international agrochemical companies from Europe or the United States.

Despite these many understandable and sincerely voiced concerns, the government of India set caution aside in 1965. Under courageous political leadership from Agriculture Minister C. Subramaniam and others, India decided in 1965–66 to import 200 tons of Mexican wheat plus appropriate quantities of high-yielding rice to launch an ambitious seed production and farm demonstration campaign. The goal was to plant 13 million hectares to the new varieties within five years. Subramaniam was told by Western experts and by India's own Planning Commission that his goal was too ambitious and that he should not try to move so fast (Subramaniam 1979). Subramaniam's plan to move ahead quickly with new Green Revolution seeds was ultimately supported by Prime Minister Indira Gandhi and then aggressively implemented, despite continued internal opposition. His approach won the policy debate on this occasion because the alternative to taking the new seeds was continued dependence on imported food aid from the United States, which had always come with unwelcome diplomatic strings attached. As Subramaniam recalls telling his critics at the time: "Would you like to continue this dependence on America for imported foodgrains? Was that preferable to raising domestic production? Instead of importing food was it not better to import fertilizer and plant protection chemicals to help raise production?" (Subramaniam 1979, 28).

When GM crop technologies first became commercially available in the 1990s, India was no longer significantly dependent on food imports from abroad, either as food aid or even as commercial purchases. The success of the Green Revolution itself had eliminated the need for such imports. GM crop advocates have therefore not been able to use Subramaniam's politically powerful argument, that it is necessary to embrace GM crops in order to free India from food import dependence. Instead of importing wheat as food aid, India's government today is burdened by surplus stocks of wheat. Several hundred million Indian villagers are still poor and poorly fed because they cannot improve the productivity of their own farmlands or protect their crops from pests and disease, and this could well be seen as a legitimate reason to move ahead quickly with GM crops. But this line of argument has been hard to develop because many of India's leading advocates for the poor within the NGO community are explicitly opposed to GM crops, just as many of them were earlier opposed to the Green Revolution HYVs. RFSTE's Vandana Shiva, the leading NGO critic of GM crops in India today, had earlier made her international career out of criticizing high-yielding non-GM crops in India (Shiva 1991). Given these political dynamics, it was perhaps to be expected that a far more cautious approach to the new technology would prevail. In the current case the caution expresses itself through controversies over the bio-safety of GM crops, but the same larger background debate about the wisdom of relying on the international private sector and of importing new agricultural technologies from the West is alive and influential just below the surface.

But what is the opinion of India's farmers about GM crops? Until farmers in India are given permission by the government to grow these crops, this important question will remain unanswered. In the 1960s and 1970s farmers in India developed strong positive views of high-yielding seed varieties once they were given access to the new seeds. Once these Indian farmers had voted in favor of high-yielding varieties by adopting the new seeds so quickly and so widely, the policy debate continued among some NGOs and non-farmers but otherwise became largely irrelevant. Today in India various self-styled farm leaders have taken pro-GM or anti-GM positions in the policy debate, but until GM crops are released for commercial use by actual farm communities the views of farmers will not be known. By slowing the movement of GM crops into farmers' fields, the government is postponing the day when the nation's own most important stakeholders in the transgenic crop revolution will be able to develop and express an informed opinion.

6 Permission Partly Granted in China

While nations such as Kenya, Brazil, and India were putting off GM crop production for various reasons, China was embracing the new technology and moving ahead. China was actually the first nation in the world to grow GM crops, having planted GM tobacco over a significant area late in the 1980s. In the 1990s China then developed its own Bt cotton varieties and approved them for planting on a commercial scale along with an imported Monsanto variety. China also approved commercial use of GM tomato and green pepper varieties it had developed, and pushed ahead with field tests of its own GM rice. Yet even in China the international controversy surrounding GM crops eventually began to breed greater policy caution.

China's Early Attraction to GM Crops

China's food and agricultural circumstances have improved dramatically since 1978, when Deng Xiaoping introduced market incentives and individual household land contracts into the nation's farming sector. Over the next two decades China's total grain output increased by 65 percent, from 305 million tons to annual averages of 500 million tons by 1999. Agricultural production overall, in value-added terms, increased at a strong 5.1 percent annual rate between 1980 and 1999 (World Bank 2000). The Chinese farmers who partici-pated in this impressive feat saw their incomes improve markedly as well: annual per capita net income for rural people in China increased from a destitute level of only 134 yuan in 1978 to 2,210 yuan (US$276) by 1999. The number of Chinese people living in poverty and unable to feed, clothe, or adequately house themselves declined as a result from 250 million in 1978 to only 34 million by 1999 (Chen 2000) despite continued overall population growth. Never before in human history have so many people escaped deep poverty and food insecurity so quickly in one country.

These two decades of success did not leave China's food and agricultural policymakers complacent, however. Food production and food prices (espe-cially in urban areas) are still a major preoccupation, since food accounts for about 50 percent of consumption expenditures by urban residents in China, and 60 percent for rural dwellers (Rozelle et al. 2000). As recently as 1994, falling public investments in agriculture plus a mismanagement of macroeconomic policy caused grain production in China to falter and urban food prices to increase, prompting authorities to arrange for the import of a record 21 million tons of grain. At this point some outsiders argued that China's capacity to continue increasing grain production had finally been exhausted (Brown 1995). But China's policymakers responded by boosting state procurement prices for grains and expanding the area planted to grains, which promptly restored the upward production trend. In 1998 and 1999, despite widely publicized conditions of first flood then drought, record or near-record harvests were recorded and, by 2000, China's officials were struggling with how to store or dispose of grain stocks that were momentarily too large. Yet with China's population still growing, total land and water resources available for farming either fixed or in decline (owing to competition from urban and industrial use), and per capita income growth pushing up food demands per person, a significant long-term challenge of increasing food output in China remained.

The promotion of improved crop technologies—including GM crops—is one obvious way for China's policy leaders to meet this challenge. China has a long history of timely technical innovation in agriculture. In the 1950s, well before the so-called Green Revolution reached other parts of Asia, China was successfully extending semi-dwarf rice varieties and drought- and pest-resistant wheat cultivars. In the 1970s, Chinese scientists were the first to develop hybrid rice. Between 1975 and 1990, new rice technologies such as hybrids and single-season varieties contributed over half (60 percent) of China's overall increase in average yields (Huang and Rozelle 1996). Not satisfied with this success, top leaders argue today that China's technology upgrade in farming must continue. China's 2010 Long Term Plan concludes that the nation must rely on new technology, particularly new crop and livestock varieties, to raise future farm production. Jiang Zemin, the president of China, is widely quoted for his saying that China's agriculture needs to be "reinvented" using a "sciences and technology revolution" (Huang, Lin, and Rozelle 2000, 8).

GM crops might prove a particularly useful response to several short-term and long-term problems in Chinese farming. In the near term, a number of problems linked to crop pests could be treatable with existing GM crop applications. In cotton production the same problem experienced in India of cotton bollworm resistance to chemical insecticide sprays has also plagued China. In 1992–93 bollworm infestations reduced cotton yields to zero in some places. This hurt farmers' incomes and forced some of China's cotton textile factories to stop production, causing an estimated US$630 million in total damages (Song 1999). GM cotton engineered to contain its own Bt insecticide is a proven response to such problems. Crop pests also threaten the sustainability of rice production in China. Per hectare pesticide use on China's rice fields has tripled in the past 20 years, causing severe human health problems (including chronic liver and kidney disease among farmers) as well as water pollution and damage to non-target species. Bt rice could give farmers a fresh start in their battle against pests. In the longer run, GM crops with improved quality traits (for example, rice enriched with vitamin A, or hybrid rice with improved eating and cooking qualities) might bring benefits directly to consumers as well as to farmers in China (Zhang 2000). Perhaps only through GM innovations will it be possible in the long run for China to engineer the drought resistance that its field crops may need to continue performing in dry areas where rapidly growing urban and industrial water use could eventually preclude irrigation. In recognition of this potential, China has fashioned a set of policies toward GM crops that have, for the most part, allowed the technology to move forward.

Intellectual Property Rights Policy

China is distinctive for its promotion of GM crops, yet in the area of intellectual property rights (IPR) China's policy posture toward GM crops must be rated as between precautionary and outright preventive. Along with many other rapidly industrializing countries, China has recently been trying to strengthen the intellectual property rights guarantees it offers innovators. Yet China is distinct from most of these other developing countries in the cultural and institutional distance it will have to travel to put minimal IPR guarantees in place. As recently as the late 1970s, China's completely state-owned and state-managed economy did not permit most kinds of private commerce, so laws to govern private property ownership and private business transactions did not even exist. The People's Republic of China did not have any trademark law until 1983 and it did not have any patent law until 1985. Since the 1980s China has moved a long way—on paper—toward providing important business law and IPR guarantees. In practice, however, these guarantees are not sufficiently well developed or enforced to increase incentives for innovation or private investment. IPRs were finally incorporated into China's basic civil law in 1987 and China acceded to the Patent Cooperation Treaty of the World Intellectual Property Organization (WIPO) in 1994, but lax enforcement persisted. Under intense pressure from the United States in 1995, China accepted a special Sino-U.S. agreement on IPR protection and then put into effect an Action Plan for Effective Protection and Enforcement of IPR, but international corporate dissatisfaction with China's IPR system has continued.

In the narrow area of plant variety protection, in October 1997 China finally put into force its current Regulations on the Protection of New Varieties of Plants, and one year later it used this regulation as the basis for acceding to the 1978 version of the Convention of the International Union for the Protection of New Varieties of Plants (UPOV).[1] This means that new plant varieties from UPOV member states supposedly can be protected in China, and Chinese varieties can be protected in UPOV member states. China's new law on plant breeders' rights (PBRs), together with the terms of its patent law, which makes microorganisms such as bacteria or fungi subject to patentability, also suffices as a *sui generis* system suitable for compliance with the Agreement on Trade-Related Aspects of Intellectual Property Rights (TRIPS) in the eyes of the World Trade Organization (WTO). China's anticipated entry into the WTO has been a strong motivating factor in moving the nation's IPR policies forward. China has even been lauded by the director general of WIPO for its efforts to move so quickly from offering no IPR guarantees at all to formally accepting the minimal world standards.

China's IPR policies do not provide much comfort for international owners of GM crop technologies, however. China's patent law is closer to the European than to the U.S. standard in that it excludes the patentability of plant or animal varieties and all inventions contrary to "public order or morality" (Pan 2000). China's PBR law, which follows the 1978 version of UPOV, allows farmers to replicate seeds of protected varieties and use them on their own land. These weaknesses on paper, together with weak enforcement in practice, have slowed the growth of private sector biotechnology investments in China. It is telling that companies specifically dedicated to biotechnology are not yet among the thousand or more private firms recently listed on China's various stock markets (Leggett and Johnson 2000). Some private companies have nonetheless been willing to bring GM crop technologies into China in spite of China's weak IPR policies.

We can illustrate the weakness of China's plant variety protection policy by examining the Monsanto company's efforts to protect its "Bollgard" Bt cotton variety in China. As Monsanto moved toward the release of this openly pollinated variety in the United States, it suspected the technology would find its way into China one way or another, so the company sought to create its own joint venture in China in order to capture at least some of the sales. Monsanto first had to overcome resistance to any venture in China from the national authorities in Beijing. When Monsanto, together with Delta and Pineland (its partner company at the time), tried to get GM cotton seeds into the Chinese market in 1993, it learned that China's national cotton research institute did not want foreign competition for China's own state-owned seed companies. The authorities in Beijing also wanted to protect the scientists at China's Bio-technology Research Institute (BRI) inside the Chinese Academy of Agri-cultural Sciences, who had been working since 1991 to develop their own Bt cotton cultivars.

---

1. This accession entered into force in April 1999.

Monsanto had better luck in 1994 negotiating directly with the provincial government in Hebei province, China's prime cotton-growing region, whose economy depended heavily on cotton and textile production. Monsanto was allowed to conduct field tests in Hebei province in 1995, and the tests revealed that Monsanto's GM variety (called 33B) controlled bollworm well enough to outyield local varieties by 30 percent. Monsanto was then permitted by the state authorities to form a US$8.4 million joint venture with Hebei's provincial seed company, JiDai. Monsanto and Delta and Pineland were to bring in the technology and would own a two-thirds share of the joint venture, while JiDai was to take responsibility for seed production, processing, and local distribution. With the impressive field trial results in hand and with strong political support from the Hebei provincial governor, in 1997 Monsanto finally won approval from the Chinese Ministry of Agriculture (MOA) in Beijing to go ahead with commercial plantings. JiDai then went on to build a state of the art seed production facility in Shijiazhuang, Hebei, and started commercial seed production in 1998.

Using what amounted to a contractual monopoly with Hebei's 5,000 separate cotton seed retailers, JiDai was able in 1998 to capture virtually the entire purchased seed market share for Monsanto's GM variety. Although this was only 17 percent of all cotton seed actually used—because most cotton farmers in Hebei were still using saved rather than purchased seed at the time—Monsanto's GM variety performed so well that in 1999 roughly 50 percent of all cotton seed used in Hebei came from JiDai sales of 33B. Cotton farmers in Hebei were enthusiastic about 33B because it allowed them to use fewer sprayings of insecticide and hence to save on both their chemical input and labor costs. One survey of 283 small farmers in 1999 found that 33B reduced total production costs per kilo by roughly 14 percent compared with non-Bt cotton, even after factoring in the higher costs of purchasing the more expensive GM seeds (Pray et al. 2000). Farmers growing 33B also reduced their exposure to some of the highly toxic insecticides used on non-Bt cotton; many were able to reduce their insecticide sprayings from 12 per crop to only 2–3 per crop. Fewer insecticide sprayings had the further advantage of permitting larger populations of non-target beneficial insects to thrive in the Bt cotton fields compared with non-Bt fields.

Although Monsanto's GM cotton seeds performed well technically and elicited an enthusiastic response from farmers, actual commercial returns to the joint venture were undercut almost immediately by widespread piracy. Only part of the rapid spread of 33B in Hebei generated revenue for the company, because much of the spread—perhaps as much as half—was a result of farmers propagating and replanting their own saved 33B seed rather than purchasing seed anew from JiDai (Pray et al. 2000). Monsanto's 33B is an openly pollinated variety, so once in the hands of farmers its use can be sustained and spread without further commercial purchase for several further growing seasons.[2] Estimates by Pray et al. show that Monsanto received only about 16 million renminbi (RMB), or US$1.9 million, in gross revenue from its joint venture with JiDai in 1999, whereas the Chinese farmers who so often saved and replanted 33B were together earning total benefits from the new technology 10–20 times as great (Pray et al. 2000).

Monsanto could not object to Chinese farmers saving and replanting 33B on their own farms, or even exchanging 33B with other farmers, since seed saving for on-farm use or exchange was permitted under the relatively weak PBR law enacted by China in 1997. But Monsanto thought it did have grounds to complain about the sizable illicit commercial sales of pirated 33B that it witnessed in Hebei in 1999. Chinese merchants were selling pirated 33B at a discount and without quality control; in some cases they were even using copied versions of JiDai's boxes, seed bags, logos, and printed coupons. Monsanto's initial complaints to the Chinese authorities regarding such practices had little effect, however, partly because the office inside China's Ministry of Agriculture that managed the nation's list of UPOV-protected varieties had not yet added cotton to the list.

Some of this Chinese indifference to Monsanto's intellectual property rights reflected the fact that China's own scientists working in government institutes were developing and promoting their own Bt cotton varieties. Yet in the case of Bt cotton China's own scientists have also been hurt financially by weak IPR protection. Scientists working to develop new GM varieties in China complain that they do not get IPR protections any stronger than those offered to foreign companies. When scientists in the Chinese Academy of Agricultural Sciences (CAAS) work independently to develop and commercialize their own varieties of Bt cotton, they must go into partnership with state-owned seed companies in order to sell their GM cotton seed to farmers, and once farmers get these CAAS seeds they can also save, replant, and exchange them, thus undercutting subsequent seed company sales. When the state seed companies then lose revenue, they often refuse to pay the royalties that CAAS is supposed to obtain from the sales (Pray et al. 2000).

Chinese scientists must compete with one another for public research grants, and this gives them a substantial incentive to conduct high-quality research, but the system does not protect their IPRs and thus leaves them significantly indifferent to the final end use of their research. Chinese scientists (a bit like Indian scientists in the Indian Council of Agricultural Research) do not have adequate incentives to "finish" their development of new tech-

---

2. Farmers using or buying saved seed in Hebei tend eventually to experience quality problems, so they continue to purchase at least some new seed. The widespread use of saved seed has nonetheless undercut Monsanto's hoped-for profits in Hebei.

nologies (GM or otherwise) in a commercial context. Unfinished technologies languish in the laboratory. Within China's crop research community, training in IPR practices has lagged along with enforcement. Chinese scientists and administrators have participated in IPR training workshops sponsored by the World Bank abroad, yet inside CAAS itself IPR awareness is low and training is minimal.

Weak enforcement of IPR policy in China also undercuts research partnership opportunities for CAAS scientists and international companies. Private firms with valuable protected GM technologies are less likely to want to bring those technologies into China for research purposes because China's institutes find it difficult to offer mutually acceptable arrangements for sharing profits or IPRs. Monsanto tried for several years in the late 1990s to enter into a transgenic crop research agreement with CAAS, but the negotiations broke down over profit sharing and IPRs. Pioneer/DuPont was able to reach an agreement to cooperate with the China Agricultural University (CAU) on the development of Bt corn, but this was not an ambitious research agreement because the CAU's role was mostly to field-test Pioneer's varieties rather than to develop new Chinese varieties. Pending a stronger IPR environment in China, international companies owning valuable GM technologies will be tempted—as in India—to bring in only hybrid varieties. The Monsanto company at one point supported an effort at the China National Rice Research Institute to develop openly pollinated herbicide-resistant (Roundup Ready) rice, but later pulled back, perhaps not wishing to repeat its disappointment with openly pollinated GM cotton.

China's IPR policies must therefore be judged as quite weak for the purpose of advancing the spread of new GM crop technologies. China's policies are at best precautionary toward GM crops, going by the weak standard of protection guaranteed on paper in the PRB law and under UPOV 1978. Because of weak enforcement, the standard of protection available in practice is often less than that. Yet several words of caution must be added. First, China's weak IPR policy does not grow out of any official hostility toward GM crop technologies. To the contrary, as we shall see below the public research investment policies of the Chinese government toward GM crops have been highly promotional. All IPR protection policies are still in their infancy in China and all tend to be weak or at least weakly enforced. This in turn reflects a more general lack of trust toward private market institutions on the part of most Chinese state authorities. Chinese officials speak with unreserved enthusiasm about high-technology applications in Chinese agriculture, and they even speak with enthusiasm about bringing those applications into China from abroad. To this end, Beijing in 2000 pledged RMB 20 billion (US$2.2 billion) to help construct a "Chinese Biotech Valley" in Yunnan, zoned for international companies to bring their research and product development activities into the country (APBN 2000c, 1). Yet China's actual IPR and foreign direct investment policies, as written and as implemented, have so far done little to advance such transfers.[3]

China can to some extent afford its weak IPR policy, because it has other ways of attracting investment and technology into the country. The size and anticipated future growth of China's vast internal seed market for crops can be a significant counterbalancing incentive to invent and invest. Private seed companies place high value on gaining a foothold in China, so they have been willing to tolerate weak IPR protections, up to a point, as part of the price of admission.

Biosafety Policies

China's biosafety policies toward GM crops have evolved from promotional to only permissive. Early in the GM crop revolution China allowed transgenic crops to be field-tested (cotton) and even grown commercially (tobacco) without any systematic case-by-case screening for biohazards. Only after 1996, when China set in place a formal biosafety regulation specifically for GM crops, did case-by-case risk-based screening come to be required. This permissive biosafety policy nonetheless allowed for a significant number of GM crop releases late in the 1990s.

China has the distinction of having been the very first country in the world to commercialize a GM crop: virus-resistant tobacco was developed in China and planted over large areas in northeastern Liaoning province and Henan province beginning in 1988, well before the GM crop revolution was launched commercially in the United States in 1995–96. China went ahead with GM tobacco without a strong biosafety policy in place at home, and without at first saying anything about its GM variety to tobacco customers abroad. Foreign buyers eventually learned the leaves were GM, and some cancelled their purchases, so in 1998 the Chinese government finally decided as a public relations gesture to disapprove commercial production of the GM tobacco, although many in the private trade believed more than 1 million hectares in China continued to be planted to GM varieties. China in any case was planting GM

---

3. China's foreign investment policies have also slowed technology transfer. On paper these policies stress the importance of bringing in companies "capable of introducing or adopting superior varieties (germplasm resources), advanced seed technology, and equipment from abroad," yet they prevent foreigners from establishing wholly owned crop seed enterprises in China. Since 1997 these investment policies have also blocked foreigners from owning majority shares in joint venture seed enterprises for basic crops such as grains, cotton, or oilseeds (China, MOA 1997). Monsanto secured a two-thirds share of its JiDai cotton seed joint venture in 1996 before this regulation went into effect, but it was more recently asked to make a "remedial application" in light of the 1997 change.

crops on a large scale well before the nation had in place any formal biosafety screening procedures for GM crops.

China's first formal biosafety regulation in the area of genetic engineering —applying to medicines and animals as well as to crops—was promulgated in December 1993 by the State Science and Technology Commission under the Ministry of Science and Technology (China, SSTC 1993). This regulation was authored by scientists actually engaged in developing GM technologies, so its tone and content were largely permissive. The regulation assigned administrative responsibility for safety to the "relevant administrative departments," and in the case of farm crops and animals this meant the Ministry of Agriculture, which finally issued its own more detailed Implementation Regulation on Agricultural Biological Genetic Engineering (hereafter, the IR) in July 1996 (China, MOA 1996).

The IR was more detailed, but it too created essentially a permissive biosafety policy for the regulation of GM crops in China. The IR was written specifically for GM, so China was not following the U.S. practice of avoiding a separate set of GM-specific biosafety regulations. The IR was nonetheless permissive because it focused exclusively on scientific demonstrations of risk. The IR did not assume GM crops were inherently any more dangerous to human or environmental health than non-GM crops, it focused on demonstrated risks rather than unknown risks, and it did not assume that uncertainty was itself a risk. Rather than presuming GM crops to be inherently more dangerous, the IR actually asserted that in some instances they might be less dangerous (for example, if genetic modification resulted in the deletion of a pathogenic trait). The IR does view scientific uncertainty as potentially dangerous, but it specifically instructs regulators to consider the degree of safety reduction implied by uncertainty and to remain open to options for risk avoidance through safety control measures when confronted with uncertainty.

To ensure these guidelines can be followed in a suitably permissive manner, the IR assigns approval authority directly to the Ministry of Agriculture. The MOA is authorized to approve not only large-scale field trials of GM crops (what the Chinese call environmental release) but also commercial deregulation (what the Chinese call "industrial production"). Only in the rare case of GM crops with an established Class IV high biosafety risk level must the MOA submit its work to higher authorities before it can grant approval.[4]

Two administrative structures inside the MOA have helped to consolidate agriculture's control over the GM biosafety review process. The first is an Administrative Office for the Safety of Biological Genetic Engineering (the AO), which accepts applications from those seeking to conduct research exper-

---

4. Class IV is a hypothetical category of organisms known to be harmful and known frequently to exchange genetic material with other organisms.

iments, pilot studies, environmental release (larger-scale field tests), and full commercial production of GM crops. As gatekeeper the AO accepts applications twice a year, then passes them along to the Committee on Safety of Agricultural Biological Genetic Engineering (the CS), which makes case-by-case decisions to accept or refuse the applications or to send them back with a request for additional information. The structure and composition of the CS have favored agricultural interests and science-based decisions, because the CS is chaired by China's vice minister of agriculture and a departmental director inside the MOA serves as vice-chair. Of the 33 members of the CS, roughly one-third are from the MOA and most of the rest are representatives of China's larger scientific establishments, including the Chinese Academy of Science (CAS), the Ministry of Science and Technology (MOST), the Ministry of Education, and the Chinese Society of Agro-Biotechnology. There is no representative from the Ministry of Health, and only one occasional representative from the State Environmental Protection Administration (SEPA).

There are obvious differences between China's Committee on Safety and the GM crop biosafety review committees of Kenya, Brazil, and India. China's Committee on Safety is the only one of this group to be entirely within a ministry of agriculture rather than under a ministry of science and technology (as in Kenya and Brazil) or chaired by an environment ministry (as with the Genetic Engineering Approval Committee in India). China's CS process is also more limited in scope, since it is responsible only for the biosafety of GM crop production and does not make separate food safety or trade policy decisions on GM crops.

Some CS procedures are bothersome to applicants. For example, separate applications to the Committee on Safety are required for pilot experiments with GM crops (no more than two sites, and the whole area not larger than 2 mu, or one-eighth of a hectare), for environmental release in field trials (no more than 10 sites, and the whole area not larger than 20 mu), and then finally for commercial production; moreover, applications for commercial production must be made separately for each province.[5] Still, a simple numerical count of all separate applications to the Committee on Safety for 1997–99 shows a high rate of eventual success, as indicated in Table 6.1.

A significant number of these approvals by the Committee on Safety have been for commercial ("industrial") production of GM crops. Between 1997 and 1999 the Committee on Safety gave 26 separate commercial production approvals for a total of five different kinds of GM plants (see Table 6.2).

Beginning in 1999, with the growing international controversy over GM crops—especially GM food crops—the rate of new approvals in China slowed. As of September 2000, according to an official on the Committee on

---

5. Monsanto was frustrated to have initially received approval for the commercial release of 33B in Hebei province only.

TABLE 6.1 Applications to the Committee on Safety and approvals for pilot experiments, environmental release, and commercial production of GM crops, 1997–99

Year	Total applications	Total approvals[a]	Success rate (%)
1997	53	45	85
1998	68	51	75
1999[b]	59	53	90

SOURCE: Private industry accounting, Beijing.

[a]Some of these approvals were for re-applications, so the total eventual success rate per technology is actually higher than these numbers imply.

[b]First 59 applications only for 1999.

Safety, there was a backlog of nearly 200 applications for various kinds of release that had not yet been approved by the committee (He 2000). Many of these delayed approvals were for food crops, which aroused greater social and political sensitivities than did industrial crops such as cotton.

Although denied by officials, the Committee on Safety quite naturally favors projects where Chinese universities or institutes are co-applicants. Of the 26 cumulative commercial production approvals noted above, 6 went to Monsanto for Bt cotton whereas 20 went to BRI/CAAS, or to Beijing University, or to Huazhong Agricultural University, or to the China National Rice Research Institute. Monsanto believes it has provided more than enough information from field trials that were originally approved in 1997 to justify a

TABLE 6.2 Plants approved by the Committee on Safety for commercial production, 1997–99

Plant	Separate GM traits or functions approved	Applicants
Cotton	Bollgard Bt	Monsanto
	Bt (single Bt gene)	BRI, CAAS
	Insecticidal double gene	BRI, CAAS
Green pepper	CMV virus resistant	Beijing University
Tomato	CMV virus resistant	Beijing University
	Delayed ripening	Huazhong Agricultural University
Petunia	Chalcome synthase	Beijing University
Rice	Herbicide-resistant hybrid	CNRRI, CAAS

SOURCE: Private industry accounting, Beijing.

NOTE: BRI = Biotechnology Research Institute; CAAS = Chinese Academy of Agricultural Sciences; CNRRI = China National Rice Research Institute.

commercial approval for its Bt corn application, but the Committee on Safety has moved slowly, possibly to await development of a Pioneer/DuPont Bt corn variety being tested with assistance from researchers at the China Agricultural University. Chinese scientists do not get a free pass from the Committee on Safety, however. The application procedures are burdensome (10 copies must be submitted detailing results from the experiments conducted at each stage, plus duplicate copies of official written replies to earlier safety approvals). A fee is charged for each application (together with the substantial cost of conducting the required safety experiments, this actually imposes a selective disadvantage on China's budget-constrained institutes). And not until after CS approval can an applicant begin the process of seeking normal varietal registration within the MOA. When refusals are given by the Committee on Safety, substantive reasons are usually provided. In the case of Bt corn, for example, the Committee on Safety told Monsanto it was going slow on approval pending more and better information on pest population resistance problems, because some of the insects that would attack Bt corn in northeast China also attack Bt cotton and are already somewhat resistant to Bt.

These permissive biosafety screening procedures did not change with the approval, in July 2000, of a new national seed law in China. This new law governing seed production, seed management, and seed quality did not in most cases single out GM seeds for differential treatment, and the several clauses in the new law that refer to GM crops mostly reinforce the terms of the 1996 Implementation Regulation—reasserting that screenings must be done stage by stage and that regulatory control does not end once commercial production approval has been given (CIB 2000). The 2000 Seed Law does explicitly give the State Council in Beijing managerial authority over all new introductions of GM plant varieties into the country (Seed Law of PRC 2000, Chapter 8, Article 50). This provision is partly intended to prevent Monsanto from again using the authority of a provincial governor, as it did in Hebei in 1994, to initiate field trials of GM crops.

The State Environmental Protection Administration (SEPA) was the only part of the Chinese government not initially satisfied with the operation of the nation's GM crop biosafety policies. SEPA would prefer a policy not so heavily dominated by molecular biologists and agricultural production scientists from CAAS and the MOA. SEPA has called for moving the administration of biosafety regulations for crops out of the MOA and into a "national administrative system" under SEPA chairmanship and supervision (Liu and Xue 1999). Officials at SEPA would like the Committee on Safety inside the MOA to function as a "subcommittee" of a larger national system under SEPA leadership. In addition, SEPA wants this new national biosafety system to be established in the form of a law endorsed by the State Council and issued by the Standing Committee of the National People's Congress (similar to the 2000 Seed Law), not merely a regulation (Wang and Yang 1999). On such questions SEPA has generally been isolated. Whenever SEPA attempts to put forward its proposal, State Council endorsement is blocked by objections from other ministries— particularly the MOA and MOST. There already exists in China the skeletal structure of a national biosafety committee above the MOA, but it is under the leadership of MOST, not SEPA.

The strongest supporters of SEPA's jurisdictional claims are to be found in the international environmental community abroad. China is one of 18 countries funded under a Global Environment Facility (GEF) program designed to develop "National Biosafety Frameworks." Thanks to sponsorship from the GEF and the United Nations Environment Programme (UNEP), SEPA in 1996 was appointed the lead agency and executing institution in China for the project. With international technical assistance SEPA drafted and published its own version of a National Biosafety Framework (NBF) for China; not surprisingly it endorsed the formation of a national review committee under SEPA's lead. As of 2000 this NBF had not been endorsed by the State Council, yet both SEPA and its international technical advisers at GEF/UNEP routinely describe it as a semi-official document. SEPA has also gained policy influence inside the government by virtue of having served as the lead agency representing China in the negotiations under the Convention on Biological Diversity for the new Biosafety Protocol governing transboundary movement of living modified organisms (LMOs). Through international connections such as these, SEPA has become the avenue through which foreign critics of GM crop technologies have tried to move China's biosafety policies in a more precautionary direction. At the same time, international companies and other foreign advocates of GM technologies cultivate special relationships within the MOA and MOST, hoping to keep a permissive policy in place.

Within SEPA itself, the concern over GM crop biosafety is more jurisdictional than substantive. SEPA calls for the movement of GM crop biosafety regulation out of the grip of the Committee on Safety inside the MOA, but it does not cite any specific differences with any of the decisions the Committee on Safety has made so far. It does not call for the abandonment of risk-assessment screening, in favor of an uncertainty-driven precautionary approach. SEPA officials, like MOA officials, are more comfortable stressing what is known about GM crops than what is not known. These characteristics of GM crop biosafety policy in China reflect among other things the near total absence of powerful independent environmental nongovernmental organizations (NGOs) in China. Greenpeace is active in Hong Kong but not permitted to operate in Beijing. Organizations such as the Worldwide Fund for Nature are permitted to work with the Chinese government trying to save habitat for giant pandas, but NGOs (foreign or domestic) opposing the government on GM crop policy (or on any other policy) are not allowed to operate. Some prominent individuals in China have misgivings about the country's permissive biosafety policies, and on occasion have been willing to voice these misgivings in interviews with foreign journalists. Perhaps the most visible GM crop critic in China is Qian Yingqian, a research fellow at CAS who has concluded from his work on naturally occurring biohazards that more studies are appropriate before allowing widespread planting of GM crops in China.

Individual Chinese scientists and academicians—especially those who have recently studied or traveled in Europe—are aware of international debates regarding the biosafety of GM crops, and some have encountered warnings from international GM critics about specific risks to China's environment. Among individual environmentalists and even within SEPA rumors circulate that Bt cotton and Bt corn have already been responsible for killing butterflies in China. In China, however, there is little political space for independent critics to challenge state policy directly. Challenge is possible in countries where genuinely independent environmental NGOs can operate, where an independent press gives these NGOs a means to publicize their case, where an independent judiciary creates room for public interest litigations and legal challenges, and where opposition parties are always eager to join in a challenge to government policy, but none of these factors is present in China.

Trade Policy

China has a long history of maintaining complete state control over agricultural trade, internal as well as international. Prior to 1978 the right to import agricultural commodities was completely monopolized by just a handful of state-owned foreign trade corporations. These trading monopolies were subsequently decentralized and in the 1980s some private firms did win direct trading rights as well. However, import tariff rates remained high (averaging 47.2 percent overall as recently as 1991), and for many key commodities import quotas could not be exceeded and import licenses had to be separately arranged (Huang, Chen, and Rozelle 2000). This state-managed system was mostly just an extension to China's borders of the extremely tight internal system of commodity market controls maintained by the government.

Particularly since the 1990s, China has begun to allow more room for private commodity markets to operate, both internally and at the border. It reduced its restrictions on commodity imports dramatically: average tariffs on agricultural commodities were cut in 1997 to just 23.6 percent and the number of items subject to import quotas or licensing was reduced. Then in a landmark 1999 agreement over terms of accession to the World Trade Organization (WTO), China promised to cut its average import duties to just 17.5 percent, and promised even deeper cuts to 14 percent for agricultural import products of special interest to leading exporters such as the United States.[6] China still protects its state-owned seed companies by in effect blocking all commercial seed imports (foundation seed only can be imported in most cases, and to protect Chinese germplasm from foreign crop diseases some countries are not allowed to export even foundation seed). Yet China's overall commodity import policy trend has been in the direction of liberalization.

As of 2000, China had not drawn any formal regulatory distinction between imports of GM versus non-GM commodities. When commodities arrive at ports of entry into China, they are routinely inspected by commodity inspection quarantine (CIQ) agents from China's Office of Customs Tariffs, but these have been only for product quality characteristics, such as moisture or trash content, or for sanitary and phytosanitary (SPS) compliance in the area of crop disease. The CIQ agents conducting these inspections have so far drawn no distinctions between GM commodities (for example, soybeans from the United States) and non-GM commodities. There are not yet any legal grounds for drawing such a distinction, since the only regulation that singles out GM agricultural commodities—the 1996 Implementation Regulation—makes no reference to imports or to trade. As regards GM commodities, then, we may classify China's import policies as "permissive." In the case of GM seeds intended for planting China does now require labels, but not in such a way as to inconvenience importers since the seed bags in question are already segregated as to identity.

China may eventually move in the direction of a more precautionary import policy, and increasing imports of GM soybeans from the United States and Argentina could become the occasion for such a policy shift. China is a substantial producer of soybeans (all non GM) but in recent years the soybean meal requirements for China's growing livestock feed industry have run ahead of domestic production and the difference has been made up through imports. In 1998/99 China imported an all-time high of 3.85 million tons of soybeans from abroad. Just then, however, China's livestock industry went into a slump, so soybeans from its own new harvest began piling up. At this point officials in the MOA, with an eye to protecting China's own soybean producers from a surplus, began seeking ways to cut down on the future growth of imports. They proposed several different means of limiting imports, including initiating more restrictive policies on imports of GM commodities, which would affect soybeans from both the United States and Argentina. Roughly two-thirds of China's imports of soybeans come every year from the United States, and

---

6. Under this WTO accession agreement, China even promised to establish significant and growing tariff rate quotas to allow substantial quantities of wheat, corn, cotton, rice, and soybean oil into the country with only nominal duties of 1–3 percent. For soybeans and soybean meal, China agreed to fix its tariffs for an unlimited quantity of imports at low levels of 3 percent and 5 percent respectively (USDA 2000a).

roughly half of all bulk exports of U.S. soybeans have recently been GM. This restrictive suggestion was not accepted in 1999, but by 2000 agents from CIQ had begun to signal to the private trade that some kind of GM-specific treatment of soybean imports was looming, perhaps in the form of testing for GM content, or perhaps labeling requirements. Customs officials on one occasion seized a shipment of GM rapeseed on the grounds that it was a variety not yet approved in the country.

China may also be nudged in the direction of a GM-specific import policy by procedures called for under the international Biosafety Protocol (BP) negotiated in Montreal in January 2000. Officials from the State Environmental Protection Administration led China's delegation to the BP negotiations, and SEPA officials joined the Like-Minded Group of developing countries calling for a precautionary approach to imports of LMOs. Other members of China's negotiating team, including officials from the MOA, were not happy with SEPA's endorsement of the BP's precautionary language and procedures, but were not in a position to challenge the SEPA stance. Partly because of this opposition from the MOA and some other key ministries such as MOST, China delayed signing the BP in Nairobi. Eventually, however, SEPA is likely to emerge as China's primary "focal point" agency for receiving notifications and granting assent under the various terms of the new BP, so GM skeptics may for the first time gain a formal role in the conduct of China's commodity import policy. Because the terms of the BP permit importers to require cautionary notifications whenever transboundary movements of commodities "may contain" LMOs, U.S. shipments of soybeans into China may soon have to be labeled accordingly and SEPA may use this new international labeling requirement as justification for a parallel Chinese labeling requirement on GM imports.

If events do push China's import policies in this direction, the end result would not have to be a fully precautionary policy. Internal consumer anxieties in China are not yet pushing food importers to look for GM-free options. State sector provincial grain and oil companies in China as of 2000 had shown no great interest in finding GM-free soybeans, and the major private importers still routinely bought from the United States. Consumer resistance to GM foods was not yet a factor in China, in contrast to Europe and Japan where it had emerged as the single largest policy factor. Even if China does some day embrace a Japanese- or European-style policy regulating GM soybean imports for food use, its trade would not have to be much affected because soybean imports in China are not used for human food. China makes its tofu entirely from domestic (non-GM) soybeans. Virtually all of the soybeans imported by China are intended for processing and then primarily for use as animal feed. Some of the soybean oil that is produced by this processing is used for direct human consumption, but oil from GM soybeans contains no detectable trace of its GM content.

China has tried to avoid a fully precautionary import policy toward GM crops partly to protect its own future options to go forward with domestic GM food crop production, and perhaps someday to become a GM food exporter in its own right. This approach is now under reconsideration. In April 2001, Chinese officials cited international consumer resistance to GM foods as one reason to halt, at least temporarily, any further release of new GM food crops for planting within China. The planting of GM cotton (an industrial crop) would continue, but official approvals for the commercial planting of major GM food crops such as soybeans, corn, rice, and wheat might be held up for the next three to five years. This evolving policy stance was a reaction to the increasing preference of consumers inside so many other food-trading states in the region (especially Japan and Korea) to avoid GM foods. China is an occasional exporter of corn to Korea, so a commercial release of GM corn at home could now compromise export options. Even European aversions to GM were having an impact. On at least one occasion a shipment of Chinese soy sauce produced in Shanghai from GM soybeans that had been purchased from the United States was turned back by European importers.

If officials do now decide to implement a freeze on new approvals of GM food crops at home in order to protect access to export markets abroad, this will mark a major change in China's hitherto permissive approach toward GM crop approvals. Calculations of commercial trade advantage abroad will have trumped the once-permissive posture of farm development advocates and technology regulators at home.

Food Safety and Consumer Choice Policy

In the past, China's food policymakers were preoccupied almost exclusively with the total quantity of food and farm production in the country. More recently, as the income and sophistication of urban consumers have grown, officials have begun to pay closer attention to food quality, including food safety. China's current 1995 food safety law empowers the Ministry of Health to regulate food ingredients, sanitation, packaging, and labeling. The many diverse and (to Western tastes) somewhat daring regional cuisines of China do not yield easily to central regulation in this regard, yet efforts are being made. Under China's current basic food law, the Ministry of Health officially approves of 1,040 different spices and 431 separate food additives (Zhao 2000). Since the 1980s, the Ministry of Health, assisted by the MOA, has also set standards for chemical pesticide residues on foods, and China has even promulgated rules for the labeling of organic or "natural" foods presumably unpolluted by farm chemicals, primarily with export markets in mind. Up through 2000, however, China's various laws and regulations had not made separate reference to the safety of GM foods or to the right of consumers to know whether the food they are consuming is GM or not.

This promotional policy toward GM foods was finally changed into a permissive policy in May 2001, when China's State Council considered and passed a new Regulation Concerning the Biotech Safety Management of Agricultural Gene Alteration. This new regulation did not impose any tighter food safety screening on GM products, but it did require labeling for those products in the interest of a consumer's right to know. Early official explanations for this change emphasized not just the possible concerns of domestic consumers but also the interest that foreign consumers might have in knowing whether China's food products were or were not GM.

China's rules for food safety previously had not mentioned GM, just as its original rules for GM barely mentioned food safety. The 1996 MOA Implementing Regulation (IR) covering GM crops did stipulate that GM technologies should be assessed for their level of risk to "human health," and it did require assessments of whether the recipient plant being used in any transformation is "toxic to human beings and other organisms," but there were no references to other conventional food safety issues such as allergenicity or digestivity. Prior to granting a commercial release, the Committee on Safety does require that GM food crops must be separately screened in one of two laboratories under the Ministry of Health, and given 30 days of standard toxicity testing. Applicants are warned they must be able to provide "materials concerning safety of the food made of the genetic engineering organisms in question, e.g., reports on toxicity tests, reports on analyses of the nutritive elements of the transgenic and non-transgenic organisms, etc." (China, MOA 1999). This does not, however, imply a significantly higher food safety hurdle for GM crops in China compared with non-GM crops.

The policy debate in China over GM food labeling has not so far been led by any one ministry. A long list of ministries and agencies have an interest in this issue, including the MOA (especially its marketing and information department), the Ministry of Health, MOST, the Customs Office (specifically the import and export inspection office that handles SPS issues), the Ministry of Light Industry (which regulates food processing), and the Bureau of Domestic Commerce. One of the few ministries willing to admit it does *not* have jurisdiction in the area of GM crop food safety is actually SEPA, which does not address food safety directly in its National Biosafety Framework.

Internal pressures to label GM foods in China were slow to develop partly because the government denied that any GM foods were yet on the market inside the country (He 2000). In Hong Kong, Greenpeace activists with close ties to the United Kingdom have staged labeling actions in supermarkets (placing death's head stickers on bottles of soy sauce) to alert consumers to the hidden presence of GM ingredients in foods on the shelf, but such actions had little impact and were not permitted on the mainland (CIB 2000). China's leading skeptic toward GM crops, scientist Qian Yingqian, had called for the labeling of GM products and this demand was echoed by the parastatal Chinese

Consumer Association, but regulators resisted any GM labeling rule up until 2001 by restating their official claim that GM foods are not yet in China. They based this somewhat dubious claim on the facts that China's commercial GM cotton and tobacco production had never been for food, its commercially approved GM tomato and pepper varieties are still not widely planted, and China's imports of GM soy from the United States and Argentina so far had not gone for direct human food use, only for animal feed. This resistance to labeling finally broke in May 2001.

By adopting this public relations denial strategy, China's officials may have further complicated the problem of eventually releasing the GM food crops—such as Bt rice and Bt corn—that their own laboratory scientists have been working so hard to produce. Nor will it be easy for China, if it ever begins growing GM food crops widely, to take the Japanese approach to labeling and market segregation. Countries that grow no GM foods can implement a permissive or precautionary market segregation and labeling policy simply through border controls on imports. China, if it begins growing GM food crops internally, will not have that option. Understandably, Chinese officials are now struggling with the implications of these labeling policy dilemmas, in anticipation of the day when Bt corn or Bt rice might be approved for commercial production by China's own farmers. Chinese officials had watched GM-specific food labeling policies sweep through other advanced countries in the East Asian region and clearly began to worry about appearing less progressive in the food safety area than Japan, South Korea, or even some other states in Southeast Asia. When Chinese leaders finally yielded on GM labeling in 2001, it seemed a further indication that they were not planning a domestic commercial release of new GM food crop varieties any time soon.

Public Investments in GM Crop Research

It is in the area of public research investments that China's policies toward GM crops have been most promotional, and this should be no surprise. China has a long history of relying on public sector resources to promote the innovation and adoption of new and more productive farm technologies. Chinese authorities employed state-funded agricultural researchers and state-owned seed companies to develop and extend semi-dwarf rice varieties and new hybrid maize varieties in the 1950s and 1960s, then hybrid rice in the 1970s and 1980s. When China's leaders first became attracted to the unique promise of GM crop technologies in the 1980s and early 1990s, it was natural for them to choose their own national agricultural research system as the politically preferred vehicle for promoting this technology. China's faith in the independent scientific capacity of its own national research establishment even helps to explain some of the earlier noted weakness in China's IPR policies toward GM crops. Believing it is desirable and possible to promote a GM crop revolution by using the resources and incentive systems of their own public sector, Chinese officials have naturally placed lower priority on IPR policies tailored to the preferences of the private sector. China has encountered some difficulties following its largely state-led approach, especially in the area of GM crop technology dissemination, but in the area of innovation China's large state investments have generated a significant pipeline of potentially valuable GM crop applications.

State-sponsored applied work in plant genetic engineering in China dates to the early 1980s, with the establishment in 1983 of a Molecular Biotechnology Research Laboratory at CAS. This laboratory was elevated to the status of a Biotechnology Research Centre (BRC) in 1986, when China's State Council responded positively to a direct petition from the nation's top scientists for more state support in several high-technology fields, led by biotechnology. The State Council created a new National Program for Developing High Technologies (known as the 863 Program) and six new National Key Laboratories in different locations in north, central, and south China, all equipped to do biotechnology and molecular biology research. In addition, existing laboratories under CAS and the ministries of Education and Agriculture were encouraged through competitive grants to move into biotechnology research. According to one official count, by the end of the 1990s more than 80 state-funded institutions in China were involved in research on agricultural genetic engineering (Li and Liu 1999). By 1996, Chinese scientists were engaged in research on 47 different kinds of transgenic plants and claimed to be using more than 100 different genes to transform those plants (Zhao 2000).

One of China's most visible and successful institutes working in the area of transgenic crops is a renamed successor to the BRC, the Biotechnology Research Institute (BRI) within the CAAS in Beijing. BRI employs 78 scientific researchers, 59 percent of whom have Ph.D. or Master's degrees. Many of these advanced degree holders were originally sent abroad for advanced training in molecular biology and genetic engineering with an expectation that they would bring their knowledge back to China. In 1991, China's internationally trained scientists at the BRI launched a major program to develop Bt cotton, funded initially with only a modest grant of RMB 500,000 (US$60,000) from the 863 Program. By 1993 these BRI scientists had successfully synthesized (and patented) a new pesticidal Bt gene and had used that synthesized gene to transform cotton plants. Field testing began in 1995 and seeds for this new GM cotton variety were given to farmers on a small scale in 1996. In 1997 the Committee on Safety approved four different CAAS Bt cotton cultivars for commercial-scale planting in nine provinces (Pray et al. 2000). By 1999 roughly 100,000–200,000 hectares of cotton land in China were successfully planted to this home-developed Bt variety, roughly the same area planted that year to Monsanto's imported 33B variety. Also in 1999, BRI scientists received permission from the Committee on Safety to begin commercial production of a new double-gene variety of insecticidal cotton, which they had produced by combining a Bt gene with a trypsin inhibitor gene in the hopes of gaining even longer effectiveness against bollworm.

By 1999 China's GM crop scientists had also secured permission from the Committee on Safety to go ahead with commercial production of a delayed-ripening tomato produced at Huazhong Agricultural University, a virus-resistant tomato, a virus-resistant green pepper, and a chalcome synthase petunia all produced at Beijing University, and a herbicide-resistant restoring line of hybrid rice, produced by the CAAS and the China National Rice Research Institute (CNRRI).[7] China's scientists had several other potentially useful GM varieties in the pipeline as well. By introducing the coat protein gene of the yellow dwarf disease into wheat, a disease-resistant wheat was developed, and by synthesizing and inserting antibacterial polypeptide genes into potatoes a wilt-resistant GM tomato variety was produced (Zhao 2000).

The success of China's GM crop researchers is not entirely home grown. Particularly in the area of rice biotechnology, as early as 1985 China's NRRI began receiving grants—initially for 20 different projects—from the Rockefeller Foundation's Rice Biotechnology Program. China was the first developing country to join this program. The Rockefeller Foundation took a lead in sponsored international training opportunities in molecular biology for Chinese scholars, helped equip laboratories in China, and brokered research contacts between China's NRRI and the International Rice Research Institute (IRRI) in the Philippines from which China has received some of its best rice germplasm. Thanks in part to these Rockefeller efforts, Chinese scientists at the BRI not only synthesized their own Bt genes in 1991 but then went on to transform the elite lines of hybrid rice now widely used in China so as to carry Bt. If successfully tested and released, this Bt hybrid rice will be better protected against the yellow stem borer pests that attack rice plants from the inside and are thus normally untreatable with chemical insecticides. As of 2000, successful pilot studies of these transformed varieties of Bt hybrid rice had been reviewed by the Committee on Safety and permission had been granted to move to the environmental release stage, raising hopes that approval for commercial production could be won in several more years' time. Local varieties of ordinary non-hybrid rice were also transformed by Chinese scientists thanks to provincial government support and help from university partners in Canada. The Monsanto company at one point also provided assistance to the CNRRI for the development of glyphosate-resistant (Roundup Ready) ordinary rice, including financial assistance and IPR permission to use Monsanto's transgene for research purposes, although IPR and profit-sharing differences eventually

---

7. The difficult and costly job of producing high-quality hybrid seed could be made easier by this rice breakthrough by permitting the use of herbicides on restoring lines at the seedling stage, thus killing the pseudohybrids that will lack the resistance trait.

led Monsanto to pull back from this initiative. In the area of maize, researchers at China Agricultural University made progress developing Bt maize partly thanks to a research partnership with the private international seed company Pioneer (later part of DuPont).

These international connections have been important, yet the capacity of China's scientists to develop and deploy GM varieties largely on their own—going all the way back to the original work on virus-resistant tobacco in the 1980s—remains noteworthy. Financial incentives from the state have been one key to this success. Resources come from many different ministries and flow through many different competitive grant programs, but the most important single source of support has been the 863 Program, launched in 1986. The original program was designed to run for 15 years and dispensed RMB 10 billion for high-technology research work in all areas. Roughly 15 percent of that total went for biotechnology. A 10-year renewal of this program was agreed to in 2000, called the Super-863 Program (or S-863) because it is scheduled to allocate three times as much as the original program over a 10-year period.

Not all of the biotechnology money in the 863 Program goes to agriculture or to GM crops, but in recent years GM crop research outlays have nonetheless been substantial. Annual nationwide 863 Program allocations for GM crop research have averaged roughly RMB 100 million (about US$12 million). Individual scientists conducting GM crop work that is near completion under this program are eligible for grants worth RMB 2 million (roughly US$250,000) for three years, and scientists working at earlier stages are eligible for RMB 1 million grants.

These substantial 863 Program grants represent only one part of China's total state resource commitment to GM crop research. Researchers can also get non-863 grant support through a so-called Key Technology Program, which is focused more on technology applications, or from various other sources within the Ministry of Science and Technology or the National Planning Commission, or directly from the Ministry of Agriculture itself. The Ministry of Finance approves research budgets overall, with allocation decisions then made primarily by the Ministry of Science and Technology and its National Center for Biotechnology Development. In October 2000 China's minister of science and technology announced a still more ambitious set of goals in science and technology development for agriculture as a part of China's new Tenth Five Year Plan (2001–2005), including a speed-up in construction of high-tech "development parks" and further investments in advanced overseas training for Chinese scientists (APBN 2000d).

This high official attention to GM crop research is interesting because of China's larger pattern of modest spending for agricultural research overall. Public spending on agricultural science and technology as a percentage of agricultural GDP has often been quite low in China—estimated at less than

0.4 percent in the mid-1990s. China's leaders have promised on numerous occasions to increase this "investment intensity" level to 1 percent or more, but actual performance has lagged. In constant 1985 prices, government investments in agricultural research and development in China were no higher in 1996 (at just less than RMB 1 billion) than they had been in 1985. The state has attempted to supplement its core research spending by giving institutes greater freedom to earn their own revenues by selling their technologies and their services directly to seed companies and farmers, and revenues from such ventures did increase after 1990, but little of this commercial income went directly to fund research (Rozelle, Pray, and Huang 1997). China's latest plan for strengthening public research without spending more money overall has been to reduce sharply—perhaps by as much as two-thirds—the co-funded research personnel within CAAS. Some reduced funding of non-performing staff is overdue at CAAS and it should ease the problem of giving adequate salaries and research budgets to top-performing researchers at the better labs and in the better institutes, but agriculture research overall may remain underfunded as before.

Of the state resources that China does devote to agricultural research, however, a surprising share now goes to GM crops and other applications in advanced agribiotechnology. Agricultural scientists doing more conventional work complain that the only way to get their work funded now is to put a GM or "high-tech" label on the grant application. China's authorities do not want their generous funding of GM to create harmful disconnections from other related research activities, so as one part of their plan to reform and streamline the structure of CAAS they have awarded RMB 100 million to build a new combined research facility, bringing together GM crop researchers at BRI with scientists from China's germplasm and breeding institutes. Even so, it will be the GM crop research activities in this new facility that will ensure its fundability in the eyes of the state.

One possible drawback to China's emphasis on state-led research in GM crops is weak dissemination capacity. The Chinese authorities have found a way (even absent strong IPR protections) to give public sector researchers an incentive to develop new GM technologies, but China's publicly owned seed companies do not yet have sufficient incentive to extend these new GM technologies to farmers. China's seed industry for major field crops such as rice, wheat, maize, and cotton is composed almost entirely of state-owned enterprises, including approximately 2,200 separate county-level companies. These companies tend to have high cost structures and few financial resources because they are continuously subject to pressures from local political leaders to supply seed at a low price. When researchers at state institutes produce new GM varieties, the companies cannot be trusted to respond quickly. In the case of cotton, CAAS made its newly approved Bt variety available in 1998, but the state companies did not have the resources or the incentive to undertake a timely seed multiplication and distribution effort, so in the first year only 10,000 hectares of the new CAAS variety were planted. Not until CAAS formed its own private joint venture with a Shenzhen-based real estate company and with the Ministry of Science and Technology did it see its own variety begin to spread (Pray et al. 2000).

Working around these state enterprises is normally difficult, however, since they have traditionally enjoyed state-enforced monopolies over the local production and distribution of seed (Huang, Rozelle, and Hu 2000). In the case of GM tomatoes, researchers at Beijing University received approval for commercial release of their virus-resistant GM variety in 1998, but two years later the total area planted to this new GM variety in China was a trivial 20 mu, all planted by the researchers themselves. Monsanto had a better experience extending Bt cotton into Hebei province because from the start it used its own private resources and its position as the controlling partner in a private joint venture to promote rapid seed production and distribution. China reacted to Monsanto's success in a somewhat defensive manner, however. Rather than noticing and welcoming what private international seed companies can offer in the way of timely technology introduction and dissemination, China adopted a new rule blocking any further foreign majority ownership of seed company joint ventures for major crops, and then it wrote more restrictive measures for imported GM seeds into its new Seed Law. Although top leaders in China have recently been working hard to dismantle inefficient state-owned companies in many sectors of the economy often against fierce local resistance, in the area of seed distribution, including GM seed distribution, the liberalizers have a distance yet to travel.

Summary

Table 6.3 summarizes China's policies toward GM crops. This summary shows that China's policies in key areas such as biosafety and trade have been more permissive than those of the other three countries examined in this study.

For advocates of GM crop applications in developing countries, China thus emerges as a source of hope. Whereas GM crop development policies have been slowed or temporarily blocked elsewhere owing to consumer and environmentalist anxieties, GM crop development and commercialization in China have moved ahead. The contrast to India is instructive. Cotton farmers in both India and China faced bollworm infestation problems in the early 1990s. In both countries the Monsanto company entered into a private joint venture with a local seed company to introduce Bt cotton as one remedy to the pest problem; in both countries the Bt cotton performed well in field trials; and in both countries technical opinions on biosafety grounds were favorable. Yet China went ahead in 1997 to allow the commercial planting of Bt cotton (not only Monsanto's variety, but its own independently developed Chinese

TABLE 6.3 Policies toward GM crops in China, 1999–2001

Policy	Promotional	Permissive	Precautionary	Preventive
IPR			Since 1997 China has provided plant breeders' rights protection and has joined UPOV 1978; regulations are weak and enforcement is weaker still	
Biosafety		China screens GM crops for demonstrated risks on a case-by-case basis. GM varieties of five plants were released commercially in 1997–99		
Trade		No formal distinction is drawn between GM and non-GM commodity imports		
Food safety and consumer choice		GM foods not tested by a separate or higher standard, but labeling will now be required in the name of consumer choice		
Public research investment	China spends significant public resources on independent development as well as on adaptations of GM crops			

NOTE: UPOV = International Convention for the Protection of New Varieties of Plants.

variety) whereas India as late as mid-2001 had not yet done so. The early response to Bt cotton from China's small farmers in Hebei province was enthusiastic. They were able to reduce chemical insecticide use, reduce labor costs, increase their profits, reduce damage to non-target insects and pollution of local water supplies, and reduce their own health risks that had been associated with chemical spray exposure. Chinese officials claimed publicly that cost savings in some cases as high as US$451 per hectare had been realized by Chinese farmers who had switched to growing GM cotton (He 2000). Farmers in India were prevented from enjoying any such GM crop gains.

Advocates of GM crop usage in the developing world may seek reassurance from the example of China's successful experience with GM cotton so far, yet the Chinese case is not that simple. The Chinese model is one that most other countries would have difficulty adopting, and in some cases might not wish to adopt. What sets the China model apart has been the lack of any opportunity, within China, for GM crop critics to use independent nongovernmental organizations, independent news media coverage, or an independent judicial system to challenge the official views and policy choices of Chinese leaders, agricultural scientists, and technocrats. For the purpose of launching a potentially useful GM crop revolution, this guarantee of no opposition from an independent civil society is undeniably convenient, and for some small cotton farmers it has been highly beneficial. And this Chinese approach does not disregard issues such as biosafety entirely: even without strong independent pressures from civil society, Chinese policymakers since 1996 have moved their biosafety policies from what was initially a promotional extreme to a more prudent permissive posture, based on case-by-case risk assessments. Yet for larger public policy purposes this Chinese model of keeping authority in the hands of scientists and top leaders risks technocratic and bureaucratic abuse.

Some other features of China's approach also may not serve well as a universal example. China has opted to promote GM crops by relying heavily on its own public sector. The top scientists in China's massive state sector have so far been up to this task, thanks to the international training they earlier received at universities abroad and thanks to the substantial state resources and private international foundation resources that have been mobilized in their support. Yet most developing-country governments lack the option to rely so exclusively on public sector research capacities. Most other developing countries will have to work more often through research partnerships either with private companies, foundations, foreign donors, and universities, or perhaps with the international agricultural research centers of the Consultative Group on International Agricultural Research. Finally, because China has opted to do so much through its state sector, it has not felt the urgency of putting in place the full set of IPR protections that still might eventually be needed to attract technology transfers or cooperative research investments from the private sector. China relies on the massive size of its internal market as a motivating device for bringing in foreign companies, and this too is a strategy that smaller developing countries will not be able to follow.

In sum, although the case of China may be useful in illustrating the potential success of GM technologies in a developing-country setting, it is of less certain value in offering a model of the policies that others can or should follow. This is just as well, because China's leaders have no desire to become an international poster-boy country for GM crops. China's leaders welcome what GM crops can provide, but they do not wish to enlist with the international biotechnology industry or the government of the United States in promoting GM crops for others. China is aware of the intense international debate surrounding GM technologies and does not want to call attention to itself by being too far out of step with other countries in its region. China is sensitive to international opinion and, although it wants to develop GM technologies it can be proud of, it also wants GM crop policies that will not invite too much international scrutiny or criticism. China is sensitive to international market pressures as well. If consumers in Asia continue to shun GM foods, China may respond by not planting GM foods.

7 Comparing and Explaining Developing-Country Policies toward GM Crops

The four countries covered in this study are individually important and the policy choices they have made regarding GM crops are individually interesting, yet value can be gained from a more systematic comparison of these choices. Several of the patterns that emerge deserve comment.

Table 7.1 summarizes the policy classifications (in the period 1999–2001) that I have made here for Kenya, Brazil, India, and China. In some respects these policy choices are unsurprising. In the area of food safety, permissive or even promotional policies toward GM foods were found in all four of these countries. In one sense this was to be expected because consumers in developing countries have more serious food safety risks to worry about than the GM versus non-GM content of food. The still hypothetical consumer risks associated with GM foods are naturally less likely to trigger precaution in developing countries than in rich countries. A somewhat less expected discovery, however, was the basis on which three of these governments justified their promotional or permissive food safety policies toward GM foods. When questioned, the governments of Kenya, India, and China each said they did not yet need a precautionary policy toward GM foods in part because such foods were not yet on the market within their borders, officially at least. The governments of these countries are not, therefore, promoting GM foods as safe, or even safe enough. Instead, they are dodging the food safety issue by describing GM foods as not yet on the market. This dodge is likely to weaken consumer confidence in GM foods as time goes on. Even in Brazil, where the government has tried to reassure consumers regarding the safety of GM foods, political pressure in 1999 forced a retreat from a promotional policy stance to a permissive stance, accompanied by a mandatory labeling law designed to provide consumer choice. China did the same in 2001.

The IPR policy choices made by these four countries can also be seen as largely conforming to expectations. None of these developing countries should have been expected to embrace the fully promotional U.S. policy of genetic and GM crop patenting, since not even the other industrial countries of Europe follow this approach. Each of the countries in this study instead opted for a

TABLE 7.1 Policies toward GM crops in Kenya, Brazil, India, and China, 1999–2001

Policy	Promotional	Permissive	Precautionary	Preventive
IPR		Brazil	Kenya China	India
Biosafety		China	Kenya Brazil India	
Trade		China	Kenya Brazil	India
Food safety and consumer choice	Kenya	Brazil India China		
Public research investment	Brazil India China		Kenya	

more common plant breeders' rights (PBR) approach allowing farmers and breeders more generous access to protected varieties. And all four of these countries moved toward an acceptance of plant variety protection in the 1990s primarily for the purpose of satisfying their minimum obligations under the Agreement on Trade-Related Aspects of Intellectual Property Rights (TRIPS) within the World Trade Organization, rather than for the independent purpose of promoting research or investments in GM crops or any other kinds of crops. There were some important IPR variations between these countries, as Table 7.1 indicates, but these were not surprising either. Brazil's policies went somewhat beyond the minimal 1978 version of PBRs in the International Convention for the Protection of New Varieties of Plants (UPOV)—as might be expected given Brazil's recent interest in attracting private international investment to its agribusiness sector—and India's PBR law had not yet worked its way through parliament by 2000, partly reflecting India's stronger suspicions about the international private sector. China's plant variety protection policies were much stronger on paper than they were in practice, yet this too is not surprising, since it is a pattern found in other areas of IPR protection in China as well.

The public research investment policies in these countries also conform to expectations. Brazil, India, and China have all maintained traditionally strong national agricultural research systems capable of generating independent farm technology innovations, not just adaptations. It is thus not surprising that all three of these countries were using at least some treasury resources seeking a capacity to develop their own GM crops within these national systems. Nor was it surprising that Kenya would be attempting less, given the relatively high costs of GM crop development and given Kenya's weaker budget resources.

What did not so nearly conform to prior expectations in this study were the decisions of Kenya, Brazil, and India to impose highly cautious—or even preventive—biosafety and trade policies toward GM crops. It was specifically because of highly cautious national biosafety policies that farmers in these countries had not yet by mid-2001 been given official permission to grow any GM crops. The authorities in Brazil tried to release herbicide-tolerant soybeans for commercial use in 1998 but were blocked when a federal court judge concluded that a full environmental impact assessment would first be required. Biosafety authorities in India tried at first to take a permissive approach toward the testing and release of Bt cotton, but when field trials were attacked by anti-GM activists the approval process slowed down, and as of 2000 only large-scale field trials had yet been approved. In Kenya, the National Biosafety Committee took nearly two years to approve a request from the nation's own agricultural research institute to import transgenic sweet potato materials into the country, initially for research purposes only, and as of 2000 only field trials were under way.

The cautious biosafety policies of these three governments tended to generate equally cautious trade policies. So long as biosafety authorities had not cleared any GM crops for internal production, trade policy authorities felt constrained from approving GM commodities for import, except in exceptional circumstances owing to occasional food emergencies (in Kenya and India) or temporary animal feed shortages (in Brazil).

This sort of policy caution toward GM crops in biosafety and trade is surprising in several respects. First, it actually exceeds the official caution shown so far by most industrial-country governments. Even in most of Europe and in Japan it has been permissible since the mid-1990s for farmers to plant at least some GM crops and for food and feed industries to import at least some GM commodities without segregation or a higher level of screening. Yet in Kenya, Brazil, and India such actions were not yet officially permitted as of mid-2001. It is uncommon to see developing-country governments imposing product standards of any kind that are tighter than those in place in the industrial world; more often the developing countries fight for international permission to maintain lower standards (Sykes 1995). It is all the more surprising to find these higher standards emerging in the area of rural biological safety. Many developing countries have for years had serious problems with rural biosafety, owing to unchecked damage from bioinvasions by exotic species, habitat loss from the expansion of cropped areas and grazing lands, toxic pollution or damage to non-target species from pesticide sprays, and growing resistance to those sprays within pest populations. Yet these damaging farming practices have seldom received priority attention from government regulators. So the question arises as to why hypothetical biosafety threats from GM crops would be attracting so much attention.

It would be understandable for poor countries to resist GM crops on biosafety grounds if the specific GM applications in question had never been tried out in the industrial world. Developing countries are sensitive to being used as an experimentation site—as guinea pigs—and they do not want to be a dumping ground for unproven or dangerous technologies being exported for profit by industries that are banned from selling those same technologies in rich countries. But the GM crops that farmers have not yet been allowed to plant in Kenya, Brazil, and India are not officially classified as dangerous by regulators in the industrial world. The herbicide-tolerant soybeans that were not released in Brazil in 1998 had been planted widely and safely without incident since 1995–96 in both the United States and Argentina, and it was legal to plant them in Europe and Japan as well. The Bt cotton that was not yet released to farmers in India in 2000 had been planted widely and without incident for several years previously in both the United States and Australia. Far from generating new biohazards, the best evidence so far is that these herbicide-tolerant and insect-resistant GM crops have been reducing rural biohazards by allowing farmers to engage in less damaging soil tillage practices, to spray herbicides less frequently and use herbicides that are less toxic and less persistent, and to reduce sprays of chemical insecticides that tend to damage non-target species and poison farm workers. Field trials with Bt cotton in India indicated that these would be among the benefits of the new technology, yet commercial approval continued to be delayed on biosafety grounds.

The danger of unwanted geneflow to wild relatives was not the problem either in at least two of these countries. Kenya could not have been worried about geneflow in the case of the GM sweet potato because there are no wild relatives of the sweet potato anywhere in Africa (it is a plant that comes from Ecuador) and it is in any case a plant that is propagated vegetatively rather than through pollen drift. Brazil could not have been worried about geneflow in the case of Roundup Ready soybeans because there are no wild relatives of the soybean anywhere in the Western hemisphere.

Adding to the puzzle is the fact that two of these countries—Brazil and India—were operating highly cautious biosafety policies toward GM crops while at the same time supporting, at public expense, a significant national research program designed explicitly to promote such crops. The promotional public investment policies of countries such as China or India may not be in direct conflict with their precautionary or preventive IPR policies, because sufficient public investments can make the luring in of private investments less important. But expensive public sector promotion and paralyzing biosafety policy caution do not so clearly fit together. In Brazil, India, and also Kenya, national agricultural research scientists routinely complain about the slow-down in GM crop development being imposed through biosafety regulations or owing to biosafety disputes.

It might be imagined that government leaders in the developing world would be eager to get their hands on the latest and most powerful agricultural production technologies, and would then be frustrated by the reluctance of their own cautious and highly traditional farming communities to take up those technologies. In Kenya, Brazil, and India the opposite seems to be happening. Rather than working to gain access to GM crops, a number of governmental authorities in these countries have worked—especially through biosafety and trade policy actions—to keep those technologies at bay. Developing-country participants in the negotiations that led to the 2000 Biosafety Protocol constructed a mechanism designed to slow down rather than speed up the transfer of this technology into their countries. Meanwhile a number of farmers in these developing countries seem eager to plant GM crops but were prevented by their own governments from doing so. In Brazil, soybean growers were so attracted to GM varieties that they smuggled seeds in from Argentina, risking harassment or arrest by planting and replanting them illegally. And in China, where farmers were permitted to plant Bt cotton, they did so eagerly and successfully.

Further puzzles arise. Developing countries sometimes complain about their inability to get flexible and affordable access to the latest or most powerful technologies in use by rich countries because of tightly guarded IPR claims. Yet, in all four of the cases examined here, IPR was not the most important barrier to technology transfer. In Kenya, private international companies with protected GM technologies were willing to share those technologies on a royalty-free basis. It was the biosafety issue, not an IPR issue, that kept Monsanto's GM sweet potatoes out of the hands of Kenyan researchers and farmers. In Brazil, too, the Monsanto company was willing and even eager to bring its GM soybean technology into the country, and it was a paralysis of the biosafety approval process rather than a disagreement over IPRs that frustrated that desire. In India, despite an extremely weak local IPR environment, private companies eager to move their technologies into the country decided to do so by concentrating on hybrids. The size of India's market was by itself a sufficient lure to private companies to justify the IPR risk. It was not the reluctance of the international companies but rather the slow progress of India's own biosafety approval process that kept Bt cotton out of the hands of farmers. In China as well, despite blatant IPR piracy, private companies attracted by China's market size looked for ways to bring in GM crops, including even openly pollinated varieties. What makes the China case distinct is that the biosafety approval process actually went forward.

Nor can we say from this study that developing countries are keeping the GM crops sold by foreign companies at bay simply for protectionist reasons, to preserve their domestic seed markets for local or national companies. In the case of Kenya, the GM sweet potato that had such trouble gaining biosafety approval did not compete significantly with any local commercial varieties. Nor did Monsanto's Bt cotton seeds compete with seeds sold by local competitors in India, because Monsanto had arranged in advance to use its most likely local seed company competitor, the Mahyco company, as a local partner. In Brazil, although national scientists were developing their own varieties of herbicide-tolerant soybean, they were not pleased to see the release of Monsanto's varieties delayed by anti-GM crop activists because they knew this opposition to GM crops could eventually block their own efforts as well. And in China, where a competitive dynamic did develop between Monsanto's Bt cotton seed and nationally developed Bt varieties, Monsanto still found a way, through a provincial governor's influence and a local joint venture partner, to sell its seeds in the country.

If highly cautious biosafety policies caused the slowdown in GM crop technology movement into Kenya, Brazil, and India, what brought on these cautious policies? Recall that in Brazil and India the original political intent was to adopt a permissive rather than a highly cautious biosafety policy toward GM crops. In Brazil, the National Technical Commission on Biosafety (CTNBio) was initially structured (complete with corporate representation) and tasked to pursue a permissive policy in this area; CTNBio tried at first to play this role by issuing a favorable technical opinion on GM soybeans in 1998 almost as soon as its procedures would allow. In India, the Review Committee on Genetic Manipulation was also originally designed to reflect the interests and preferences of the technology promoters. In these two countries biosafety policy shifted toward a more cautious posture only after GM crops became controversial among consumer and environmental advocacy groups in the industrial world. Local nongovernmental organizations (NGOs) in Brazil and India took up the criticisms of GM crops they heard being made by their counterparts in the industrial world, and the approval processes in their countries slowed accordingly.

In some cases, such as that of Greenpeace in Brazil, the local NGOs were direct institutional extensions of their European counterparts. The industrial-country NGOs such as Greenpeace that opposed GM crops had failed to mobilize in time to block biosafety approval of these crops in rich countries, but they hoped they could make up for that failing by blocking approvals in poor countries. Their objections to GM crops were usually part of a larger set of concerns about the dangers of globalization, as pushed by U.S.-based multinational corporations and neoliberal institutions such as the World Trade Organization. This larger ideological agenda was a core feature of the anti-GM appeals made by NGOs to urban constituencies in developing-country societies. It was convenient, given this agenda, that so many of the GM crop technologies being offered to the developing world had been developed by a U.S.-based multinational giant, the Monsanto company. If GM crops had come out of public sector laboratories in the developing world, or even out of the publicly funded Consultative Group on International Agricultural Research, it would not have been as easy for international anti-GM activists to raise anxieties about them.

Several other international influences have helped push GM crop policies in developing countries in a more cautious direction. Most consumers in developing countries are not yet concerned about GM foods, but international commodity markets transmit the aversion of consumers elsewhere, especially in Europe and Japan, into the developing world. In export-oriented agricultural countries such as Brazil, decisions about the biosafety release of GM crops are now being made, in part, on the basis of likely consumer acceptance in markets abroad. Given the high costs of segregating a GM-free supply of bulk commodities for export once some farmers within a country begin planting GM varieties, it is best perhaps to keep an entire nation GM free until international preferences become more certain. And what better way to keep an entire nation GM free than to refuse the commercial release of GM crops on biosafety grounds. There are limits, of course, to this approach. Some in Brazil have advocated remaining GM free to capture export market price premiums, yet sophisticated foreign customers have been slow to provide those premiums for soybeans because their testing has told them Brazil is anything but a GM-free country, owing to illicit plantings of GM soybean seeds smuggled in from Argentina.

Yet another international source of biosafety caution toward GM crops in the developing world has been the negotiation of the 2000 Biosafety Protocol within the Convention on Biological Diversity. The years that it took to negotiate this agreement slowed biosafety approvals in some countries, because GM crop critics could argue that national regulatory actions regarding GM crops in the developing world should first await a clarification of international obligations. Now that the Protocol is in place, further caution on biosafety approvals is being encouraged by the tone and terms of the agreement, which implicitly likens the transboundary shipment of genetically modified organisms to the international shipment of hazardous waste. The negotiation of the Protocol also tended to strengthen environment ministry authority over GM crops within developing countries at the expense of agricultural ministry authority.

A final international source of biosafety caution in developing countries has been the donor community. In low-resource countries such as Kenya in particular, biosafety policy can easily become donor driven. Wealthy donor governments have good reason to want to help poor countries promulgate effective biosafety policies before introducing GM crops. Yet too often these wealthy governments have helped developing-country governments draft regulations and guidelines that set standards for testing and data evaluation that poor countries do not have the capacity to meet. Donors work hard to help poor countries set out strict biosafety standards on paper, but they invest much less in building the technical and administrative capacity needed within those countries to implement those strict standards properly on a case-by-case basis. Knowing they lack the technical capacity to implement their own biosafety regulations with complete self-confidence, and knowing they will be closely questioned by NGOs and in the media if they release any GM crops for commercial use, biosafety regulators in these low-resource countries then have every incentive to move slowly.

Of the four countries examined here, only China had embraced a more permissive biosafety policy toward GM crops. One reason was its greater insulation from some of the international influences that were promoting caution elsewhere. In contrast to Kenya, China did not depend so heavily on donor funding so it was under less external pressure and scrutiny when it initially went ahead with some GM crop field trials without having any formal biosafety screening process in place. When China finally did set a formal process in place it was permissive rather than precautionary, and located within the production-oriented Ministry of Agriculture rather than under a more cautious ministry such as health or environment. And, in contrast to Brazil and India, China does not have to shape its biosafety policies in response to internationally connected NGO critics of genetic engineering. This is because China does not allow such organizations to operate freely within the country. Nor does China yet allow rival political parties, independent journalists, or an independent judiciary to operate. This lack of open political space for civil society to challenge government policy in China has been one reason for China's ability to go ahead with some GM crops while others in the developing world have not.

One international influence that China must accept is international consumer skepticism toward GM crops in export markets. Because China is a food-exporting as well as a food-importing country, and because some of its exports go to nations in East Asia and the Pacific (such as Korea or Australia) where consumer skepticism regarding GM foods is high, it has reason to think twice before releasing GM varieties of crops such as corn or rice into its agricultural system. This helps explain why China's strongest early efforts with GM were with two non-food commodities, tobacco and cotton.

Making policy under international constraint is nothing new in the developing world. In the face of these new international constraints against adopting GM crops, do the developing-country officials who might want these technologies have any options? In particular, are there steps they can take to break away from the bottleneck of an excessively cautious biosafety policy? China's policy insulation approach should not and probably could not be imitated by others. Insulating biosafety policy approvals from all internal political challenge and from all international NGO pressures and media scrutiny is a dangerous practice, as it undermines accountability and risks inviting technocratic abuse. Yet some other features of the Chinese approach could usefully be considered by others. For example, China was able to operate a permissive biosafety review process (screening only for evidence of demonstrated risk) rather than a precautionary process (screening for scientific uncertainties as well as demonstrated risks) in part because it had located its review committee inside its Ministry of Agriculture. This has helped China balance hypothetical biosafety risks from GM crops against the nation's real food production needs. In Kenya, by contrast, the National Biosafety Committee was located within the Ministry of Science and Technology and had a membership institutionally removed in most cases from farm productivity problems. In Brazil, CTNBio was also located under a Ministry of Science and Technology. CTNBio was eager to be permissive, but it lacked the statutory or constitutional authority to make its judgments stand up in court, and it could easily be caricatured as being closer to international agribusiness interests than to the needs or interests of Brazil's own poor farmers. In India, the final decision over biosafety approval was left to the Genetic Engineering Approval Committee, a committee chaired by the Ministry of Environment. Once again, agricultural productivity imperatives were certain to be underemphasized. Nations seeking to balance real production needs more effectively against hypothetical biosafety risks would be well advised to strengthen the agricultural ministry links to their approval committee.

A second lesson also grows from the Chinese experience. Governments in the developing world that wish to move ahead with the GM crop revolution and shape its potential to their own individual national needs must be prepared to invest more of their own treasury resources in developing an independent national scientific capacity in crop transformation. China's State Council began making substantial GM crop research investments in 1986, and by 1993 Chinese scientists were successfully synthesizing (and even patenting) their own insecticidal Bt gene for use in transforming cotton plants. So when the time came in 1997 for China's biosafety committee to review Bt cotton for commercial release it was not only looking at a Monsanto variety introduced by a multinational company from abroad, but also reviewing four different varieties developed nationally by the Chinese Academy of Agricultural Sciences. This eased the approval process considerably.

Nationalism still shapes policy in the developing world, far more in fact than in the developed world. It is naturally easier for regulatory authorities under pressure from GM crop critics to defend a biosafety approval if the crop in question has been developed by national scientists with public sector resources, rather than by foreign companies. Several other probable advantages flow from placing heavier emphasis on public sector research. Public sector GM crop development efforts are less likely to neglect the "orphan crops" grown by the poorest farmers in tropical countries. Private companies do not see poor farmers as good customers, so the profit-making private sector is unlikely to invest in GM varieties of cassava or cowpeas. It is the public sector, working perhaps with nonprofit foundations, that will invest the needed resources here. Developing GM crops through the public sector is also less likely to leave new innovations encumbered by restrictive IPR claims.

The private marketplace, left to itself, is not likely to work much GM crop magic for the poorest farmers of the developing world. The lead role that so far has been played by private international companies in the GM crop revolution is arguably the main reason this revolution has not yet reached the poorest farmers of the tropics, and one reason GM crops have encountered such strong political and social opposition in some quarters. During the successful Green Revolution of the 1960s and 1970s, nobody waited for the profit-making private sector to take the lead, which it never did. Instead, national and international public sector research institutes, philanthropic foundations, agricultural ministries, and extension agencies developed and moved new high-yielding seed varieties to farmers. Too often in the current "gene" revolution public sector agencies have abdicated this role.

If public sector institutions, especially governments in both the developed and developing world, were willing to invest more financial resources in shaping this new technology, the benefits would more often be targeted toward poor farmers and reach those farmers at an affordable price. Social resistance could then diminish as well, since it would be easier to view GM crops as the products of a national development strategy rather than as alien technologies introduced by profit-hungry foreign companies.

GM crops have been planted commercially for only half a decade, so all of the developing-country policies described in this book are of recent origin and most are still rapidly evolving. The international debate over GM crops is also still rapidly evolving. Estimating the further spread and most likely future direction of this technology is thus a difficult task. This study provides only a snapshot of policies toward GM crops at one moment in time, in 1999–2001. As policy toward this new technology evolves in the years ahead, we have to hope that the views of the real stakeholders in the developing world—consumers, farmers, and rural communities—will eventually come to be heard as loudly as the various and conflicting opinions of the outsiders, the GM crop critics and advocates from the developed world who too often dominate the policy debate.

References

ABSF (African Biotechnology Stakeholders Forum). 1999. RE: Biotechnology and Kenya's socio-economic survival. Open letter to policy makers in Kenya, Nairobi, October.

ABSP (Agricultural Biotechnology for Sustainable Productivity). 1998. *Cooperating to enrich earth's capacity.* East Lansing, Mich., U.S.A.

ADA (American Dietetic Association). 1995. Position of the American Dietetic Association: Biotechnology and the future of food. *Journal of the American Dietetic Association* 95 (December):1429–1432.

APBN. 2000a. *Asia-Pacific Biotech News* 4 (24):455.

———. 2000b. *Asia-Pacific Biotech News* 4 (8):168.

———. 2000c. Yunnan to build Chinese biotech valley. *Asia-Pacific Biotech News* 4 (10):15 May.

———. 2000d. China sets goals for science and technology. *Asia-Pacific Biotech News* 4 (23):430.

Balasubramanian, D. 2000. Biotechnology in India: An introduction. *Biotechnology in India* (Special Issue of *Asia-Pacific Biotech News*) 4 (February):47–52.

BGE (Biotechnology Global Update). 2000. Farmers too are knowledge workers. 2 (January):1.

Birchard, K. 2000. European Commission to end de facto moratorium on GM products. *Lancet* 356:320–322.

Brazil. 1995. Law Number 8974, January 5 (National Biosafety Law).

Brazil, Ministry of Environment. 1998. First national report for the Convention on Biological Diversity—Brazil. Brasilia: Federal Republic of Brazil.

Brazil, Ministry of Justice. 1999. Consulta publica No. 02, De 1 De Dezembro de 1999. Brasilia: Federal Republic of Brazil.

Bright, Christopher. 1999. Invasion species: Pathogens of globalization. *Foreign Policy* 116 (Fall).

Brown, L. R. 1995. *Who will feed China? Wake-up call for a small planet.* New York: W. W. Norton.

Burnquist, H. L. 1996. Biotechnology and agriculture in Brazil: Social and economic impacts. International Development Research Center. http://www.idrc.ca/books/focus/789/burnquis.html.

Byrne, D. 2000. Food safety: Continuous transatlantic dialogue is essential. *European Affairs* 1 (2):80–85.

Cantley, M. F. 1996. International instruments, intellectual property and the collaborative exploitation of genetic resources. Paper presented at conference on Phytochemical Diversity: A Source of New Industrial Products, April 14–17, University of Sussex, U.K.

CBD (Convention on Biological Diversity). 1992. June 5, Rio de Janeiro.

CE (Centro Ecologico/CAPA/CETAP Consortium). 2000. For a Brazil free of transgenics. Newsletter No. 1 (Brazil), June.

CENARGEN (Center for National Genetic Resources). 1995. Program for basic biotechnology research. http://www.cenargen.embrapa.br/embrapa/programs/ingles/program3/impac.html.

Chang, Ha-Joon. 2001. Intellectual property rights and economic development: Historical lessons and emerging issues. Background paper prepared for *Human Development Report, 2001,* Cambridge, U.K., Faculty of Economics and Politics.

Chen, X. 2000. The status quo and prospect of China's agricultural development. China Development Forum, conference on China 2010: Charting the Path to the Future, March 27–28, Beijing.

China, MOA (Ministry of Agriculture). 1996. Safety administration implementation regulation on agricultural biological genetic engineering. Issued July 10. Beijing.

———. 1997. Administration of the examination, approval and registration of foreign-invested crop seed enterprises provisions. Effective 8 September 1997.

———. 1999. An explanation of the regulations for applying for safety assessment of agricultural biological genetic engineering. October.

China, SSTC (State Science and Technology Commission). 1993. Safety administration regulation on genetic engineering. Regulation No. 17. Beijing, December 24.

CIB (China International Business). 2000. Easy pickings: China promises rich harvest for "frankenfood" business. 151 (May):14–18.

Conway, G. 1999. Statement of Gordon Conway, president of the Rockefeller Foundation, to the Monsanto board of directors, July 24, Washington, D.C.

———. 2000. Crop biotechnology: Benefits, risks, and ownership. Speech at conference on GM Food Safety: Facts, Uncertainties, and Assessment, the Organisation for Economic Co-operation and Development (OECD) Edinburgh Conference on the Scientific and Health Aspects of Genetically Modified Foods, March 28, Edinburgh, Scotland.

CoP CBD (Conference of Parties to the Convention on Biological Diversity). 2000. Draft Cartagena Protocol on Biosafety. Final draft text submitted by the Legal Drafting Group, January 24–28, Montreal.

CTNBio (National Technical Commission on Biosafety). 1998. Transgenicos. Ministerio da Ciencia a Tecnologia, Brasilia.

———. 1999. Processos de liberacao planejada no meio ambiente de organismos geneticamente modificados: Resumo dos eventos por cultura liberados pela. Unpublished summary, Brasilia, December.

Cullet, P. 1999. Plant variety protection in the TRIPS: Towards the development of *sui generis* protection systems. Background paper prepared for regional workshop on

Biotechnology Assessment: Regimes and Experiences, organized by Africa Centre for Technology Studies (ACTS), September 27–29, Nairobi, Kenya.

DeCola, D. 2000. U.S.–Japan corn deal lifts prices. *Wall Street Journal,* December 19:C15.

DePalma, A., and S. Romero. 2000. Crop genetics on the line in Brazil. *New York Times,* May 16:C1.

DeVries, J. 1999. Rockefeller Foundation's initiatives to build Africa's capacity in biotechnology. Background paper prepared for the regional workshop on Biotechnology Assessment: Regimes and Experiences, organized by the African Centre for Technology Studies (ACTS), September 27–29, Nairobi, Kenya.

Dhar, B., and C. Niranjan Rao. 1999. Plant breeders and farmers in the new intellectual property regime: Conflict of interests? In *Biotechnology, biosafety, and biodiversity: Scientific and ethical issues for sustainable development,* ed. S. Shantharam and J. Montgomery. Enfield, N.H., U.S.A.: Science Publishers.

Dutfield, G. 1999. *Intellectual property rights, trade and biodiversity: The case of seeds and plant varieties.* IUCN Background Paper, Intersessional Meeting on the Operations of the Convention on Biological Diversity, June, Montreal. Oxford, U.K.: Oxford Centre for the Environment, Ethics, and Society.

Embrapa. 1998. Embrapa Cerrados and Cerrados region. Embrapa Cerrados (CPAC), Ministry of Agriculture, Planaltina, DF.

Enriquez, J., and R. A. Goldberg. 2000. Transforming life, transforming business: The life-science revolution. *Harvard Business Review* (March–April):96–104.

ESCOP (Experiment Station Committee on Organization and Policy). 2000. Agricultural biotechnology: Critical issues and recommended responses from the land-grant universities. Mimeo, January.

European Commission. 2000a. Economic impacts of genetically modified crops on the agri-food sector: A synthesis. Directorate-General for Agriculture Working Document. Brussels.

———. 2000b. Regulation (EC) No. 49/2000.

Evenson, R. E., C. E. Pray, and M. W. Rosegrant. 1999. Agricultural research and productivity growth in India. Research Report 109. Washington, D.C.: International Food Policy Research Institute.

Falck-Zepeda, J. B., G. Traxler, and R. G. Nelson. 1999. Rent creation and distribution from biotechnology innovations: The case of Bt cotton and herbicide-tolerant soybeans. Paper presented at Transitions in Agbiotech: Economics of Strategy and Policy, NE-165 Conference, June 24–25, Washington, D.C.

Fan, S., P. Hazell, and S. Thorat. 1999. Linkages between government spending, growth, and poverty in rural India. Research Report 110. Washington, D.C.: International Food Policy Research Institute.

Ghosh, P. K. 1997. Transgenic plants and biosafety concerns in India. *Current Science* 72 (February):172–179.

———. 1999. Biosafety guidelines: International comparisons. Paper presented at Workshop on Genetically Modified Plants: Benefits and Risks, June 24. Proceedings published by TERI, New Delhi.

Ghosh, P. K., and T. V. Ramanaiah. 2000. Indian rules, regulations and procedures for handling transgenic plants. *Journal of Scientific & Industrial Research* 59 (February):114–120.

Government of India. 1999. *The protection of plant varieties and farmers' rights bill, 1999.* Bill No. 123 of 1999, as introduced in Lok Sabha. New Delhi.

Gupta, A. 2000. Creating a global biosafety regime. *International Journal of Biotechnology* 2 (1–3):205–230.

Hall, A., M. V. K. Sivamohan, N. Clark, S. Taylor, and G. Bockett. 1998. Institutional developments in Indian agricultural R&D systems: Emerging patterns of public and private sector activities. *Science, Technology & Development* 16 (December): 51–76.

He Sheng. 2000. GMO research stirs hot debate. *China Daily* (Beijing), September 25.

Hoffmann, Jose Hermeto.1999. Transgenicos: Um tema politico. *Reportagem* 1 (November):37–39.

Huang, J., and S. Rozelle. 1996. Technology change: Rediscovering the engine of productivity growth in China's rural economy. *Journal of Development Economics* 49:337–369.

Huang, J., C. Chen, and S. Rozelle. 2000. Trade liberalization and China's food economy in the 21st century. Center for Chinese Agricultural Policy (CCAP) Working Paper WP-00-E1. Beijing.

Huang, J., J. Y. Lin, and S. Rozelle. 2000. What will make Chinese agriculture more productive? Center for Chinese Agricultural Policy (CCAP) Working Paper No. WP-00-E3. Beijing.

Huang, J., S. Rozelle, and R. Hu. 2000. Reforming China's seed industry: Transition to commercialization in the 21st century. Center for Chinese Agricultural Policy (CCAP) Working Paper WP-00-E6. Beijing.

IBAC (Independent Biotechnology Advisory Council). 1999. Economic implications of a first release of genetically modified organisms in New Zealand. Discussion Paper. Wellington: Government of New Zealand, December 31.

ICRISAT. 1992. The medium term plan. Patancheru, Andra Pradesh, India.

IDRC (International Development Research Centre). 2000. *Seeding solutions:* Volume 1. *Policy options for genetic resources: People, plants, and patents revisited.* Ottawa, Canada.

India, DBT (Department of Biotechnology, Ministry of Science and Technology). 1990. Recombinant DNA safety guidelines. New Delhi, January.

———. 1994. Revised guidelines for safety in biotechnology. New Delhi.

———. 1998. Revised guidelines for research in transgenic plants and guidelines for toxicity and allergenicity evaluation of transgenic seeds, plants, and plant parts. New Delhi, August.

———. 1999. *Annual report 1998–99.* Delhi.

Inside U.S. Trade. 1999. Japan announces GMO labeling in the face of U.S. opposition. *Inside U.S. Trade* 17 (August 20):1, 18–19.

———. 2000. 18 (February 4).

IPE (Institute for Public Enterprise). 2000. Andhra Pradesh Netherlands biotechnology programme. Hyderabad, India: IPE, Biotechnology Unit, Osmania University.

ISAAA (International Service for the Acquisition of Agri-Biotech Applications). 2000.

The intellectual and technical property components of pro-vitamin A rice. ISAAA Brief No. 20-2000. Ithaca, N.Y.

ISNAR (International Service for National Agricultural Research). 1999. Assessing the feasibility of a regional initiative on biotechnology for agricultural research in the Eastern and Central Africa region. ISNAR Project RAF320. The Hague.

James, C. 2000a. *Global status of commercialized transgenic crops: 1999.* ISAAA Briefs No. 17-2000. Ithaca, N.Y.: International Service for the Acquisition of Agri-Biotech Applications.

————. 2000b. *Preview: Global review of commercialized transgenic crops: 2000.* ISAAA Brief No. 21-2000. Ithaca, N.Y.: International Service for the Acquisition of Agri-Biotech Applications.

Jayaraman, K. S. 2001. Indian regulatory system stifles industry growth. *Nature* 19 (February):105–106.

Juma, C. 1989. *Biological diversity and innovation: Conserving and utilizing genetic resources in Kenya.* Nairobi: African Centre for Technology Studies.

Kenya, Ministry of Environmental Conservation (MOEC). 1999. Sessional Paper No. 6 of 1999, on Environment and Development. Nairobi.

Komen, J. 1997. International initiatives in agri-food biotechnology. Unpublished manuscript. The Hague: ISNAR.

Korwek, E. L. 2000. Labeling biotech foods: Opening Pandora's box? *Food Technology* 54 (March):38–42.

Laws of Kenya. 1980. The food, drugs and chemical substances act. Chapter 254. Revised edition. Nairobi: Government of Kenya.

Leggett, K., and I. Johnson. 2000. China bets the farm on promise (and glory) of genetic engineering. *Wall Street Journal,* March 29:A17.

Lele, U., W. Lesser, and G. Horstkotte-Wessler. 2000. Summary and implications for the World Bank. In *Intellectual property rights in agriculture: The World Bank's role in assisting borrower and member countries,* ed. U. Lele, W. Lesser, and G. Horstkotte. Washington, D.C.: World Bank.

Li, N., and X. Liu. 1999. Safety administration and agricultural biological genetic engineering in China. In *Regulation and practice on biosafety,* ed. D. Xue and I. Virgin. Proceedings of the International Workshop on Biosafety, November 2–5, 1998, Nanjing, China. Beijing: China Environmental Science Press.

Liu, B., and D. Xue. 1999. The structure and content of the proposed national biosafety regulation in China. In *Regulation and practice on biosafety,* ed. D. Xue and I. Virgin. Proceedings of the International Workshop on Biosafety, November 2–5, 1998, Nanjing, China. Beijing: China Environmental Science Press.

Lynam, J., and R. M. Hassan. 1998. A new approach to securing sustained growth in Kenya's maize sector. In *Maize technology development and transfer: A GIS application for research planning in Kenya,* ed. R. M. Hassan. New York: CAB International.

McCammon, S. 1999. Testimony before U.S. House of Representatives Subcommittee on Basic Research hearing on Plant Genome Research: From the Lab to the Field to the Market, Part III. October 19, Serial No. 106-60. Washington, D.C.: Government Printing Office.

Mishra, J. P. 1999. Plant-variety protection including UPOV convention and biodiversity: An Indian perspective. Paper presented at the International Seminar on Implications of New IPR Regime under TRIPS for Developing Countries, May 19–20, Habitat Centre, New Delhi.

Moi, D. T. arap. 2000. Open letter to U.S. President Bill Clinton. Nairobi, August 21.

Mugabe, J., et al. 2000. *Global biotechnology risk management: A profile of policies, practices and institutions*. Nairobi: UNEP and ACTS.

Mugo, S. N. 2000. Presentation of IRMA project goals, objectives, and activities. Remarks at IRMA stakeholders' meeting, March 3, Nairobi, Kenya.

Murthyunjaya, and P. Ranjitha. 1998. The Indian agricultural research system: Structure, current policy issues, and future orientation. *World Development* 26 (6): 1089–1101.

NCST (National Council for Science and Technology). 1998. Regulations and guidelines for biosafety in biotechnology for Kenya. NCST No. 41, February. Nairobi, Kenya.

Ndiritu, C. R. 2000. Kenya: Biotechnology in Africa: Why the controversy? In *Agribiotechnology and the poor: An international conference on biotechnology*, ed. G. J. Persley and M. M. Lantin. Washington, D.C.: Consultative Group on International Agricultural Research (CGIAR).

Nelson, G., T. Josling, D. Bullock, L. Unnevehr, M. Rosegrant, and L. Hill. 1999. The economics and politics of genetically modified organisms in agriculture: Implications for WTO 2000. Bulletin 809, University of Illinois College of Agricultural, Consumer and Environmental Sciences, Urbana-Champaign, Ill., U.S.A.

Netherlands, Ministry of Foreign Affairs. 1992. Biotechnology and development cooperation: Priorities and organisation of the special programme. Directorate General for International Cooperation. The Hague.

Nuffield Council on Bioethics. 1999. Genetically modified crops: The ethical and social issues. London, May.

Obure, C. M. 2000. Insect resistant maize for Africa (IRMA) project. Opening remarks at IRMA stakeholders' meeting, March 3, Nairobi, Kenya.

OECD (Organisation for Economic Co-operation and Development). 1993. *Safety considerations for biotechnology: Scale-up of crop plants.* Paris: OECD Publications.

———. 2000. Modern biotechnology and agricultural markets: A discussion of selected issues. Directorate for Food, Agriculture and Fisheries, Committee for Agriculture. Paris.

Paarlberg, R. L. 1994. *Countrysides at risk: The political geography of sustainable agriculture.* Washington, D.C.: Overseas Development Council.

Pachauri, R. K. 1999. Welcome address. Delivered at Workshop on Genetically Modified Plants: Benefits and Risks, June 24. Proceedings published by TERI, New Delhi.

Padmanabhan, A. 2000. Transgenic seeds: Key to green revolution, Version 2.0. *India Abroad,* August 4.

Pan, A. 2000. Patent protection in the field of biotechnology in China. Paper presented at conference on China Agriculture and Food Biotechnology, April 4–5, Great Wall Sheraton Hotel, Beijing.

Paroda, R. S. 1999. Keynote address: Biotechnology and future Indian agriculture.

Paper presented at Workshop on Genetically Modified Plants: Benefits and Risks, June 24. Proceedings published by TERI, New Delhi.

Persley, G. J. 2000. Agricultural biotechnology and the poor: Promethean science. In *Agribiotechnology and the poor,* ed. G. J. Persley and M. M. Lantin. Washington, D.C.: Consultative Group on International Agricultural Research (CGIAR).

Pollack, A. 2000. Is everything for sale? Patenting a human gene as if it were an invention. *New York Times,* June 28:C1.

Potrykus, I. 2000. Email correspondence (Re: Hungry for Biotech) from Dr. Ingo Potrykus to C. S. Prakash, June 26.

Prakash, C. S. 1999. Relevance of biotechnology to Indian agriculture. Paper presented at Workshop on Genetically Modified Plants: Benefits and Risks, June 24. Proceedings published by TERI, New Delhi.

Pray, C. E. 1999. Exploiting the multinationals: LDC policies toward the life science giants. Rutgers University Department of Agricultural, Food, and Resource Economics, New Brunswick, N.J.

Pray, C. E., D. Ma, J. Huang, and F. Qiao. 2000. Impact of Bt cotton in China. Rutgers University Department of Agricultural, Food, and Resource Economics, New Brunswick, N.J. Unpublished manuscript.

Qaim, M. 1999. Assessing the impact of banana biotechnology in Kenya. ISAAA Brief No. 10-1999. Ithaca, N.Y.: International Service for the Acquisition of Agri-biotech Applications.

Raj, N. Gopal. 1999. GMOs: Promise and danger. In *The Hindu: Survey of the Environment '99,* Hyderabad, India.

Rao, S. R. 1999. Building public acceptance of genetically modified products in India. Paper presented at Workshop on Genetically Modified Plants: Benefits and Risks, June 24. Proceedings published by TERI, New Delhi.

RFSTE (Research Foundation for Science, Technology and Ecology). 2000. Stop dumping GE food! Using disasters to create markets. RFSTE Memorandum, June.

Roberts, D. 1998. Preliminary assessment of the effects of the WTO Agreement on Sanitary and Phytosanitary Trade Regulations. *Journal of International Economic Law* 1: 377–405.

Roseboom, J., and P. G. Pardey. 1993. Statistical brief on the national agricultural research system of Kenya. No. 5, November. The Hague: ISNAR.

Rozelle, S., C. Pray, and J. Huang. 1997. Agricultural research policy in China: Testing the limits of commercialization-led reform. *Comparative Economic Studies* 39 (2):37–71.

Rozelle, S., A. Park, J. Huang, and H. Jin. 2000. Bureaucrat to entrepreneur: The changing role of the state in China's grain economy. Center for Chinese Agricultural Policy (CCAP) Working Paper WP-00-E5, Chinese Academy of Agricultural Sciences, Beijing.

Sahai, S. 1999. Intellectual property rights and community rights. In *Bioresources and biotechnology: Policy concerns for the Asian region,* ed. S. Sahai. New Delhi: Gene Campaign.

Sampaio, Maria Jose Amstalden. 1999. Biotechnology and agriculture in Brazil: Facing the present challenges. Unpublished paper presented to CGIAR/World Bank Conference on Agribiotechnology, October, Washington, D.C.

————. 2000. Perspectives from national systems and universities: Brazil. In *Intellectual property rights in agriculture*, ed. U. Lele et al. Washington, D.C.: World Bank.

Seed Law of People's Republic of China. 2000. Approved at the sixteenth meeting of the Standing Committee of the ninth National People's Congress, July 8. Unofficial English translation, Beijing.

Sehgal, S. 1999. IPR controversy and the Indian seed industry. In *Biotechnology, biosafety, and biodiversity: Scientific and ethical issues for sustainable development*, ed. S. Shantharam and J. F. Montgomery. Enfield, N.H., U.S.A.: Science Publishers, Inc.

Selvarajan, S., Dinesh C. Joshi, and John C. O'Toole. 1999. *The India private sector seed industry*. Manila: Island Publishing House, for the Rockefeller Foundation.

Serageldin, I. 2000. The challenge of poverty in the 21st century: The role of science. In *Agribiotechnology and the poor*, ed. G. J. Persley and M. M. Lantin. Washington, D.C.: Consultative Group on International Agricultural Research (CGIAR).

Serageldin, I., and G. J. Persley. 2000. *Promethean science: Agricultural biotechnology, the environment, and the poor*. Washington, D.C.: Consultative Group on International Agricultural Research (CGIAR).

Sharma, D. 2000. Selling out: The cost of free trade for food security in India. New Delhi: The Ecological Foundation.

Sharma, M. 1999. India: Biotechnology research and development. In *Agricultural biotechnology and the poor*, ed. G. J. Persley and M. M. Lantin. Proceedings of an International Conference, October 21–22. Washington, D.C.: CGIAR.

Shiva, V. 1991. *The violence of the green revolution: Third world agriculture, ecology and politics*. London: Zed Books.

Singh, H. P., and B. Venkateswarlu. 1999. Rainfed farming: Turning grey areas green. In *The Hindu: Survey of Indian Agriculture '99*, Hyderabad, India.

Song, Y. 1999. Introduction of transgenic cotton in China. *Biotechnology and Development Monitor*, No. 37 (March):14–17.

Soule, E. 2000. Assessing the precautionary principle. *Public Affairs Quarterly* 14 (4): 309–328.

Stave, J. W., and D. Durandetta. 2000. New diagnostics track the identity of agricultural products. *Today's Chemist at Work* 9 (6):32, 33, 37.

Stout, D. 1999. Study puts U.S. food-poisoning toll at 76 million yearly. *New York Times*, September 17: A14.

Subramaniam, C. 1979. *The new strategy in Indian agriculture: The first decade and after*. New Delhi: Vikas.

Swaminathan, M. S. 1999. Genetic engineering and food security: Ecological and livelihood issues. In *Agricultural biotechnology and the poor*, ed. G. J. Persley and M. M. Lantin. Proceedings of an International Conference, October 21–22. Washington, D.C.: CGIAR.

Sykes, A. O. 1995. *Product standards for internationally integrated goods markets*. Washington, D.C.: Brookings Institution.

Tewolde Behran Gebre Egzhiaber. 2000. Letters from Tewolde: Using the South to promote GE in Europe—Once again! Open letter to colleagues, April 3.

Thompson, L. 2000. Are bioengineered foods safe? *FDA Consumer Magazine* (January–February).

Thomson, J. A. 2000. Opinion: Poor nations can't afford debate on gene-altered crops. *Christian Science Monitor,* November 13.

UNEP (United Nations Environment Programme). 1995. UNEP international technical guidelines for safety in biotechnology. Nairobi, Kenya.

UPOV (International Convention for the Protection of New Varieties of Plants). 1978. *International Convention for the Protection of New Varieties of Plants, as revised at Geneva, October 23, 1978.* Geneva.

———. 1991. *International Convention for the Protection of New Varieties of Plants, as revised at Geneva, March 19, 1991.* Geneva.

USDA (United States Department of Agriculture). 2000a. The U.S.–China WTO accession deal. Foreign Agriculture Service, USDA, February 9.

———. 2000b. Segregating nonbiotech crops: What could it cost? *Agricultural Outlook* (April):32–33.

———. 2000c. Agricultural biotechnology: Frequently asked questions; http://www.aphis.usda.gov/biotechnology/faqs.html, September 2.

U.S. Congress Committee on Science. 2000. Seeds of opportunity: An assessment of the benefits, safety, and oversight of plant genomics and agricultural biotechnology. Report prepared by Chairman Nick Smith, Subcommittee on Basic Research, April 13, Committee Print 106–B.

Van Der Walt, W. J. 2000. Biotech likely to spark trade disputes. *Biosafety News* (Nairobi), No. 11 (August):12–15.

Wafula, J. S. 1999. Agricultural biotechnology in Kenya. Background paper prepared for the Regional Workshop on Biotechnology Assessment: Regimes and Experiences, September 27–29, African Centre for Technology Studies (ACTS), Nairobi, Kenya.

Wafula, J., and C. Falconi. 1998. Agribiotechnology research indicators: Kenya. ISNAR Discussion Paper No. 98-9. The Hague: ISNAR, September.

Wambugu, F. 2000. Message on "GM sweetpotatoes in Kenya," posted on http://www.agbioview@listbot.com, December 22.

Wang, D., and C. Yang. 1999. The Chinese national biosafety framework project. In *Regulation and practice on biosafety,* ed. D. Xue and I. Virgin. Proceedings of the International Workshop on Biosafety, November 2–5, 1998, Nanjing, China. Beijing: China Environmental Science Press.

Warren, G. F., Jr. 1998. The spectacular increases in crop yields in the United States in the twentieth century. *Weed Technology* 12.

Winrock. 2001. *Transgenic crops: An environmental assessment.* Policy Studies Report No. 15, Winrock International, Arlington, Va., U.S.A.

World Bank. 1999 *Knowledge for development.* New York: Oxford University Press.

———. 2000. *World development report 2000/2001: Attacking poverty.* New York: Oxford University Press.

Yudelman, M., A. Ratta, and D. Nygaard. 1998. *Pest management and food production: Looking to the future.* 2020 Discussion Paper 25. Washington, D.C.: International Food Policy Research Institute.

Zhang, Q. 2000. China: Agricultural biotechnology opportunities to meet the challenges of food production. In *Agricultural biotechnology and the poor,* ed. G. J. Persley and M. M. Lantin. Proceedings of an International Conference, October 21–22, 1999. Washington, D.C.: CGIAR.

Zhao, T. 2000. Food safety control and inspection in China. Paper presented at conference on China Agriculture and Food Biotechnology, April 4–5, Great Wall Sheraton Hotel, Beijing.

Index

Page numbers for entries occurring in figures are followed by an *f;* those for entries occurring in notes, by an *n;* and those for entries occurring in tables, by a *t.*

About the Author

Robert L. Paarlberg is professor of political science at Wellesley College and an associate at the Weatherhead Center for International Affairs at Harvard University. He has published books on the reform of U.S. agricultural policy (*Policy Reform in American Agriculture*, University of Chicago Press, with David Orden and Terry Roe), U.S. foreign economic policy (*Leadership Abroad Begins at Home*, Brookings Institution Press), sustainable agriculture (*Countrysides at Risk*, Overseas Development Council), international agricultural trade negotiations (*Fixing Farm Trade*, Council on Foreign Relations), and the use of food as a weapon (*Food Trade and Foreign Policy*, Cornell University Press).